Question&Answer
FAMILY LAW

Develop your legal skills with Longman

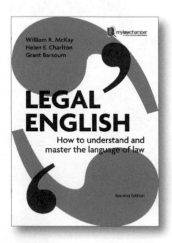

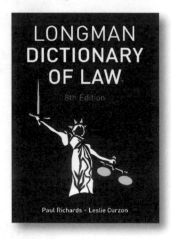

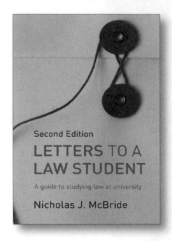

Question&Answer

FAMILY LAW

Jonathan Herring
Exeter College, University of Oxford

Longman
is an imprint of

Harlow, England • London • New York • Boston • San Francisco • Toronto • Sydney • Singapore • Hong Kong
Tokyo • Seoul • Taipei • New Delhi • Cape Town • Madrid • Mexico City • Amsterdam • Munich • Paris • Milan

Pearson Education Limited
Edinburgh Gate
Harlow
Essex CM20 2JE
England

and Associated Companies throughout the world

Visit us on the World Wide Web at:
www.pearson.com/uk

First published 2012

© Pearson Education Limited 2012

ISBN: 978-1-4082-4127-1

British Library Cataloguing-in-Publication Data
A catalogue record for this book is available from the British Library

Library of Congress Cataloging-in-Publication Data
Herring, Jonathan.
  Law express question and answer : family law / Jonathan Herring.
      p. cm. -- (Law express question and answer series)
  Includes bibliographical references and index.
  ISBN 978-1-4082-4127-1 (pbk.)
  1. Domestic relations--England--Examinations, questions, etc. 2. Domestic relations--
Wales--Examinations, questions, etc. I. Title. II. Title: Family law.
  KD750.H473 2011
  346.4201'5076--dc22

10 9 8 7 6 5 4 3 2 1
15 14 13 12 11

Typeset in 10pt Helvetica Condensed by 30
Printed and bound in Great Britain by Ashford Colour Press Ltd, Gosport, Hampshire

Contents

Supporting resources

Visit the **LawExpress Question&Answer** series companion website at
www.pearsoned.co.uk/lawexpressqa to find valuable learning material including:

- Additional **essay and problem questions** arranged by topic for each chapter give you more opportunity to practise and hone your exam skills.
- **Diagram plans** for all additional questions assist you in structuring and writing your answers.
- **You be the marker** questions allow you to see through the eyes of the examiner by marking essay and problem questions on every topic covered in the book.
- Download and print all **Attack the question** diagrams and **Diagram plans** from the book.

Also: The companion website provides the following features:

- Search tool to help locate specific terms of content.
- Online help and support to assist with website usage and troubleshooting.

For more information please contact your local Pearson sales representative or visit www.pearsoned.co.uk/lawexpressqa

Acknowledgements

I have been very grateful for the support and help of many people in writing this book. In particular, Zoe Botterill and Gabriella Playford at Pearson and to the anonymous reviewers of an earlier draft.

Publisher's acknowledgements

Our thanks go to all reviewers who contributed to the development of this text, including students who participated in research and focus groups which helped to shape the series format.

What you need to do for every question in Family Law

HOW TO USE THIS BOOK

Books in the *Question and Answer* series focus on the *why* of a good answer alongside the *what*, thereby helping you to build your question answering skills and technique.

This guide should not be used as a substitute for learning the material thoroughly, your lecture notes or your textbook. It *will* help you to make the most out of what you have already learned when answering an exam or coursework question. Remember that the answers given here are not the *only* correct way of answering the question but serve to show you some good examples of how you *could* approach the question set.

Make sure that you regularly refer to your course syllabus, check which issues are covered (as well as to what extent they are covered) and whether they are usually examined with other topics. Remember that what is required in a good answer could change significantly with only a slight change in the wording of a question. Therefore, do not try to memorise the answers given here; instead use the answers and the other features to understand what goes into a good answer and why.

Many law students feel that they do not do themselves justice in the exams. They have understood the legal principles and are aware of the leading cases, but struggle to put it all together in the exam room. If that sounds like you, then this is the book for you.

It is designed specifically to help you use what you know to improve your exam performance. It goes through 50 questions and answers, giving you a good answer and highlighting the things that examiners look for when marking the essays. Hopefully this will give you an insight into what examiners are looking for and help you get the marks you deserve.

Of course, it is important you listen carefully to the advice you are given by your lecturers. They will be able to tell you about the particular guidance offered by your college or University. This book provides general guidance about what examiners look for.

Family Law is commonly examined by essays, although problem questions can be used too. To reflect that, there are more essay questions than problem questions in this book. You should check with your university about what format the exam will take.

Guided tour

What you need to do for every question in Family Law

What to do for every question – Find out the key things you should do and look for in any question and answer on the subject in order to give every one of your answers a great chance from the start.

Themes in family law

How this topic may come up in exams

Family law exams often contain essay questions which raise general themes in family law. These do not fall within a particular topic, but require you to show a good knowledge across the subject. Students can find these questions rather frightening. They are not quite sure what the examiner expects and it may involve thinking about questions which they have not considered before.

The good news is that examiners realise that these broad questions can be hard to tackle and so can be generous when marking them. Even more good news, there is usually no right way of tackling these questions. Examiners usually don't expect a particular structure or list of topics. Indeed, you are expected to come up with your own way of dealing with the questions. That might sound scary, but it means you can't really go wrong!

It may help if I give you an example. Let us say there was an essay asking you to discuss whether family law should used fixed rules or a more discretionary-based

How this topic may come up in exams – Learn how to tackle any question on this topic by using the handy tips and advice relevant to both essay and problem questions. In-text symbols clearly identify each question type as it occurs.

 Essay question

 Problem question

Attack the question – Attack attack attack! Use these diagrams as a step by step guide to help you confidently identify the main points covered in any question asked.

Answer plans and Diagram plans – Clear and concise answer plans and diagram plans support the planning and structuring of your answers whatever your preferred learning style.

■ **Attack the question**

Is there a marriage?

No → Is there a civil partnership?

Yes → Consider whether the marriage is void or voidable

Yes

No

Answer plan

→ Are Anne and Brian associated people? If so, can Anne get a n[...]

→ What section of the Family Law Act can Anne use to get an occ[...] sections 33 and 36.

→ Are the courts likely to make an occupation order? The balance of [...] discussion.

Diagram plan

Are Anne and Brian associated people?

No → No remedy under FLA

Anne c[...] non-mole[...]

Do[...]

Answer with accompanying guidance – Make the most out of every question by using the guidance to recognise what makes a good answer and why. Answers are the length you could realistically hope to produce in an exam to show you how to gain marks quickly when under pressure.

3. DOMESTIC VIOLENCE

[1]The question asks you specifically to consider the parties separately. As we will see there is no need simply to repeat points of law already made in relation to one party when they come up later in relation to another.

[2]You have been asked in the question *only* to consider the remedies under the FLA so do not be sidetracked into discussing other remedies that may be available.

Answer

In this answer Anne's and Brian's claims will be considered separately.[1] Each might want to apply for a non-molestation order or an occupation order under the Family Law Act 1996. Remedies may also be available under the Protection from Harassment Act 1997 or the law of tort.[2]

Anne can apply for a non-molestation order as long as she and Brian are 'associated people'. This phrase is defined in section 62 of the Family Law Act 1996.[3] This list includes 'cohabitants and former cohabitants' and so there seems little doubt that Anne and Brian are associated.[4] Under section 42(5) the court will decide whether or not to make a non-molestation order after considering all the circumstances of the case, including the health, safety and well-being of Anne and the children.[5] Given the threats of violence and the push the court may well make a molestation order and specify that Brian must not assault Anne or threaten violence against her.[6]

[6]You need to emphasise the strictness that the courts have taken here, at least traditionally.

this. The other comment 'I owe you' is also probably insufficient as it is not a clear statement that ownership will be shared. In **James v Thomas** ([2007] 3 FCR 696) it was held the statement 'You will be well provided for' was not sufficient for a constructive trust.[6] And Barbara's statement seems just as vague as that one.

If the court decides there is insufficient evidence of an express agreement to share, it may be willing to infer one. Lord Bridge in **Rossett** suggested that only a direct contribution to the purchase price or a mortgage instalment would be sufficient. More recently in **Lightfoot v Lightfoot-Brown** [2005] EWCA 201 Arden LJ suggested a slightly broader approach that payments that were 'referable to the acquisition to the house' may be sufficient to lead to an inference of sharing of ownership. Tom might argue that although he did not make a direct contribution to the purchase price or to the mortgage the fact he paid for all of the other bills enabled Barbara to buy the house. This argu-

Case names clearly highlighted – Easy to spot bold text makes those all important case names stand out from the rest of the answer, ensuring they are much easier to remember in revision and in the exam.

Make your answer stand out – Really impress your examiners by including these additional points and further reading to illustrate your deeper knowledge of the subject, fully maximising your marks.

✓ Make your answer stand out

- You could expand the discussion on the nature of equality in this context. See Eekelaar (2000) 'Post-divorce financial obligations' in S. Katz, J. Eekelaar and M. Maclean, *Cross Currents*, Oxford: OUP.
- The interests of the state could be discussed further. See Herring (2005) 'Why financial orders on divorce should be unfair' *International Journal of Law Policy and the Family* 218.
- There could be more discussion of whether the law should be more predictable or whether discretion is beneficial. See Miles (2005) 'Principle or pragmatism in ancillary relief' *International Journal of Law, Policy and the Family* 242.
- More could be made of feminist approaches to this issue. See O'Donovan (2005) 'Flirting with academic categorisations' *Child and Family Law Quarterly* 415.

Don't be tempted to – Avoid common mistakes and losing easy marks by understanding where students most often trip up in exams.

! Don't be tempted to...

- Confuse cases where children seek to be represented in cases between adults, with cases where they wish to instigate their own litigation.
- Assume that children have a right to bring litigation.

Bibliography – Use this list of further reading to really explore areas in more depth, enabling you to excel in exams.

Bibliography

Anitha, S. and Gill, A. (2009) 'Coercion, Consent and the Forced Marriage Debate in the UK' *Feminist Legal Studies* 295.
Archard, D. (2004) *Children, Rights and Childhood*, London: Routledge.
Argent, H. (2009) 'What's the problem with kinship care?' *Adoption and Fostering Journal* 6.
Autchmuty, R. (2008) 'What's so special about marriage? The impact of Wilkinson v Kitzinger' *Child & Family Law Quarterly* 479.

Guided tour of the companion website

 Book resources are available to download. Print your own **Attack the question** and **Diagram plans**.

 Additional **Essay and Problem questions** with **Diagram plans** arranged by topic for each chapter give you more opportunity to practise and hone your exam skills. Print and email your answers.

 You be the marker gives you a chance to evaluate sample exam answers for different question types for each topic and understand how and why an examiner awards marks. Use the accompanying guidance to get the most out of every question and recognise what makes a good answer.

All of this and more can be found when you visit
www.pearsoned.co.uk/lawexpressqa

Table of cases, statutes, statutory instruments and conventions

Cases

▓ Statutes

▮ Statutory Instruments

▮ Conventions

Themes in family law

1

How this topic may come up in exams

Family law exams often contain essay questions which raise general themes in family law. These do not fall within a particular topic, but require you to show a good knowledge across the subject. Students can find these questions rather frightening. They are not quite sure what the examiner expects and it may involve thinking about questions which they have not considered before.

The good news is that examiners realise that these broad questions can be hard to tackle and so can be generous when marking them. Even more good news, there is usually no right way of tackling these questions. Examiners usually don't expect a particular structure or list of topics. Indeed, you are expected to come up with your own way of dealing with the questions. That might sound scary, but it means you can't really go wrong!

It may help if I give you an example. Let us say there was an essay asking you to discuss whether family law should used fixed rules or a more discretionary-based approach. There are many topics you could discuss: financial orders on divorce; the welfare principle; child protection etc. Well, the good news is that you can choose which topics to focus on. The examiner will not mind which ones you use as long as you discuss them in a way which answers the essay question.

I would suggest that with this broad essay you start by discussing some of the general themes raised by the question. Then look at two or three particular issues and see how your general discussion relates to concrete scenarios.

■ Attack the question

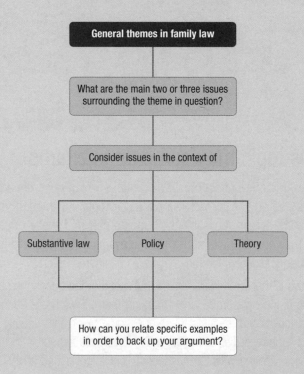

🖋 Question 1

What is a family for the purposes of family law?

Answer plan

→ Explain how family law used to centre on marriage.

→ Trace the way that there has been increased recognition of cohabitation.

→ Discuss the growing acknowledgement of same-sex couples and their legal rights.

→ Set out the growing importance attached to parenthood.

→ Consider alternative ways of looking at families.

Diagram plan

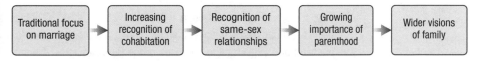

| Traditional focus on marriage | → | Increasing recognition of cohabitation | → | Recognition of same-sex relationships | → | Growing importance of parenthood | → | Wider visions of family |

A printable version of this diagram is available from www.pearsoned.co.uk/lawexpressqa

Answer

[1]The examiner will like the fact that you are emphasising that we are not talking about just a change in the law, but also a change in social attitudes. Changes in the law to a large extent reflect changing social attitudes.

The traditional focus of family law was marriage and the legal consequences of marriage. However, as we shall examine in this essay society and the law have moved well beyond that narrow understanding. Rates of cohabitation outside marriage are increasing and same-sex relationships are now accorded virtually all the same legal rights as opposite sex couples.[1]

Looking first at the case law in 1950 in **Gammans v Ekins** [1950] 2 KB 328, it was said to be 'an abuse of the English language' to describe a cohabiting couple as a family. A court would never take that line today. In **Fitzpatrick v Sterling** [2000] 1 FCR 21 two men (Mr Thompson and Mr Fitzpatrick) had shared a flat for 18 years in a gay relationship. The House of Lords were asked to rule whether they should be regarded as a family for the purposes of the Rent Act 1997. Lord Slynn firmly rejected the view that only married couples or those connected by blood could be family members. He, instead, suggested that the hallmarks of family life were 'that there should be a degree of mutual inter-dependence, of the sharing of lives, of caring and love, or commitment and support' and that the relationships should not be 'transient'. Applying these criteria to the case at hand the majority of their lordships were able to conclude that Mr Thompson and Mr Fitzpatrick were indeed members of a family. However, their lordships rejected a view that the couple should be seen as spouses or equivalent to spouses.[2]

[2]This is an important point to make, because it shows that the decision is not quite as liberal as might at first appear.

The significance of this decision is that the House of Lords no longer saw the hallmark of a family in terms of formal status: marriage, parenthood or blood tie; but rather in the nature of the relationship: is there mutual caring and love? This shift being based on relationship rather than status or form, has been a consistent theme in recent case law on the meaning of family.[3]

[3]The examiner will like you drawing the distinction between formal status and relationship. This is a major theme in the academic debates and it will show you have understood the material on this.

Fitzpatrick v Sterling also heralded increasing acceptance in family law of same-sex relationships. It has been followed by two major developments. First in **Mendoza v Ghaidan** [2004] UKHL 30, it was held that a same-sex couple could be treated as living together 'as husband and wife' for the purposes of the Rent Act 1977. Notably the House of Lords in reaching this conclusion relied on the Human Rights Act 1998, arguing that the law must not be interpreted in a way which discriminated against same-sex couples.[4] Second, the Civil Partnership Act 2004 has enabled same-sex couples to enter a civil partnership which has virtually all the legal rights of marriage. Indeed the President of the Family Division has described it as 'marriage in all but name' (**Wilkinson v Kitzinger** [2007] 1 FCR 183).[5]

[4]It is important to show the examiner that you are aware of the context of a decision. Noting that in *Fitzpatrick* the Human Rights Act was not yet in force shows that you are aware that the Human Rights Act can make a significant difference to how the law develops.

[5]When thinking about changes in family law the examiner will expect you to consider both changes by statute as well as in the case law.

So we have now reached the position where the law is willing to recognise as a family a couple living together in a mutually inter-dependent way, even if they are not married and even if they are of the same sex.

Some commentators (e.g. Dewar (1998)) have argued that over the past few decades we have witnessed a shift away from the primary obligations for family law focusing on marriage or cohabitation, towards parenthood. Increasingly the legal consequences of the end of a relationship depend on whether the couple have children, rather than whether the couple are married on not.[6] This is particularly so following the Child Support Act 1991, where the support obligations apply to married and unmarried parents alike. There are certainly some cases where the marital status of the couple is

[6]This shift from the focus of the law on marriage to being on parenthood is another theme that the examiner will be pleased to see you raising because it shows you are able to take a broad look at the way family law is studied.

very important in financial cases, but for less well-off couples, the central issue is often child support, rather than spousal support. The point can also be made that while in the past textbooks on family law were dominated by the law of marriage, nowadays there is more focus on the children.

[7] *Burden* is a good case to rely on in exams when considering what a family is.

It will be interesting to see where the future understanding of families goes. Consider, for example, **Burden *v* UK** [2008] ECHR 357 which involved two sisters living together for over thirty years.[7] They were not permitted to marry or enter a civil partnership. They claimed that this disadvantaged them, especially in terms of inheritance tax. They argued that their relationship was exactly the same as any other couple, save there was no sex. So should the sexual element really have a significant impact on the legal status of the relationship?

[8] Impress the examiner with your knowledge of influential commentators.

Some commentators (e.g. Fineman (2004)) argue that the focus of family law should be on relationships of care, rather than relationships involving sex or blood ties or marriage.[8] That might bring within the idea of a family an adult looking after an elderly parent or a person looking after a disabled adult. Fineman (2004) makes the powerful point that it is caring relationships which really help society and contribute to it, rather than sexual ones. That might mean that a marriage between two healthy employed people without children would not be a family, as there is no caring or dependency relationship. That would be quite a turn about for the law to take!

[9] This conclusion brings together the main themes in the essay and reminds the examiner of the key points you want to make.

To conclude, we are witnessing a change in the understanding of the family. In the past it was determined by status: were a couple married or not? Increasingly the law's focus is on the nature of the relationship: were the couple dependent on each other; are they living mutual lives? The shift should not be exaggerated. Where the couple are married it is highly unlikely that at the moment the law would say they were not family, because they did not love each other. The law, however, now recognises that there is a wide range of ways of 'doing family' and there is no rule book you have to follow.[9]

✓ **Make your answer stand out**

■ Refer to the shift from approaches based on status to those based on the reality of the relationship: see Glennon (2008) 'Obligations between adult partners: Moving from form to function?' *International Journal of Law Policy and Family*, **22**, 22.

■ Consider whether the notion of care and dependency is taking over from sex as the marker of a family relationship. This is discussed in Herring (2010c) 'Sexless Family Law' Lex Familiae **11**, 3.

■ Examine whether parenthood is now more important than marriage in family law.

■ The *Burden* decision raises some interesting issues. You might have time to discuss further the different arguments over whether this couple should be able to have a civil partnership or whether we need some other legal category to describe relationships like this. Note that gay activists have expressed concern that if friends or relatives living together are allowed to be civil partners, this will weaken the significance of the notion of civil partnership.

! **Don't be tempted to...**

■ Just to discuss the theory without reference to legal specifics. You must give practical examples of the points you are making.

■ Suggest that marriage is now legally irrelevant. Although its significance has lessened there are still plenty of cases where it has a major impact on the legal consequences of a relationship.

📝 Question 2

What contribution does feminism offer to a study of family law?

Answer plan

→ Explain how feminism challenges disadvantage to women.

→ Explore the way that feminists have challenged the norms of family law.

→ Feminists have spoken of the power of the law, discuss what this means.

→ Consider whether there are 'male' and 'female' forms of reasoning.

→ Assess the value placed on care by the law.

Diagram plan

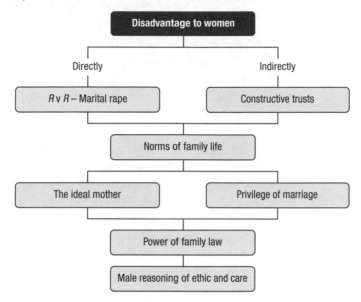

A printable version of this diagram is available from www.pearsoned.co.uk/lawexpressqa

Answer

[1]This is an important point to make early on. You need to show the examiner that you realise that feminism is a way of asking questions and approaching issues, but does not necessarily pre-determine a particular answer.

[2]You will want to show the examiner you are aware of the range of feminist opinions in order to show you have read widely.

A major theme in academic writing on family law has been the use of feminist approaches to analyse family law. It is not possible in this essay to bring out all of the contributions from this school of thought, but we will pick out a few key themes. Before doing so it should be emphasised that there is not a single 'feminist approach'.[1] A uniting theme is that feminists seek to ask 'the gender question': how will this policy or approach impact on men or women differently? A major division within feminism is between those who espouse 'feminism of difference' and those who favour 'feminism of equality'.[2] For the former the law should accept that men and women are different, but we should make sure that no disadvantage flows from those differences. For the latter we should seek to treat men and women equally and the ideal world will be one where there are no real differences between men and women. So feminists of difference might encourage good support and recognition of childcare so that women who undertake childcare are not disadvantaged. Feminists of equality will strive to ensure that the childcare burden is shared equally between men and women. Of course, on that issue it may be possible to try to peruse both approaches.

A major theme of feminist writing has been to point out ways in which family law operates to the disadvantage of women. Historically the forms of discrimination against women were blatant: for example, a husband could divorce his wife if she committed adultery, while she could not divorce him unless there was aggravated adultery (e.g. that the adultery was with her sister). Another notorious example is marital rape. It was not until 1992 and the decision of **R v R** [1991] 4 All ER 481 that the rule that on marriage a wife was taken to irrevocably consent to sex with her husband at any time during the marriage was abolished. The marital rape exemption meant that the rape of huge numbers of wives went unpunished by the law, not only that, but the law told them they were consenting. Quite rightly feminists have been outraged that it took so long for this decision to be reversed.

[3]The examiner will want to see that you have understood this distinction between direct and indirect discrimination.

[4]It is good to use concrete examples in the law to make your points.

It is rare now for law to explicitly discriminate against women, but there are still those who do indirectly.[3] A good example is the law on property dispute between unmarried couples, which is now dealt with by the law on constructive trusts and proprietary estoppel.[4] This law has drawn a sharp distinction between contributions which are financial and those which are non-financial (e.g. by housework or childcare). While not directly referring to women, this approach would, in effect, work against the interests of women who are more likely to contribute through childcare or housework than men. Hillary Lim (1996) argues, therefore, that the law in this area indirectly discriminates against women.

[5]This point about terminology having laden meaning is a good one to make because it shows that you are thinking carefully about the meaning behind words. You may be able to think of other examples.

Feminist writing has also done much to reveal norms that are sometimes hidden behind familiar terms. So terms such as 'mother' or 'family' may appear to be neutral or non-contentious, but are laden with meanings.[5] It has been claimed by Smart, for example, that mothers are expected to live up to a higher standard than fathers. A good mother is meant to sacrifice everything for her child, while less is expected of the father. An example might be that a mother who does not allow her child to see its father is strongly criticised for harming the child; but a father who does not want to see the child faces no opprobrium from the court. Yet each is harming the child in the same way.

[6]Referring to leading academic writers shows the examiner that you have been reading around the issue.

Some feminists (e.g. Carol Gilligan (1982)) have controversially suggested that there is a difference between 'male' and 'female' reasoning.[6] Male reasoning focuses on abstract principles and binding rules; while female reasoning seeks to resolve issues by focusing on flexible solutions and results that work for the particular individuals and the particular relationships in question. 'Male reasoning' is based on an 'ethic of justice'; while female reasoning is based on an 'ethic of care'. In relation to family law an ethic of care would argue in favour of a discretionary-based approach that enables a result to be tailored to those involved, rather than a rights- or rules-based approach, appealing to abstract principles of justice. It does not matter too much whether you buy into this being a difference between male and female reasoning, but this distinction between an ethic of justice and an ethic of care has proved a valuable tool in analysing the decisions of courts in family cases.[7]

[7]The examiner will be looking out for a discussion of the differences between an ethic of care and an ethic of justice. In fact, this distinction is one you can use in a lot of family law essays and so is well worth revising.

This links too into a wider feminist argument about the value of care. Martha Fineman (2004) and others have argued that for too long our society has not adequately valued the practice of care. Looking after vulnerable people (e.g. children) has been labelled private and therefore not recognised for the value it provides. Similarly in family cases the actual day-to-day care provided by a parent is downplayed where the biological link is emphasised and it is said that parents should be treated equally even where one of them has been involved in significantly more care work than the others.[8]

[8]This theme too: the valuing of childcare and other care work is a useful one for essays looking at family law in general.

So, we have seen in this essay some very useful forms of analysis from feminist commentators. Not only do they provide a way of critiquing the current law. They also suggest new ways that family law could develop in the future.

 Make your answer stand out

- Bring out the difference between an ethic of care and an ethic of justice. This is discussed in Smart and Neale (1999) *Family Fragments?* Cambridge: Polity Press.
- Consider the importance attached to the realities of family life for feminist commentators. Look at some of the essays in Diduck and O'Donovan (2007) *Feminist Perspectives on Family Law*, London: Routledge.
- Look at ways that terminology in family law can convey preconceived ideas about gender or family life: Diduck (2008) *Law's Families*, ch. 1, London: LexisNexis, Butterworths.

> **!** ## Don't be tempted to...
>
> ■ Assume there is a single feminist position on issues.
> ■ Only see feminism as about discrimination issues.

✒ Question 3

Assess the impact of the Human Rights Act 1998 on family law.

Answer plan

→ Discuss the key articles in the ECHR.

→ Consider how an approach based on human rights would deal with child protection issues.

→ How might human rights be relevant in cases of domestic violence?

→ Analyse how human rights might challenge the welfare principle.

→ Explain how the right to marry might affect the law on marriage.

Diagram plan

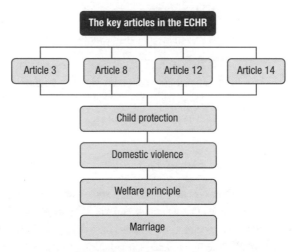

A printable version of this diagram is available from www.pearsoned.co.uk/lawexpressqa

Answer

When the Human Rights Act 1998 was passed there was considerable debate among family lawyers over the impact it would have on family law. Generally, it seems that the impact has been significantly less than might have been expected. It is perhaps the area of child protection where the difference is most significant, but in other areas decisions of the courts have lessened its potential impact.

To start we will look at four of the key articles that have relevance for family lawyers.[1] First, there is article 3. This protects the right not to suffer torture, inhuman or degrading treatment. It covers not only physical maltreatment, but also serious psychological abuse. In **A v UK** [1998] 3 FCR 597 it was accepted that the article requires the government to protect citizens from conduct which will infringe article 3 whether that conduct comes from the state or other individuals.[2] Hence in **E v UK** [2002] 3 FCR 700 it was held that the state under article 3 had a duty to protect children from abuse at the hands of their parents. Second, article 8 protects the right to respect for private and family life. Notably this is a conditional right.[3] That means that there are circumstances in which it is justifiable to interfere in someone's private or family life, which are set out in paragraph 2 of article 8. To justify an interference it is necessary to show that the interference in family life was in accordance with law and was necessary in order to peruse a list of aims. That list includes the interests of others. So, it could be justifiable to interfere in family life and remove a child from its parents, if that was necessary to protect the child from harm. Third, there is article 12 which protects the right to marry. However, that has been interpreted in the English courts only to cover heterosexual couples (**Wilkinson v Kitzinger** [2007] 1 FCR 183). Finally there is article 14 which protects citizens from discrimination. This can only be used in conjunction with another right. So, you cannot say in the abstract that you have been discriminated against, but you must argue that one of your convention rights (e.g. article 8) has been interfered with in a discriminatory way. It is very difficult to justify discrimination.

Turning to look at particular issues.[4] First, the area where the courts have used human rights the most is that of child protection. There are two main themes. First, it is now well established that the state has a duty to protect children from abuse at the hands of their

[1] Here, show the examiner that you are aware that while article 8 deals with family life, other articles are relevant for family lawyers.

[2] This is an important point that the examiner will want to see you have picked up. Human rights are not only relevant for relationships between the state and citizens, they can also be relevant for relationships between individuals.

[3] The examiner will want to make sure you have appreciated this point. Some articles in the ECHR are absolute and it is not possible to justify their breach. Others are conditional and their breach can be justified. You need to explain that in essays on human rights.

[4] There are lots of areas of family law you could use as examples. There is no need to choose the ones I have chosen.

parents. Where the public authority knows or ought to know about the abuse and fails to take reasonable steps to protect children it can face a claim under section 7 of the HRA by the children (**E v UK** [2002] 3 FCR 700; **Z v UK** [2001] 2 FCR 246). Second, where children are removed from parents this can be justified under article 8(2), but it must be shown that the intervention is 'proportionate'. This means that it needs to be shown that there was no less interventionist measure which could have been used to adequately protect the children (**Re L** [2004] 1 FCR 289). If, for example, a care order is sought, it must be shown that a supervision order would not adequately protect the child.[5] Third, any intervention in family life must use procedures which ensure that the parents are sufficiently involved to protect their interests. This has an impact on the procedures used when children are taken into care: parents must be kept informed and must have a chance to put their case and must be given copies of all the relevant information.[6]

[5]Giving a practical example is useful here. The examiner will want you to apply your analysis to particular concrete issues.

[6]Although this point relates to procedure rather than substantive law the examiner will be pleased to see a discussion of this because it is very significant in practice.

Domestic violence is another area where Human Rights could be relevant. As we have already seen articles 3 and 8 can be used to state that there is a duty on state to protect victims of domestic violence from abuse, where the state authorities are aware of the risk of abuse and can take reasonable steps to protect them (**Opuz v Turkey** Application no. 33401/02). If the state fails to protect victims then the victim could bring proceedings under section 7 of the HRA to obtain damages. This is particularly relevant for the police called to incidents of domestic violence. They must take reasonable steps to ensure that the victim will be safe.

One area where it was thought that the HRA would have a noticeable impact was in the interpretation of the welfare principle, which applies to all cases concerning the upbringing of children. It had been argued that after the HRA the courts would have to take into account the rights of adults and so it would not be possible simply to use the welfare principle, which only considers the interests of children (Herring and Taylor, 2006). However, the courts have rejected this analysis. They argue that the results are the same whether you use a human rights analysis or whether you use the welfare principle (**Payne v Payne** [2001] 1 FCR 425). In either case the interests of the child will always trump those of the adults. As there is no difference between them the courts have said they are entitled to continue relying on the welfare principle. Indeed

[7]The examiner will be pleased that you have noticed that the cases where HRA analysis has not been used can be as significant as cases where it has been.

[8]This is a good example of an area where it might have been thought that the HRA would have a significant impact, but it has not.

in the recent Supreme Court decision of **Re B** [2009] UKSC 4 on residence disputes, the Court focused on the welfare principle and there was not a single mention of the HRA.[7]

Another area where it might have been thought that the HRA would have an impact would be on same-sex marriage. However, in **Wilkinson v Kitzinger** [2007] 1 FCR 138, Sir Mark Potter, stated that the UK law which does not permit same-sex marriage was compatible with the ECHR.[8] The right to marry in article 12, he argued, only applied to opposite sex couples, because the word 'marriage' was to be understood in its traditional, historical sense. He also denied that not being able to marry was an interference in the couple's article 8 rights because they had the option of entering a civil partnership which would give them the same legal rights as being married. Finally, he denied that there was any discrimination, and even if there was it could be justified in the name of preserving the traditional understanding of marriage.

To conclude, the HRA has not had the impact on family law that it might have. The impact it might have had on the welfare principle and on marriage has been avoided by the way the courts have interpreted it. However, it has had an impact in some areas, particularly those relating to child abuse. It seems the courts have preferred to keep the discretion available through the welfare principle and are concerned that a rights-based approach will restrict their freedom to make the order which best promotes the welfare of the children.[9]

[9]This conclusion provides a good summary of the main issues raised in the essay.

 Make your answer stand out

■ Show a good knowledge of the relevant ECHR articles. For a detailed discussion of how the HRA can be used in family law see Choudhry and Herring (2010) *European Human Rights and Family Law*, Oxford: Hart.

■ You could do more to discuss whether the HRA challenges the welfare principle. The courts has said it does not but academics have largely rejected this analysis. See, for example, Herring and Taylor (2006) 'Relocating relocation' *Child and Family Law Quarterly* 517.

> **!** **Don't be tempted to...**
>
> ■ Only consider the relevance of article 8 and the right to respect for family life.
> ■ Suggest that article 14 is a freestanding claim. A claim of discrimination must be made in relation to another convention right.
> ■ Only think about claims against the Government arising from the HRA.

Question 4

Should family life be regarded as a private matter in family law?

Answer plan

→ Explain how privacy has been used traditionally.
→ Set out the role of privacy in article 8 of the ECHR.
→ Examine the challenges of feminists to the concept of privacy.
→ Consider how privacy operates in cases of domestic violence and child abuse.
→ Should pre-marriage agreements be enforced in the name of privacy?

Diagram plan

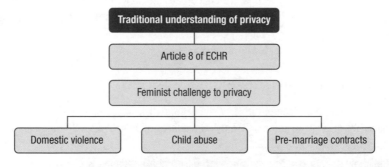

A printable version of this diagram is available from www.pearsoned.co.uk/lawexpressqa

Answer

A common way of understanding family life until the twentieth century was to see family life as a private matter. The father (the paterfamilias) was seen to have domain over his house, while the

[1]Although this is a historical point, the examiner will be impressed, because it explains how privacy has traditionally been seen as a justification for non-intervention in family life.

state had domain over the streets. This was reflected in the fact that fathers were given the authority to administer corporal punishment to their wives, children and, if they had them, servants. The role of the law was to protect the father's rights. Nowadays no one would, of course, support the notion of family privacy in this way, but aspects of it linger on in the public imagination.[1]

Article 8 of the European Convention on Human Rights protects the right to respect for private and family life. This reflects a widespread concern that there are areas of private and family life which are none of the government's business. When the state does seek to regulate domestic affairs, there are cries of 'nanny state' or 'seeking to police the nation's bedrooms'. John Eekelaar (2006a) has argued that people need a sphere of intimacy, free from legal intrusion, in which love and friendship can develop. A slightly different point can be made that where the state does try and intervene in family life it often gets things wrong. The state has failed many children in care and the history of family policy is littered with examples of the government seeking to intervene to promote children's welfare, but in fact harming them. The evacuation of children from England to Canada and Australia during wartime is an example which has recently attracted considerable attention.[2] History warns us against well-minded state attempts to intervene in family life. We should intervene in family life with caution.

[2]This is one example, but others could be used, of where attempts to help children by intervening in family life have backfired.

The argument that family life should be regarded as a private matter has been subject to considerable criticism, particularly from feminist writers (see especially Nicola Lacey (1993), Michael Freeman (1985)). They note, first, that the notion that non-intervention is the law acting neutrally is misleading. Where the law does not intervene it leaves the existing power structures in play. So, where, for example, the law does not intervene in a case where a husband is abusing his wife, the law is allowing him to continue doing that.[3] Second, there have been challenges to the division between private and public matters. Some private matters can have significant public consequences. Child abuse causes huge public costs, both financial and social. Just because it usually occurs in people's homes, does not mean it does not have an impact on the general community.

[3]This is an important point which the examiner will want to see in an essay about privacy. When deciding not to intervene we must consider what situation we are thereby allowing to continue.

[4]Referring to a leading academic is a good way of showing you have read widely on the issue and makes your answer sound more authoritative.

Elizabeth Schneider (1994) has made an interesting point about the role of privacy in family law.[4] She notes that the reason why we think that privacy is important is that we think people should be able to develop their own characters, way of life and interests free from interference from others. However, she argues that intervention in family life is sometimes necessary so that people can develop in these ways. Her example is of domestic violence, where without intervention a victim will have their freedom infringed.

Turning now to consider three areas where privacy has been used in the debates. First, domestic violence. Traditionally the law has regarded domestic violence as a private matter. It was not regarded as a proper crime and the police noted it as a 'domestic' rather than as a serious crime. It was thought of as best left as a private matter for the parties to sort out between themselves. However, the attitude of the police in more recent times has changed. Home Office guidance now recommends that the police take domestic violence seriously and an assault in the living room is to be regarded as seriously as an assault in the pub. This, it is submitted, is correct. Domestic violence can have a significant impact on women's lives and on society and the economy generally.[5]

[5]Domestic violence is a particularly good issue to discuss when looking at privacy in family law.

Considering child abuse next, again it is now recognised that this is not simply a private matter. The state should intervene to protect children from abuse. Indeed following **Z v UK** [2000] 2 FCR 245 the courts now recognise that the European Convention on Human Rights, Article 3, requires the state to intervene to protect children. So far from child abuse being 'out of bounds' for the state because it is private, it is seen rather as an obligation on the state to protect vulnerable children.[6]

[6]This is a good point to make. The HRA has meant that non-intervention can in some cases be seen as a breach of a citizen's rights.

The issue of pre-marriage contracts is more controversial. The Supreme Court in **Radmacher v Granatino** [2010] UKSC 42 has held that the courts will give effect to pre-marriage agreements as long as they are entered into fairly and meet the needs of the parties. One argument in favour of doing this is that if the parties have decided between themselves what should happen to their property in the event of a divorce the state should not intervene in that. Indeed the majority of the Supreme Court suggested it would be paternalistic for the state not to give effect to a pre-marriage contract. Supporters of pre-marriage contracts refer to the notion of autonomy and privacy to justify them. Opponents question whether pre-marriage contracts should be regarded as just private matters. If there are children involved there may be their interests

[7]It is useful to present both sides of the argument here, so that you discuss both the benefits but also disadvantages of privacy.

to consider. Herring (2005) has argued there are state interests involved in the way property is dealt with on divorce and the issues should not be regarded as being private.[7]

[8]This conclusion brings together the main themes in the essay so that the examiner can see the major points you are seeking to make.

To conclude, an approach that states that the law should not intervene in private matters but may in public matters, is outdated and simplistic. That is not to deny that there are some areas of life where it is better for the state not to regulate. Each issue must be considered separately. There may be some areas of private life where there should be legal intervention and some areas of public life where there should not be. In deciding whether there should be legal intervention or not the question should not focus on the public or private nature of the issues, but rather the nature of the interests involved and what the state could effectively do.[8]

 Make your answer stand out

- Use a good range of examples to show how many different areas of family law can be seen as private.
- Refer to the feminist critiques of the notion of privacy. Schneider (1994) 'The Violence of Privacy' in M. Fineman and R. Myktiuk (eds) *The Public Nature of Private Violence*, London: Routledge, is a helpful article on this point.
- Consider why it is that privacy can be seen as a good thing. There is an excellent discussion on this in Eekelaar (2006a) *Family Life and Personal Life*, Oxford: OUP.

! Don't be tempted to...

- Assume that privacy is a good thing.
- Just consider the issue of domestic violence.

 # Question 5

To what extent is, and should, family law be involved in making moral judgments?

Answer plan

→ Explain the difficulties in avoiding making a moral judgment.

→ Discuss the concept of pluralism.

→ Consider the role moral judgments play in divorce law.

→ Explore the role fault plays in financial orders.

→ Is fault relevant in cases where the welfare of children is the paramount consideration?

→ Explain the relevance of fault in the law on domestic violence and child abuse.

Diagram plan

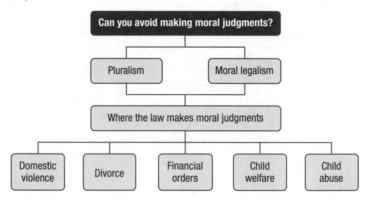

A printable version of this diagram is available from www.pearsoned.co.uk/lawexpressqa

[1]Don't let the question mislead you. The examiner may like it if you challenge the assumption behind the question. This shows you have thought about the question and not been misled into thinking there is a choice between the moral and amoral in relation to family law.

Answer

The question asks to what extent does, and should, family law make moral judgments. The first point to make in answering this is that it is impossible to avoid making a moral judgment. That is because a decision not to make a moral judgment is itself a form of moral judgment! So, perhaps the better question to ask is what role the court sees for itself in issues of morality. It cannot avoid expressing a moral judgment.[1]

In the past the courts were very willing to make moral judgments. The law required the proof of clear fault before a divorce could be granted, in relation to financial matters the blameworthiness of the parties could be a very significant issue, and the moral standing of the parents played a significant role in cases involving disputes over the raising of children. However, we have seen over the past few decades a reduction in the number of cases where the courts are willing to make bold statements about the morality of the individual's behaviour.[2] There are several reasons for this. First, there is a realisation that there is no longer a shared morality among the people of the UK. If ever there was consensus over moral and religious issues there is little nowadays. So questions on what is a good way to bring up a child or what makes a good marriage will find widely differing responses. Second, the courts often take the view that it is necessary to be forwards looking rather than backwards looking. We should be less interested in the past and most interested in the future. Of course, it may be that the bad conduct of the past is an indication of bad conduct in the future, but it need not be.[3] Third, the courts have realised that mistakes were made in the past about what was or was not morally acceptable. So, it was not that long ago when a court was able to deny residence orders to same-sex couples on the basis that their relationships were not normal and would harm children, whereas today a judge would not say that. The fact the courts made errors in the past, makes them more wary about bold assertions nowadays.

Looking now at some particular areas of family law. The area of divorce is one where it does appear that moral judgment can play a role. The court can find that a husband committed adultery or the wife engaged in unreasonable behaviour and on that basis grant a decree for divorce. However, while that is how it appears, it should be recalled that the actual ground for divorce does not relate to fault (the ground for divorce is that the marriage has irretrievably broken down: section 1 Matrimonial Causes Act 1973). Further, in reality, despite the wording of the 1973 Act, the Special Procedure that is used on divorce means that if the divorce is undefended the judge will not require proof of the fault and there will be no public hearing. Nevertheless it is still true that this is an area where a finding of fault can, at least on the paperwork, be found.[4]

[2] It is helpful here to put the issue in its historical context.

[3] This is a difficult issue in this essay and it is one the examiner will be pleased to see you have picked up on. You will need to explain carefully the difference between the use of bad conduct in the past as evidence of how a person will behave in the future, and the punishment of previous bad conduct.

[4] The examiner will be pleased you have picked up the point that in family law the law in the textbooks is not always matched with how the law works in practice.

In relation to financial orders the blameworthiness of a party used to be an important factor. A wife who had behaved badly would expect to get her maintenance reduced. However, nowadays it will be very rare indeed for conduct to be taken into account. It must be such that it would be 'inequitable' to take into account (s. 25(2)(g)).[5] The fact that the husband might have committed adultery, will not now be considered sufficiently serious to be taken into account when the court makes a financial order (**Miller v Miller** [2006] 2 FCR 213).

[6]Even though the essay is a fairly general one refer to specific examples in the case law to back up your points.

In relation to children the position is a little less clear. On the one hand there is **Re W** [1999] 3 FCR 274, a case where a mother, after separation from the father, cohabited with a naturist. The couple were nude in front of the children and the father objected to this.[6] Butler Sloss P held that the issue of nudity in families was an issue about which there was a wide range of opinion and practice. It would be wrong for the court to take a particular line. This is a common theme in cases where a reasonable case can be made on both sides of an issue. The courts will not side with one view or another. It is particularly prevalent in cases of religious upbringing (e.g. **Re J** [1999] 2 FCR 345) where the courts are very reluctant to be seen as siding with one religion over another. However, the courts are willing to use the past misconduct of a party as evidence that they may behave in the future in an undesirable way. In **Re S (A Minor)** [1995] 3 FCR 225 the fact the father had been convicted of possessing obscene paedophilic literature was taken as evidence he posed a risk to the child and could not have a contact order.[7]

[7]There is an important distinction here. The court were more concerned about whether he posed a risk to the child than whether his conduct was blameworthy.

Two areas where the courts seem willing to make judgments is in relation to child protection and domestic violence. We have seen the law becoming increasingly willing to intervene in cases of domestic violence and ensure it is treated as seriously as any other crime. Similarly in relation to child abuse the courts now recognise that there is a positive duty on local authorities to protect children (**Z v UK** [2000] 2 FCR 245). However, in both these cases the concern of the court is to protect children or vulnerable adults, rather than a moral judgment. This can be seen by the fact that even where the abusive conduct is not the fault of the abuser (e.g. **Re G** [2001] Fam Law 727) the courts will still intervene to protect the child.[8]

[8]Here again we have used case law to back up the specific points. The examiner will like that.

So we can see that in family law the courts are reluctant to pass moral judgment on conduct. They are however willing to intervene in cases where a person is facing violence or where a person's past conduct indicates that they may pose a risk in the future. Then the court will see a person's past conduct as relevant.

✓ Make your answer stand out

- An excellent article on the role played by fault in family law is Bainham (2001) 'Men and women behaving badly: Is fault dead in English family law?' *Oxford Journal of Legal Studies* 219.
- Another angle to look at this issue is the role that multiculturalism should play in family law. This is discussed in Freeman (2003) 'The State, Race and Family in England Today' in J. Dewar and S. Parker (eds) *Family Law Processes, Practices, Pressures*, Oxford: Hart.
- Emphasise that the decision not to assess blame can itself be seen as a moral judgment.

! Don't be tempted to...

- Say that the ground for divorce is fault based.
- Suggest that the courts will readily take conduct into account in financial orders.

Marriage and civil partnership

How this topic may come up in exams

In 2004, after considerable debate, the government passed the Civil Partnership Act. This enables two adults of the same sex to enter a civil partnership. A question which has troubled law students ever since is whether there are any differences between a civil partnership and a marriage. This is part of a wider debate: what is marriage for? You should consider this question carefully. Should marriage be regarded as purely a religious or social matter? Why should it matter to the courts whether a couple are married or not? An indication of what the law thinks is important about marriage can be found in the grounds upon which a marriage or civil partnership can be found void or voidable: these indicate the factors the law thinks are central to the idea of marriage. So although it might seem a rather obscure part of the law nullity is important.

Attack the question

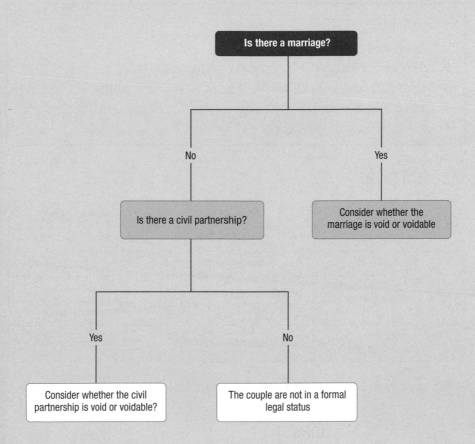

Is there a marriage?

No

Yes

Is there a civil partnership?

Consider whether the marriage is void or voidable

Yes

No

Consider whether the civil partnership is void or voidable?

The couple are not in a formal legal status

A printable version of this diagram is available from www.pearsoned.co.uk/lawexpressqa

Question 1

What are the legal differences between marriage and civil partnership?

Answer plan

The following are the key issues to cover:

➡ Set out the grounds on which a marriage or civil partnership is void.

➡ Discuss the grounds on which a marriage or civil partnership is voidable.

➡ Consider the differences in the legal consequences of marriage.

➡ Examine the Human Rights Act issues that might arise.

Diagram plan

	Marriage	Civil partnership
Who can enter	Opposite sex couples MCA s. 11	Same-sex couples CPA s. 1
When created	Exchange of vows	Signature of registrar CPA s. 24
Grounds of annulment	Includes non-consummation and venereal diseases s. 12 MCA	Does not include non-consummation or venereal diseases
Facts to establish ground of divorce or dissolution	Adultery included s. 1 (2)(a) MCA	Adultery not included

A printable version of this diagram is available from www.pearsoned.co.uk/lawexpressqa

Answer

The Civil Partnership Act 2004 was a compromise between those who wanted same-sex couples to be able to marry and those who did not want same-sex couples to receive the same legal status of marriage. Civil partnership gives a couple virtually the same legal rights as marriage, while not giving their relationship the name of marriage. The easiest way of doing this would have been to produce a statute which simply stated that civil partners had all the same rights as a married couple. Parliament chose not to do that and instead the Act goes through the legal provisions dealing with marriage separately and declares that each applies to marriage. This

¹It is useful to start by setting out the general approach of the Civil Partnership Act.

²This is a good example of referring precisely to the relevant statutory provisions.

³You will impress the examiner by using your knowledge of the law on parenthood in an essay on civil partnership.

makes it an Act of over 250 sections and 30 schedules. However, in doing this it left a small number of areas where there is a difference between a married couple and civil partners.¹

First, a marriage can only be entered into by a man and a woman (s. 3(1) Matrimonial Causes Act 1973), while a civil partnership can only be entered into by a couple of the same sex (s. 3(1) Civil Partnership Act 2004).²

Second, a civil partnership is formed at the moment the two parties sign the register (s. 2(1) Civil Partnership Act 2004), while it is on the exchange of vows that a marriage is formed. This may be of some symbolic difference, but is not of practical significance.

Third, a marriage can be annulled on the grounds of non-consummation of the relationship (s. 12 Matrimonial Causes Act 1973). However, a civil partnership cannot be annulled on the basis of non-consummation. If, therefore, a civil partnership was not consummated and one of the partners was unhappy about that they would have to seek a dissolution of the partnership. An application for nullity could not be made on that basis.

Fourth, a marriage can be annulled on the grounds that the respondent suffered from a venereal disease (s. 12 Matrimonial Causes Act 1973). However, a civil partnership cannot be.

Fifth, adultery is a fact which establishes the ground for divorce in the case of a marriage (s. 1(2)(a) Matrimonial Causes Act 1973). However, that is not a fact which could form the basis of an application for a dissolution of a civil partnership.

There used to be two further differences. One was abolished by the Human Fertilisation and Embryology Act 2008. That was that if a woman received assisted reproduction and was married, then her husband would be regarded as the father of the child born as a result of the treatment. However, if she had a civil partner, her partner would not be. However the Human Fertilisation and Embryology 2008 Act, section 42, now allows a civil partner to be treated as a parent of the child born.³

The other difference which has since been removed is that originally a civil partnership could not contain a religious element, although a marriage can (s. 2(3) Civil Partnership Act 2004). There was nothing to stop civil partners having a religious ceremony before or after the

[4]This is a recent development in the debate and referring to it shows the examiner you are keeping up with current issues.

civil partnership. By contrast a marriage can take place during the course of a church service. However, since the Equality Act 2010 religious groups who wish to have a religious service as part of a civil partnership ceremony can do so.[4]

There is much dispute as to whether these differences are of much significance. Sir Mark Potter in **Wilkinson v Kitzinger** [2006] EWHC 2022 (Fam) described a civil partnership as 'marriage in all but name'.[5] Certainly the differences described earlier are unlikely to be significant for most civil partners. The differences in voidability are mitigated by the fact that the partner can seek a dissolution of the partnership instead. The one difference which might appear significant is the fact that adultery is not a ground for dissolution. However, the significance of that is greatly reduced by the fact that unreasonable behaviour is a ground for dissolution and a court is likely to find sexual unfaithfulness to be unreasonable behaviour. It seems therefore that only very rarely indeed will the legal differences have any practical significance.[6]

[5]You cannot be expected to remember long quotes from cases but remembering a choice phrase will reassure the examiner that you have read the cases!

[6]The point you must get across to the examiner is that although in practical terms there is little difference, there may be a symbolic difference.

On the other hand it is argued by some that the differences are of symbolic importance. In particular they indicate that the law does not want to consider the sexual side of a relationship between same-sex couples because it ignores consummation and adultery issues. That might reveal a prejudicial attitude towards same-sex sexual activity.

The crucial symbolic difference may lie in the name. The fact that civil partnership and marriage do not have the same name strongly suggests that the law regards there to be something different about the relationships of legal note. But what is that? Cynics claim that by not allowing same-sex partners the title of marriage there is an implied message that they are not quite worthy of that title.

In **Wilkinson v Kitzinger** a lesbian couple sought the right to marry, and claimed that only being able to enter a civil partnership infringed their human rights. The application failed because Sir Mark Potter said that they could not point to an area of their private or family life where they were disadvantaged by being civil partners, rather than spouses. Their argument that society treated spouses and civil partners differently was rejected because there were no legal differences between the relationships and that was all the court could consider. If members of the public thought that civil partnership was lesser than marriage that was an error and was not the fault of the law. However, in response it might be said that the

[7]Notice here you have told the examiner what the judge decided, and then referred to criticisms of his reasoning.

fact that different names are used supports the view that the law regards same-sex and opposite sex relationships as different.[7]

In conclusion, there are differences between a civil partnership and a marriage, but they are few and rarely arise. For the vast majority of civil partners their legal rights will be exactly the same as if they were married. However, the tiny differences may be of symbolic value. They may indicate that civil partnerships are equal, but different. Given that there is so little legal difference it might be thought easier just to allow same-sex couples to marry. That would be politically controversial. But, attitudes towards same-sex couples are changing and it can only be a matter of time before two men or two women are allowed to marry.[8]

[8]This conclusion brings together the main points raised during the essay and points to the possible future of same-sex marriage.

✓ Make your answer stand out

- Include a detailed discussion of *Wilkinson* v *Kitzinger*. See Harding (2007) 'Sir Mark Potter and the Protection of the Traditional Family: Why Same Sex Marriage is (Still) a Feminist Issue' *Feminist Legal Studies* 223.
- Consider whether the current law is discriminatory on the grounds of sex or sexuality. There is an excellent discussion in Bamforth (2007) 'The benefits of marriage in all but name?' Same-sex couples and the Civil Partnership Act 2004' *Child and Family Law Quarterly* **19**, 133.
- You could note that under Human Fertilisation and Embryology Act 2008, section 42, although a husband will be a father, the female partner will be a parent, but not a mother.
- A key issue here is religious attitudes to marriage. There was relatively little opposition from religious groups to civil partnership because it did not use the word marriage. Discuss whether this is a good reason against allowing same-sex marriage.
- Note that some same-sex activists do not want the title marriage for their relationships, so that they can forge their own understanding of intimate relationships. Consider whether that is an argument against allowing same-sex marriage.

! Don't be tempted to...

- Get carried away with your own views on what the law should be.
- Make generalised comments about marriage and civil partnership being the same.
- Assume that all gay couples want to marry.

❓ Question 2

Alf and Sue married three months ago. At the reception Alf got drunk and fell off a podium. He suffered an injury which has meant he has been unable to have sexual intercourse since the marriage. During his medical examinations Alf's doctor discovers that Alf has an intersex condition. Sue has discovered that Alf fathered a son with his former girlfriend a few weeks before the marriage. This means that she does not fancy the idea of having sex with Alf, even if he gets better. Consider whether Alf or Sue can use nullity proceedings to bring the marriage to an end.

Answer plan

➜ Consider whether the parties are respectfully male and female.

➜ Is this a case of incapacity to consummate?

➜ Is this a case of wilful refusal to consummate?

➜ Is the fact Alf has fathered a child relevant?

➜ Are any of the bars applicable?

Diagram plan

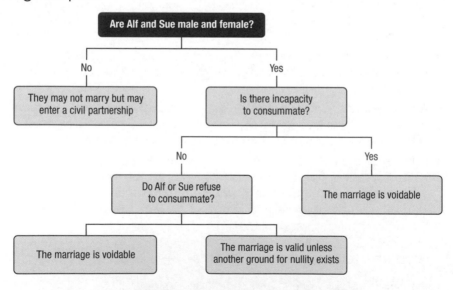

A printable version of this diagram is available from www.pearsoned.co.uk/lawexpressqa

Answer

[1]Start by setting out the key legal concepts that apply to the problem.

[2]It is best to start by considering if the marriage is void, before considering whether the marriage could be voidable because if the marriage is void it is irrelevant whether it is also voidable.

[3]Note the difference between an intersex person whose sex is ambiguous at birth and a transsexual person where it is said that at birth the physical characteristics all suggested one sex.

[4]Note that in the case of incapacity either the person suffering the incapacity or their spouse can rely on it as a ground for voidability. The examiner will want to see that you appreciate this difference.

There are two forms of nullity that may be relevant in relation to marriage. The first is a claim that the marriage is void. The grounds on which a marriage is void are set out in Matrimonial Causes Act 1973, section 11. The second is that a marriage is voidable. The grounds for these are found in section 12 Matrimonial Causes Act 1973.[1]

The only ground on which the marriage could be void is that the parties are not respectively male and female because Alf has been found to have an intersex condition.[2] The legal definition of sex was set down in **Corbett v Corbett** [1971] P 83. In that case it was held that a person's sex is determined at birth and depends on an assessment of the person's chromosomal, gonadal and genital tests. Once a person's sex is determined at birth it cannot be changed unless there is an order under the Gender Recognition Act 2004. The leading case on intersex is **W v W (Nullity)** [2000] 3 FCR 748. There Charles J accepted that if an individual's sex based on the Corbett test was uncertain then the court could also take into account psychological factors, hormonal factors and secondary sexual characteristics. It seems from his judgment that if a person suffers from an intersex condition it is likely that the law will accept whatever sex they have chosen to live in. So, in this case as long as Alf wishes to be regarded as male it is likely the courts will accept that as his legal sex in which case the marriage will not be void.[3]

There are several ways it could be claimed that the marriage is voidable. Either Sue or Alf could claim the marriage has not been consummated due to Alf's physical incapacity (s. 12(a) Matrimonial Causes Act 1973).[4] First, it would need to be shown that the marriage has not been consummated. It appears from the facts that it has not. It should be noted that an act of sexual intercourse can only be consummation if it occurs after the parties have married (**P v P** [1964] 3 All ER 919). So sexual activity before the marriage cannot be relied upon as consummation. Second, it needs to be shown that the non-consummation resulted from the incapacity of either party. It must also be shown if the incapacity is permanent and cannot be corrected by surgery (**Clarke v Clarke** [1943] 2 All ER 540). Medical evidence may be needed to establish whether this is so in Alf's case. There has been some debate whether the inability must exist at the time of the marriage. There is nothing in the

[5]The law on this is far from clear and so you could legitimately conclude that there is no need to show the inability existed at the time of the marriage.

Act which says so explicitly, but all of the other grounds on which a marriage must be voidable relate to facts that exist at the time of the marriage. So, that would suggest that is so for the inability to consummate marriage too.[5] However, in this case he did have the capacity to consummate at the time of the marriage. So this ground may not be relied upon.

Either Sue or Alf could claim the marriage has not been consummated due to Sue's psychological incapacity (Matrimonial Causes Act 1973, s. 12(a)). The courts have accepted that a party's 'invincible repugnance' can amount to an inability to consummate (**Singh v Singh** [1971] P 226). However, it will be difficult to establish this because there needs to be 'paralysis of the will' and not just a dislike of the partner (**G v G** [1924] AC 349). There will need to be evidence that Sue is unable to consummate, rather than that she does not like the idea of sex. It seems unlikely that this ground can be relied upon in this case unless Sue could produce evidence from a psychologist of the strength of her feelings.[6]

[6]You need to show the examiner that you are aware that the courts will nowadays be very reluctant to find a case of invincible repugnance. Otherwise it would be too easy to use this ground to escape from a marriage.

Although one of the grounds upon which a marriage can be voidable is that the wife was pregnant at the time of the marriage. There is no equivalent ground that a husband has fathered a child prior to the marriage. So Sue cannot rely on the fact that Alf fathered a child before the marriage.

[7]Many students forget to discuss the bars to nullity in essays on this topic, and so it is worth making sure that you do consider them.

If the parties are relying on one of the consummation grounds then consideration must be given as to whether one of the bars in section 13 of the Matrimonial Causes Act 1973 apply.[7] The most likely to apply is approbation. It would need to be shown that the respondent led the petitioner to believe that he would not seek to annul the marriage and that it would be unjust to the respondent to grant the decree nisi. There is no evidence that this occurred from the problem question.

In conclusion is seems unlikely that the marriage will be void or voidable. It seems likely that Alf will be regarded as male and that the court will not accept that there was non-consummation due to the inability of the parties. Either Sue or Alf could seek a divorce, but they can only apply once one year after the marriage has passed.

Make your answer stand out

- Discuss in detail the question of whether the incapacity has to exist at the time of consummation. There is a detailed discussion in Herring (2009b) *Older People in Law and Society*, Oxford: OUP.
- For a useful discussion on non-marriages and their legal status see Probert (2002) 'When are we married? Void, non-existent and presumed marriages' *Legal Studies* 398.
- You could go into more detail on the law on wilful refusal to consummate. Borkowski (2004) 'Wilful refusal to consummate: "Just excuse"' *Family Law* 684 provides a useful discussion.

! Don't be tempted to...

- Spend too much time on the 'red herring' issue of Alf's child.
- Assume that sex before the marriage can amount to consummation.
- Confuse intersex people (who are born with mixed sexual characteristics) and transsexual people (whose genital, gonadal and chromosomal factors at birth point in the same direction).

? Question 3

Mary and Paul decide to get married, but rather than doing so 'properly' they ask Paul's brother to read out the words from a Church marriage service in front of a group of friends in a field. Two years later Mary and Paul separate. Mary's mother tells her that she will not leave her any money in her will unless Mary marries Steven, a family friend. Mary is in severe financial difficulty and is terrified of becoming bankrupt. She therefore reluctantly goes through with a registry office marriage with Steven. Paul develops a severe mental illness after the end of his relationship with Mary. He announces he is due to marry Olive, but Mary is concerned that Paul does not really know what he is doing and she wants to stop the marriage.

Advise Mary, Paul and Steven.

Answer plan

→ Is the ceremony between Mary and Paul a marriage; a void marriage or a non-marriage?

→ Is the marriage between Mary and Steven void for bigamy or voidable for lack of consent?

→ What can Mary do to stop Paul marrying Olive?

Diagram plan

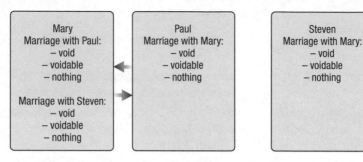

Mary	Paul	Steven
Marriage with Paul:	Marriage with Mary:	Marriage with Mary:
– void	– void	– void
– voidable	– voidable	– voidable
– nothing	– nothing	– nothing
Marriage with Steven:		
– void		
– voidable		
– nothing		

A printable version of this diagram is available from www.pearsoned.co.uk/lawexpressqa

Answer

[1]Where you have problem questions involving multiple marriages start with the earliest ones first.

[2]Most university courses do not require a detailed knowledge of the formality requirements, but check with your particular syllabus.

[3]Do not assume that because a marriage is not valid, there is nothing to discuss. The distinction between a void marriage and a non-marriage is important.

[4]Unless you have a very good memory you won't be able to remember a quote this long. But still remember the salient factors in your own words. You won't lose any marks if you cannot remember the exact words used.

The first issue to address is the legal status of Mary and Paul's marriage.[1] The marriage has failed to comply with the formalities for a valid marriage, as set out in the Marriage Act 1949.[2] These require the marriage to be undertaken by the registrar of births, marriages or deaths or according to the rites of particular churches or religious groups named in the Act. Here it is clear that Mary and Paul have not done this. Further, Mary and Paul, we can take it, knowingly and wilfully went through a ceremony which failed to comply with the formality requirements. Therefore, there can be little doubt that their marriage is not a valid marriage.

The question remains rather whether it is a void marriage or a nothing (or a non-marriage).[3] The issue is important because if the marriage is a void marriage the court still has the jurisdiction to make financial orders, whereas if the marriage is a non-marriage then no orders can be made. The leading cases on this issue are **Geris v Yagoub** [1997] 3 FCR 755 and **Hudson v Leigh (Status of Non-Marriage)** [2009] 3 FCR 401. In the latter case the following factors were listed as relevant to deciding whether or not the ceremony was a non-marriage: '(a) whether the ceremony or event set out or purported to be a lawful marriage; (b) whether it bore all or enough of the hallmarks of marriage; (c) whether the three key participants (most especially the officiating official) believed, intended and understood the ceremony as giving rise to the status of lawful marriage; and (d) the reasonable perceptions, understandings and beliefs of those in attendance.'[4] Applying those to the problem question it seems very likely that the court would conclude that this was a non-marriage. The ceremony was not in a religious building and it is hard to believe that those attending would have believed they were witnessing a lawful marriage between Mary and Paul.[5]

[5]Here consider all of the factors listed in *Hudson* v *Leigh* that appear relevant.

As it seems the ceremony between Mary and Paul was a non-marriage, it cannot be used to challenge the validity of the marriage between Mary and Steven on the basis that their marriage was bigamous.[6] However, Mary may claim that the marriage was void-able on the grounds that she did not validly consent (s. 12(d) Matrimonial Causes Act 1973). Her claim would be that the threats from her mother were such that she did not give effective consent to the marriage. In the past the law required there to be a threat of death or serious harm before the threat could negate consent to marry. However, since **Hirani v Hirani** (1982) 4 FLR 232 the Court of Appeal has recognised that any kind of threat can negate con-sent. What matters for the courts is not the kind of threat, but rather the impact of the threat (**P v R (Forced Marriage)** [2003] 1 FLR 661). That said, the courts will require evidence that the impact of the threats was such as to mean that the victim felt that they had no genuine choice, rather than that they merely feel pressurised. In this case, therefore, the judge would need to consider whether the pressures Mary felt had such an impact on her that she had no genuine choice. It is unclear whether that would be found in this case. If she did, Mary could seek to annul the marriage, assuming none of the bars are applicable. If she did not, Mary would have to consider whether or not she could prove one of the facts necessary to obtain a divorce. Although a divorce can only be applied for once a year of the marriage is over.[7]

[6]There is no point discussing bigamy in detail here because it is not relevant once we have decided that the ceremony between Mary and Paul was a non-marriage.

[7]Never forget that in cases where nullity proceedings are not available there is always the option for divorce. But you will want to make the point that divorce proceedings can only be commenced one year after the start of the marriage.

As to Paul's marriage to Olive, Mary has a number of options. She could seek an order under the Forced Marriage (Civil Protection) Act 2007. However, to obtain an order under that Act it would be nec-essary to show that Paul was in danger of being forced to enter a marriage without his full and free consent (s. 63A Family Law Act 1996). In this case although there may be questions over whether or not Paul is able to consent to the marriage, there is no sugges-tion that he is being forced into the marriage. In that case a forced marriage protection order cannot be made. If there was evidence of force then the court has a broard discretion under the Act to make orders necessary to protect those at risk, including an order prohib-iting a marriage.[8]

[8]There is not much more you can say about the act as there are no cases guiding us as to its interpretation.

She could also seek an order under the inherent jurisdiction or the Mental Capacity Act 2005 to prevent a person without capacity being married without their consent (**M v B** [2005] EWHC 1681). However, it would need to be shown that Paul lacked capacity to marry and the courts have not been strict about the degree of understanding that is required before a person is found to have capacity. In **Sheffield CC v E** [2004] EWHC 2808 (Fam) it was held that he understood the essential requirements of marriage: that the couple were to live together, be faithful to one another; and share a common life. Unless Paul's understanding has been greatly affected he may still have the capacity to understand that. Notably the courts have refused to prohibit a marriage simply in order to prevent what might be seen as a foolish marriage.[9] If the person lacks the capacity to marry the court can make orders that will protect their best interests. So, in this case unless the court is persuaded that Paul's mental illness has affected him to such an extent that he is unaware of the essence of a marriage it is unlikely an order under the Mental Capacity Act 2005 or the inherent jurisdiction preventing the marriage will be made.

[9]This means that the question is not whether the vulnerable person understands the character of the person they are marrying, but whether they understand the nature of marriage.

✓ Make your answer stand out

- Show a good knowledge of the case law on whether a marriage is a non-marriage or a void marriage.
- Discuss carefully the case law on when threats will negate consent. There is a helpful discussion in Bradney (1994) 'Duress, family law and the coherent legal system' *Modern Law Review* 499.
- Analyse the alternative jurisdictions that can be used when there is a person who is being compelled to enter a marriage. Anitha and Gill (2009) 'Coercion, Consent and the Forced Marriage Debate in the UK' *Feminist Legal Studies* 295 provides a useful discussion of the Marriage (Civil Protection) Act 2007.

! Don't be tempted to...

- Ignore the difference between a non-marriage and a void marriage. This is a crucial difference because a void marriage can still lead to financial orders being made, while a non-marriage cannot.
- Assume that whenever a person is under pressure they are not to be taken to give effective consent to marry.
- Forget the Marriage (Civil Protection) Act 2007. Examiners will expect students to be familiar with that legislation.

Question 4

What is the legal difference for a couple who are married or civil partners and a couple who are cohabiting?

Answer plan

→ Discuss the formation of the relationship.

→ Analyse the different issues that arise at the end of the relationship; financial responsibilities; inheritance.

→ What differences in taxation are there.

→ Domestic violence.

→ Set out the similarities in treatment for married and cohabiting couples.

Diagram plan

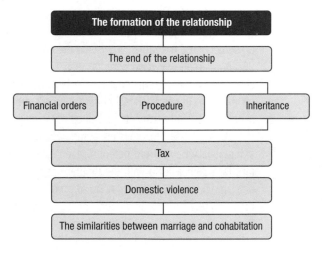

A printable version of this diagram is available from www.pearsoned.co.uk/lawexpressqa

Answer

It is commonly assumed that couples who have lived together for a while are treated as if they were married. That is wrong. Sometimes in newspapers there is talk of 'common law marriage', but that also is a fiction. The only marriages known to English law are those which comply with the formalities of marriage law. That said, as we

[1]Nor is there space in an exam to discuss all of the differences between married and unmarried couples and it is therefore sensible to focus on the major ones.

[2]This may seem an obvious point to make, but don't let that put you off making it. The examiner will want you to raise it because it is, in practice, very important.

[3]The examiner will be pleased to see you are aware of the practicalities of birth registration, as well as knowing the legal details.

[4]When explaining the differences between marriage and cohabitation the examiner will want to be sure you are aware which are particularly important and which are not.

shall see the differences between being married and unmarried are not as great as might be thought. In fact, most of the differences relate to the end of the relationship. There is not space to cover every difference in the legal treatment of married and unmarried couples, so the focus will be on the main ones.[1]

A fairly obvious difference relates to the start of the relationship. A marriage starts when a couple comply with the formalities required for a marriage. Cohabitation starts when the couple begin living together.[2] In fact, although we can be fairly confident whether there is a marriage or not (because it will be recorded in the register of marriages) there is no formal record of cohabitation. That means it can be open to dispute whether or not a couple have cohabited.

There is a difference between the children of cohabitants and married couples. A husband will automatically be presumed to be the father of any child born to his wife, and he will automatically be granted parental responsibility (s. 4 Children Act 1989). That is not so in the case of a cohabiting father. However, if a cohabiting father is registered on the child's birth certificate (as most are) he will be presumed to be the father and (since the Adoption and Children Act 2002) automatically have parental responsibility. So as long as the cohabiting father is registered on the birth certificate as the father he will be in the same position as a married father. However, if he is not on the birth certificate he will be at a significant disadvantage in that he will need to prove his paternity and even then he will not automatically be granted parental responsibility. As nowadays it is rare for a father living with the mother not to be registered on the birth certificate, the issue may be of greater significance in theory than practice.[3] It is worth noting at this point that at one time in the law there were significant differences between legitimate and illegitimate children (that is between children born in and out of wedlock). With a few very minor exceptions, there is no longer any distinction between children.

A significant difference arises between marriage and cohabitation if the relationship comes to an end.[4] Marriage can only be ended by a decree nisi of divorce issued by a court (Matrimonial Causes Act 1973); while cohabitation can be brought to an end by the parties simply going their own ways, although there may be significant paperwork involved if the couple have joint accounts, a joint mortgage or other bills. More significantly on divorce there is power in the courts to redistribute the property of the couple and to order significant periodical payments. While at the end of cohabitation the only orders available for partner support are declarations as to who owns the couple's home. On cohabitation the court can declare ownership, but cannot change it. For wealthy couples on divorce many millions of pounds can change hands (**Charman v Charman** [2007] EWCA Civ 503), while on cohabitation the most the court could do would be to order the sale of the house and division of the proceeds (**Stack v Dowden** [2007] UKHL 17). However, for the less well off, the differences between cohabitation and marriage will be much less marked. Once child support payments are made (which are made on the same basis whether the couple married or not); for many couples there is little other property available which the court could distribute.[5]

[5]It is important to emphasise that for less well-off couples, the ability of the courts to redistribute property may be of limited significance.

Death can mark another point at which marriage can be significant. If the deceased has left a will there is no difference between spouses and cohabitants. However, if the deceased has not left a will and the rules on intestacy apply a significant difference between spouses and non-spouses may arise. A spouse will automatically inherit all or most of the estate (the exact rules depend upon its size), while a cohabitant will not automatically inherit anything. All is not lost for the cohabitant who can still apply under the Inheritance (Provision for Family and Dependants) Act 1975. The court could grant them an award, but it is unlikely to be as much as a spouse would be awarded.[6]

[6]It is important to note this because it is a key difference between cohabitants and those who are married but is one that cohabitants can easily overcome if they make a will.

At one time the tax system granted significant advantages to married couples. There are still a few, although they mainly affect wealthier couples: inheritance tax exemption and capital gains tax exemptions. Currently there is little in the tax system to act as an incentive to encourage marriage, although the Conservative Party has stated that it will reward marriage in the tax system.

Rather surprisingly there is also a difference in relation to the protection from domestic violence. A wife will automatically be able to use section 33 of the Family Law Act 1996, which is the most advantageous section of the Act to use. A cohabitant can use section 33, but only if she can show that she has a property interest in the property. Otherwise she needs to rely on one of the other sections in the Act, when it is harder to persuade the court to make an order and there is a narrower range of orders available.

[7]The examiner will be looking out to see if you have noticed this point. Make sure you make this point prominently either in the conclusion (as we have) or the introduction.

Having discussed the main difference between married and unmarried couples, it is important to note that especially while the couple are happily together there is only a minimal legal difference between married and unmarried couples. The differences arise when the relationship comes to an end, be that through divorce or death. Even then it is only in the case of wealthier couples that any significant differences are experienced.[7]

 Make your answer stand out

- Refer to some of the cases dealing with property disputes between unmarried couples (e.g. *Stack* v *Dowden*) and show how the results are similar to the orders that would have been made had the couple been married. Contrast cases of wealthier couples (e.g. *Charman* v *Charman*) where the differences are dramatic.

- You could refer to the law in Australia, where when you have lived together for a certain time period you will be treated as married.

- Consider the Law Commission proposals regarding unmarried couples, where on separation they will be treated in a way which is more like married couples, but still not quite the same.

- This is a particular issue in practice in the area of state benefits where different levels are paid depending on whether a couple are cohabiting or not.

- You could also make the point that by signing a cohabitation contract the couple could even reduce that difference.

! Don't be tempted to...

- Suggest that for all couples financial orders on divorce are significant. Remember for most couples there is not enough money to meet child support payments, let alone orders for the adults.

- Believe in the 'common law myth' (that cohabiting couples are treated the same as married couples).

- Suggest that there is still a difference between 'legitimate' and 'illegitimate' children.

Question 5

Should couples of the same sex be allowed to marry?

Answer plan

→ What starting point should be used?

→ Is there a right to marry? Is the current law discriminatory?

→ Is civil partnership an adequate alternative?

→ How relevant are religious objections?

Diagram plan

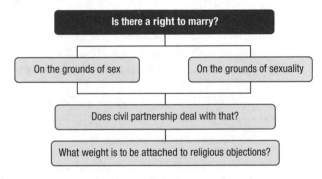

A printable version of this diagram is available from www.pearsoned.co.uk/lawexpressqa

Answer

[1] Referring to studies of public opinion will normally get extra marks.

The issue of gay marriage is a controversial one. Notably it is an idea that is gaining increasing acceptance among the British public, with over 50 per cent of the population supporting it in the most recent British Social Attitudes Survey.[1] Support is at a much higher level than that among younger age groups. Nicholas Bamforth (2007) has suggested that most countries go through a series of stages in relation to same-sex relationships. Most originate in systems in which same-sex activity is illegal. The first stage is the de-criminalisation of same-sex sexual activity. The second stage is that same-sex couples are in some circumstances given similar rights to married couples (e.g. in rent legislation). The third stage

[2]These observations from Bamforth (2007) are a useful way of presenting the background to the debate and referring to a leading academic on the subject adds weight to your answer and will get you more marks.

[3]This is an important question to pose early on because it sets out precisely what issues should be considered in the debate.

[4]In the exam you can refer to key thinkers in this way to save time.

[5]This is a useful comparison because the concept of discrimination should be the same in different contexts. It can therefore be helpful to ask whether the arguments used to justify discrimination in one context would work in analogous situations.

is that a status similar to but less than marriage (such as civil partnership) is created. The final stage is that same-sex couples are able to marry. If this is correct then England has entered the third stage, but not yet the fourth.[2] Several countries in Europe have now entered the fourth stage, while others are still at the second.

The starting point of a legal analysis is to ask how marriage is to be understood. Is marriage a status and does a couple need to show that they are 'good enough' to deserve the benefits and responsibilities of marriage? Or should marriage be regarded as a right, when there needs to be a good reason why a couple should not receive the benefits of marriage?[3] There are two reasons why it is probably correct these days to see marriage as a right. First, the right to marry is specifically referred to in article 12 of the European Convention on Human Rights. Second, the benefits provided by the state are now minimal and therefore it seems that the state cannot claim that marriage represents a status that is particularly deserving of policing. Further, it is worth noticing that there is no attempt to ensure that only suitable men and women get married (Freeman[4]). Even a child-abusing man or woman can marry! Given these points it is suggested that the burden should be on those seeking to exclude a couple that wishes to marry to provide a good reason why they should not be allowed to do so.

A strong argument can be made for suggesting that the current law is discriminatory. First, it is discriminatory on the basis of sex. A man cannot marry another man, but he could if he were a woman. That could be regarded as straight-forward sex discrimination. However, there is a ready response to that: whether a person is a man or a woman the rule is the same: you cannot marry a person of the same sex. That is true, but if we think of an analogous argument being used to support the argument that a law that forbade inter-racial marriage was not racist we would not be convinced by that.[5] Second, it can be claimed that the law is discriminatory on the grounds of sexual orientation. Sexual orientation is now accepted as a prohibited ground of discrimination under article 14 of the European Convention on Human Rights (**Da Silva Mouta v Portugal** [2001] 1 FCR 653). The law on marriage seems clearly to be discriminatory on the grounds of sex, but it might be replied that the right to marry means the right to marry in the way marriage has traditionally been understood (i.e. between a man and a woman).

It might be argued that any complaints of discrimination or unfairness are dealt with by the Civil Partnership Act 2004. That creates the status of civil partnership which same-sex couples can use. In **Wilkinson v Kitzinger** [2007] 1 FCR 183, Sir Mark Potter dismissed a claim from a lesbian couple that the fact they could not marry infringed their human rights, as civil partnership gave them the rights of marriage and, in effect, there was no difference in legal treatment which could found the basis of a discrimination claim. That argument is not completely convincing. The fact that the law gives the relationship a different name indicates that the law does not regard them as equivalent and that can be seen as giving credence to the belief that same-sex relationships are second best.

Perhaps the most common reason to give against same-sex marriage is that it will cause offence to those with conservative religious views (although it is worth noticing that there are plenty of religious people who would be willing to allow same-sex marriage and the Church of England is divided on the issue). The argument might go that marriage was traditionally a Christian concept in England. As civil partnership creates legal equality, without causing religious offence, should we not stick with that position? The difficulty is that we need to weigh up the offence caused to the religious people by allowing 'gay marriage' with the offence caused to a same-sex couple who are not permitted to marry. It is submitted that if one were to try to see whose offence is stronger, that for gay couples wishing to marry is great as it most directly affects their personal life. In any event our understanding of legal marriage has long departed from the religious sense. Perhaps the time has come to accept that legal marriage and religious marriage are two very different things.[6]

[6]There is no getting away from the religious issue because that does seem to be the main stumbling block preventing acceptance of same-sex marriage. Note that the Church of England is itself divided over whether same-sex couples should be allowed to marry. It certainly should not be assumed that all religious people object to same-sex marriage.

To conclude, civil partnership enables official recognition of same-sex relationships, without causing offence or disturbance. However, the Act, by refusing to allow same-sex couples the marriage title, sends a message that their relationship is different from marriage, which fuels discriminatory attitudes towards same-sex marriage. Now that a majority of people are willing to allow same-sex couples to marry the time is ripe for same-sex couples to marry. The arguments against are primarily based on religion, but the time is long past when religious marriage and legal marriage should be regarded as separate institutions.[7]

[7]It is important to come to a conclusion in an essay. Try not to end with a 'well it's all very difficult...' conclusion. If you are genuinely undecided tell the examiner why you find it difficult to reach a conclusion.

✓ Make your answer stand out

- Make use of the European Convention on Human Rights: articles 8, 12, 14. Bamforth (2007) 'The benefits of marriage in all but name?' Same-sex couples and the Civil Partnership Act 2004' *Child and Family Law Quarterly* **19**, 133.
- Carefully consider the question of whether marriage is a right or a status.
- Critically examine the arguments used in *Wilkinson* v *Kitzinger*. See Autchmuty (2008) 'What's so special about marriage? The impact of *Wilkinson* v *Kitzinger*' *Child and Family Law Quarterly* 479
- For an accessible summary of the case in favour of same-sex marriage see Freeman (1999) 'Not such a queer idea. Is there a case for same-sex marriage?' *Journal of Applied Philosophy* 1. For a leading article opposing same-sex marriage see Finnis (1994) 'Law, morality and "sexual orientation" *Notre Dame University Law Review* 1.

❗ Don't be tempted to...

- Get into a debate about religion.
- Get sidetracked into issues around cohabitation.
- Assume that article 12 gives people the right to marry whomever they choose.

Domestic violence

3

How this topic may come up in exams

This is a topic of enormous social importance. It is very likely that there will be an essay or problem question on domestic violence in a family law exam. Indeed, when you are writing about other family law topics domestic violence can be an important issue to bear in mind. For example, cases involving a dispute between parents over contact with a child often involve allegations of domestic violence. When you are revising domestic violence law remember the legal response falls into two categories:

- Civil law remedies (e.g. non-molestation orders; occupation orders).
- Criminal law responses (e.g. a prosecution for an assault).

You should keep both of these in mind. Running through all of the legal responses is a delicate balance between ensuring that the victim is protected, while at the same time showing due respect to the autonomy of the victim. All in all, this is a complex subject which the law has struggled to deal with.

■ Attack the question

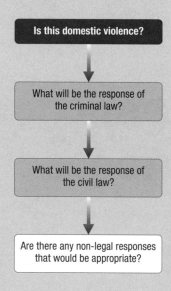

🔖 Question 1

Should the law adopt a pro-arrest or pro-prosecution policy towards domestic violence?

Answer plan

→ Explain in the opening paragraphs the meanings of the terms domestic violence, 'pro-arrest' and 'pro-prosecution'.

→ Set out the main policy arguments on either side of the debate. Emphasising the importance of protection of victims of domestic violence and their children on one side and respect for the views of the victim on the other.

→ Conclude, making sure you provide a clear answer to the question.

Diagram plan

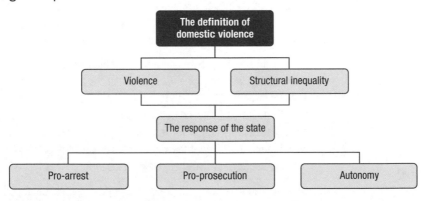

A printable version of this diagram is available from www.pearsoned.co.uk/lawexpressqa

[1] It is worth remembering a few statistics to use in family law essays. You need to show the examiner you know what the 'real world' is like; not just the cases that appear in the courts.

[2] It is always a good idea to try to explain the phrases used in the essay question before seeking to address the question.

Answer

Domestic violence is a major social problem. On average there is an incident of domestic violence reported to the police every minute of every day.[1] The term domestic violence does not have a settled definition.[2] The Government has defined domestic violence as 'Any incident of threatening behaviour, violence or abuse (psychological, physical, sexual, financial or emotional) between adults who are or have been intimate partners or family members, regardless of gender or sexuality.' However, not everyone will agree with that definition. It includes 'emotional' abuse, while some people believe

[3]It is good to refer to an academic author if you can. It shows the examiner you have read beyond the textbook.

[4]Often you can deal with explaining the terms used in the question in the opening paragraph, but there are several here and so you will need more than one paragraph.

[5]It is useful to state how domestic violence used to be dealt with in the past. This shows you understand the historical background and can explain how the law's approach has changed.

[6]You will have been directed to various articles in your reading and you can use the authors referred to there. It does not matter if you mention the academics here. It is most important that you demonstrate you have read a wide range of articles.

[7]It is good to have the arguments on both sides. Point out the weaknesses and strengths of arguments you put forward. Don't get so carried away in presenting your case that you only put the arguments in favour of your point of view. Your essay will be much stronger if you set out the arguments against your viewpoint and explain why you disagree with them.

domestic violence should be restricted to physical assaults. Madden Dempsey (2007)[3] argues that domestic violence in its strong sense should be restricted to cases where there is 'structural inequality' in the relationship (e.g. one party dominates the other). For the purposes of this essay the Home Office definition will be used.

The terms 'pro-arrest' and 'pro-prosecution' relate to how the criminal law responds to domestic violence.[4] By 'pro-arrest' is meant a policy that when the police arrive at the scene of a domestic violence incident they should arrest the perpetrator unless there is a very good reason not to. Historically the police have been rather reluctant to intervene in what were described as 'domestics'. Commonly victims of domestic violence were told by the police to use civil remedies.[5] However, the Government in its paper *Living without Fear*, has said that it wants the police to respond pro-actively to domestic violence. Her Majesty's Inspectorate of Constabulary recently confirmed that attitudes of the police towards domestic violence have been transformed. However, Burton (2008a), has argued in favour of a clear pro-arrest policy so that the approach of the police is clear.[6]

By 'pro-prosecution' is meant a policy which requires prosecution of domestic violence incidents, unless there is a good reason not to. The HM Inspectorate of the CPS found that all too often even where there is an arrest following domestic violence this does not result in a successful prosecution. Most significantly a pro-prosecution policy would mean that even if the victim did not want the prosecution to proceed the prosecution should take place.

One argument in favour of pro-arrest and pro-prosecution policies is that they can operate as a powerful deterrent against domestic violence. If a man knows that if he uses violence against his partner it is likely if the police are called that he will be arrested and prosecuted, this might deter him from using violence. However, against this it should be recalled that most incidents of domestic violence occur in the heat of an argument or when the abuser is drunk, and so the deterrent effect of the policy may be questioned.[7]

Another argument that is used in favour of the policies is that it will mean that the abuser will not have an incentive to threaten the victim into withdrawing the complaint from the police. If the police only arrest and prosecute with the victim's consent, this may encourage the abuser to use violence to persuade the victim not to proceed with the prosecution. With a pro-prosecution policy the prosecution will take place even though the victim withdraws their complaint. However, it may be argued that if the abuser is a violent man he will continue the abuse, whatever policy is used.

Perhaps the strongest argument in favour of the policy is the clear message that it sends to society that domestic violence is not acceptable and it is something society takes very seriously. This is appropriate because surveys among people indicate that there still seem to be people who regard domestic violence as acceptable, where, for example, a partner has been unfaithful. Madden Dempsey (2007) has argued that pro-prosecution policies can help combat sexism in society. It should also be remembered that there is substantial evidence that children who live in homes where there is domestic violence suffer in a wide variety of ways (see, for example, the research by Mullender (2005)). Even if the adult victim is happy for there not to be a prosecution, the state may still be justified in bringing the prosecution in order to protect the children.[8]

[8]The impact of domestic violence on children is often forgotten so it is worth emphasising.

The main argument against pro-arrest and pro-prosecution policies is that they ignore the victim's autonomy. The victim may be happy to remain in the relationship, despite the violence, and not want the state to intrude by prosecuting their partner. Indeed it has been said that aggressive pro-arrest and pro-prosecution policies infantilise victims, with the state claiming to know what is better for the victim than the victim themselves. Supporters of the policies claim that this overlooks the impact of domestic violence which can mean that the victim is not able to see what is best for themselves.[9] Choudhry and Herring (2006b)[10] have argued that often a victim who wishes to stay with an abuser has conflicting wishes: they want to stay in the relationship, but for the violence to stop. In such a case it is not obvious which of these wishes is paramount. Further, as already mentioned, it may be justified to infringe the victim's wishes in order to protect children within the household.

[9]Notice how again the essay is seeking to present both the strengths and weaknesses of the arguments.

[10]Referring to academic writers where possible assures the examiner that you are aware of the reading you have been asked to do.

[11]It is rarely the case on controversial issues that the arguments are all one way.

[12]Notice how this conclusion provides a clear answer. It also avoids taking an extreme position, but rather seeks to find a middle course. There is nothing wrong, however, in taking a more extreme position as long as you are able to consider the arguments on both sides and make a good case.

To conclude, there are good arguments on both sides of the debate.[11] It is submitted that where there has been serious violence then the state should adopt clear pro-arrest and pro-prosecution policies for three reasons: to send a clear message that domestic violence is unacceptable in our society; to protect children living in the home; and to protect other women from the abuser. Where, however, the violence is minor and does not involve 'actual bodily harm', or worse, then the victim should be entitled to have her views respected if she does not want a prosecution to take place.[12]

Make your answer stand out

■ Read Madden Dempsey (2007) 'Towards a feminist state: What does effective prosecution of domestic violence mean?' *Modern Law Review* **70**, 908 for a discussion of why the state should prosecute domestic violence.

■ Choudhry and Herring (Choudhry and Herring (2006b) 'Righting domestic violence' *International Journal of Law Policy and the Family* 1) argue that prosecution of domestic violence is required under the Human Rights Act 1998.

■ Discuss further the arguments over whether a pro-prosecution undermines the autonomy of victims of domestic violence (see Choudhry and Herring (2006b) for further discussion of this).

! **Don't be tempted to...**

■ Be very dogmatic and not see the arguments on both sides of a debate.

■ Assume that victims of domestic violence are making a free choice if they do not want prosecution.

❓ Question 2

Anne and Brian have been living together for six months in a house which is registered in Brian's name. Anne is a senior manager with a firm of accountants and has been paying most of the mortgage instalments. Brian is an unsuccessful poet. Brian finds it difficult to cope with Anne's professional success and he regularly loses his temper with her. He shouts at her and threatens violence. Anne has become terrified of him. Anne's daughter from a previous relationship, Lucy, lives with them. Her school reports that Lucy has been behaving oddly in recent weeks. One day Brian pushes Anne. She tells him to leave the flat. He refuses saying that the flat is his. Brian sees his son, Eli, from a previous relationship every weekend. He says if he leaves the flat he will have nowhere to live and that he will lose contact with Eli.

Advise Anne on what orders they may be able to obtain under the Family Law Act 1996.

Answer plan

→ Are Anne and Brian associated people? If so, can Anne get a non-molestation order?

→ What section of the Family Law Act can Anne use to get an occupation order? Consider sections 33 and 36.

→ Are the courts likely to make an occupation order? The balance of harm test needs discussion.

Diagram plan

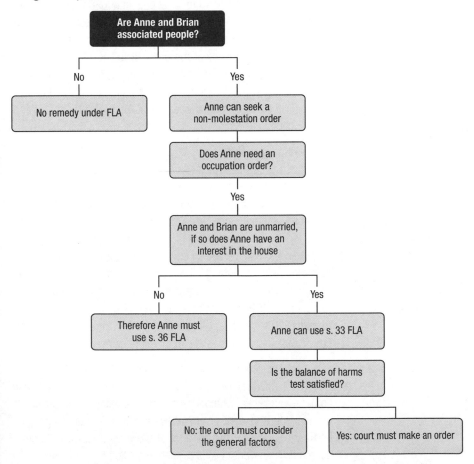

A printable version of this diagram is available from www.pearsoned.co.uk/lawexpressqa

[1]The question asks you specifically to consider the parties separately. As we will see there is no need simply to repeat points of law already made in relation to one party when they come up later in relation to another.

[2]You have been asked in the question *only* to consider the remedies under the FLA so do not be sidetracked into discussing other remedies that may be available.

[3]It is always a good idea to refer to the precise statutory provision.

[4]As this seems fairly clear, there is no point in going to greater detail on this.

[5]If you have been given the statute book in the exam there is no point writing out what it says, summarise the statute in your own words. The examiner will not give you much credit for just being able copy words from a book!

[6]Remember that under section 42 the court can specify particular acts which are to be prohibited by a non-molestation order. In family law problem questions you want to be practical and consider specifically what orders will be useful for the client.

[7]This is a problem question about domestic violence, not constructive trusts. So you don't (thank goodness) need to get bogged down in the detail of the law on trusts.

Answer

In this answer Anne's and Brian's claims will be considered separately.[1] Each might want to apply for a non-molestation order or an occupation order under the Family Law Act 1996. Remedies may also be available under the Protection from Harassment Act 1997 or the law of tort.[2]

Anne can apply for a non-molestation order as long as she and Brian are 'associated people'. This phrase is defined in section 62 of the Family Law Act 1996.[3] This list includes 'cohabitants and former cohabitants' and so there seems little doubt that Anne and Brian are associated.[4] Under section 42(5) the court will decide whether or not to make a non-molestation order after considering all the circumstances of the case, including the health, safety and well-being of Anne and the children.[5] Given the threats of violence and the push the court may well make a molestation order and specify that Brian must not assault Anne or threaten violence against her.[6]

Anne may also wish to apply for an occupation order against Brian. First, it is necessary to decide which section she will use. Section 33 can be relied upon by those who are married to the respondent or have a property interest in the house. We need to determine, therefore, whether Anne has a property interest. Although Anne is not a registered owner she has contributed to the mortgage payments, and so may be able to claim a constructive trust on the basis that she has contributed to the mortgage instalments to the property, from which the courts may infer a common intention to share ownership[7] (**Abbott v Abbott** [2007] UKPC 53; **Lloyds Bank v Rossett** [1991] AC 107).[8] It seems, therefore, that Anne has a property interest in the house and can therefore use section 33.

In considering Anne's application under section 33 of the Family Law Act 1996 the court will start by considering the 'significant harm test' in section 33(8). These require the court first to consider whether the applicant or any relevant child will suffer significant harm attributable to the conduct of the respondent if an order is not made. A relevant child is defined in section 62 as a child who is living with either party. That would suggest that Lucy, but not Eli, is a relevant child.[9] In **Chalmers v Johns** the Court of Appeal stated to amount to 'significant harm' there needed to be an exceptional

[8]Where you are using cases simply to refer to a legal proposition there is no need to state the facts of the case.

[9]The examiner will be impressed if you pick up on the precise definition of the statutory terms.

[10]It is useful to bring in here an example of what the court might regard as significant.

[11]You don't always have to reach a definitive conclusion.

[12]Keep referring back to the names of the parties. Avoid giving the impression you are just repeating your general notes on this topic.

[13]Again always good to think of practical issues.

[14]It is always good to have some cases to use to illustrate the way the courts exercise their discretion.

[15]It is important to emphasise here that if the significant harm test is satisfied the court has no option but to make the order.

[16]Don't make the mistake, as some judges have done, of thinking that because the significant harm test is not satisfied the court cannot make an order.

[17]As it is clear we are discussing the Family Law Act there is no need to keep repeating the name of the Act.

amount of harm. In that case having a long walk to school was not 'significant harm'.[10] Further in **Re Y** it was held that an occupation order was a 'draconian' order which should only be made as a last resort. The courts, it seems, have interpreted 'significant harm' at a high level. However, in this case we have not only an act of violence against Anne, but also, perhaps more significantly, evidence that Lucy is suffering harm due to the atmosphere at home. This seems to be a borderline case: it is hard to tell whether this is a case where 'significant harm' will be found. If there is evidence that Lucy will continue to suffer distress if the parties stay together it is submitted the court should find there is significant harm.[11]

If so the court must then consider whether the respondent (Brian)[12] or any relevant child will suffer significant harm if the order is made. As explained earlier Eli is not living with Anne and Brian and so would not be a relevant child for the purposes of this test. Brian will argue that if an order is made and he is required to move out this will cause him significant harm. The court will consider whether there is anywhere to live if he is ordered to leave the house, given he is an impoverished poet.[13] In **B v B** the Court of Appeal said it would be willing to make an order to remove a man from their home, even if they had no alternative accommodation; it said that in the context of a case where there was very serious violence.[14] In fact in that case, the interests of the man's child led to the court not making the order.

The court must then weigh up the significant harm that Alice or Lucy will suffer if an order is not made with the harm that Brian will suffer if the order is made. If it determines that the harm that Alice and Lucy will suffer is greater then the court *must* make an order (s. 33(7)).[15] If, however, the harm that Brian will suffer is as much or more than Alice or Lucy's harm the court has a discretion on whether or not to make an order (**Chalmers v Johns** 1999 2 FCR 110).[16] The court will consider the 'general factors' listed in section 33(6):[17]

- The housing needs and resources of the parties and relevant child.
- The financial resources of the parties.

51

■ The likely effect of making or not making an order on the health, safety or well-being of the parties and any relevant child.

■ The conduct of the parties.[18]

In this case the court will particularly pay attention to the fact that Anne has much more money than Brian and so may more easily be able to find alternative accommodation; the harm that Lucy will suffer if the order is not made; the effect on Brian if he loses contact with Eli; and the fact that Brian has used violence. If the court decides to make an order, as well it might, there is a range of possibilities listed in section 33(3). The possibilities range from removing Brian, or Anne, from the house; to dividing the house into two parts and letting each have half. This latter possibility might be an attractive option to the court if the house is big enough and it is convinced that doing so will adequately protect Anne.

In conclusion it seems very likely that Anne will be able to apply successfully for a non-molestation order. The order could specifically list some of the kinds of conduct which causes Anne to be fearful, or causes Lucy distress. The case for an occupation order is less clear cut. The court is likely to be particularly concerned about the impact of the violence on Lucy. If there is evidence that she will suffer serious harm without an order the court will make an order removing Brian from the house, or dividing the house into two parts so that Anne and Brian can live separate lives.

 Make your answer stand out

■ A really clear structure. Always be clear which order you are discussing and whose applications you are considering.
■ A good understanding of how the statutory test operates and an ability to apply it to the problem question.
■ Extra depth in knowledge of case law (e.g. refer to *Chalmers* v *Johns*, *B* v *B*).

! Don't be tempted to...

■ Add extra cases which make the same points as those you have chosen.
■ Assume facts which are not there and then answer the question based on these, e.g. asking what the position would be *if* Eli lived with the couple.

Question 3

How should lawyers define domestic violence?

Answer plan

→ Explain why lawyers need to define domestic violence.
→ Discuss what domestic means.
→ Consider the meaning of violence.
→ Is inequality in the relationship important?
→ Can women commit domestic violence?

Diagram plan

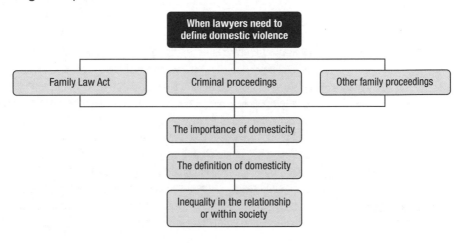

A printable version of this diagram is available from www.pearsoned.co.uk/lawexpressqa

Answer

Lawyers need to define domestic violence in a number of contexts. It has, in fact, proved a highly controversial issue. First, we will set out the circumstances in which the definition of domestic violence is important. Then we will consider the three central themes in the definition of domestic violence, building on the writing of Michelle Madden Dempsey: domesticity, violence and structural inequality. We will conclude by analysing the difficulties that arise in seeking a definition.[1]

[1]This introduction sets out clearly the way the question will be answered.

53

[2]It is helpful to put the issue in its historical context. The reasons why domestic violence is a difficult issue for the law is best understood if the history is appreciated.

[3]It is true that for a long time the police did not take domestic violence seriously, but there has been a significant change in police attitude in just the past few years.

[4]It is easy to pigeon hole domestic violence into just a topic that is relevant for essays on domestic violence. You will get credit for showing it is in fact relevant in a wide range of different family disputes.

[5]This article is well worth reading, and becoming familiar with, as it is very helpful in answering questions about how domestic violence should be defined.

Historically domestic violence was regarded as less important than other kinds of violence because it was seen as taking place in private and was therefore none of the law's business.[2] That is not an approach which is accepted today. There is legislation which provides specific civil law remedies for those suffering domestic violence (Family Law Act 1996). In the context of criminal law the police and Crown Prosecution Service have made investigation of domestic violence a priority.[3] Domestic violence can also play a role in other kinds of family proceedings, particularly contact disputes where the Court of Appeal in **Re L, V, M, and H** [2000] FCR 404 made it clear that the fact there had been violence in the relationship was a factor to take into account in determining a contact dispute.[4]

It is important for lawyers to have a clear picture about what domestic violence is for three main reasons. First, if we decide to have special policies under which the police or prosecution authorities are to respond to domestic violence (e.g. a pro-arrest or pro-prosecution policy) then we need to know what domestic violence is. Second, if there are to be civil remedies designed to deal with domestic violence, again we need to know who should have access to them. For example, in section 62 of the Family Law Act 1996 we have a list of 'associated people' who can apply for non-molestation orders. They are notably a wider category of people than those who would fall within Madden Dempsey's analysis (e.g. it includes relatives). Indeed Helen Reece has objected to the fact that the remedies for domestic violence are available to too broad a range of people. Third, if we are looking more broadly at the response of society to domestic violence and the range of legal and non-legal remedies that are available we need to know who is the 'target group'.

Michelle Madden Dempsey (2006) in a leading article on the definition of domestic violence has suggested three aspects which make up domestic violence.[5] First, there is domesticity. The argument is that if there is violence in a public place it is different from when it takes place in a person's home. If the violence is entirely in public places then this is dealt with by stalking legislation (Protection from Harassment Act 1997). Why should this be so? One argument is that if the violence is in a domestic setting it indicates that there is a close relationship between the parties because they are living together. This makes the violence more serious because it is not as easy to escape from. Further, the emotional attachment to the abuser may mean the victim does not want to leave the relationship

[6]It is good to show awareness of the practical issues in this area.

[7]This is a useful case to know about. The victim suffered emotional and psychological abuse, but it seems there was no physical violence. However she was reduced to an 'emotional wreck' and eventually killed herself. At her husband's trial he was acquitted of manslaughter as the court could not find a criminal offence he had committed.

[8]Notice here how the examiner is reminded of the basic structure of the essay and is helped to see how the argument is developing.

even if it is a violent one. It also means that the victim is going to find it harder to prove that violence has taken place.[6]

Second, there is the question of violence. It might be thought that domestic violence only includes cases where there is an assault or crime of violence of some kind. However, some social scientists think it is necessary to include not just violence, but also emotional, financial or psychological abuse within the definition. Madden Dempsey (2006) suggests that we should distinguish between domestic violence and domestic abuse to mark the distinction between cases which involve physical harm and other forms of harmful conduct. However, some commentators are not happy with making such a distinction. They point out that emotional and psychological abuse can be just as harmful as domestic violence (see Schneider (1994)). A person could be held as a prisoner in their house, purely by virtue of psychological and emotional abuse (see **R v Dhaliwal**, where this seems to have occurred, leading eventually to the victim's tragic suicide).[7] Those who wish to emphasise the importance of the distinction, however, argue that once we depart from violence, the concepts of emotional abuse are so slippery we are in danger of depriving domestic violence of a concrete meaning. Perhaps there is, therefore, wisdom in Madden Demspey's distinction between domestic violence and domestic abuse which recognises that both are serious, while maintaining a distinction between them.

The third aspect of domestic violence on this model is the notion of 'structural inequality' within the relationship.[8] This refers not only to the inequality within the relationship, but also to the wider inequalities within society. So a relationship where the person being violent is generally in a much more powerful position than the other, both in terms of the relationship and in terms of the broader society, is one where there is a particularly strong form of domestic violence. This might suggest that if a violent act is committed by the weaker party in the relationship it may not be domestic violence or at least not domestic violence in the normal sense. This factor might enable us to distinguish between a woman who hits out at a man who is generally dominating and a man who hits a woman whom he generally dominates. Both incidents might occur in a domestic setting and involve violence but the broader context will shape our description of the acts.

It is not possible to produce a single definition of domestic violence. The intersection of violence, domesticity and structural inequality within the relationship are the hallmarks of domestic violence in its strongest sense. However, there may be cases where there is an intersection of domesticity and structural inequality which may be regarded as sufficiently serious to count as domestic abuse in a weaker sense.

 Make your answer stand out

■ Be as precise as possible in your definitions.

■ Be aware of the different legal situations where a definition would be useful.

■ Read Madden Dempsey (2006) 'What Counts as Domestic Violence? A Conceptual Analysis' *William and Mary Journal of Women and the Law* **12(2)**, 301.

■ Note the concerns raised by Reece if domestic violence is defined too widely: Helen Reece (2006) 'The End of Domestic Violence' *Modern Law Review* **69**, 770.

! **Don't be tempted to...**

■ Think there is a single correct answer as to defining domestic violence: there is a range of factors that must be considered.

■ Ignore the importance for lawyers of this question.

Question 4

How might an approach based on the European Convention on Human Rights affect the law's response to domestic violence?

Answer plan

→ Discuss the significance of article 2 (the right to life).

→ Assess the significance of article 3 (the right to protection from torture and inhuman or degrading treatment).

→ Debate the relevance of article 8 (the right to respect for private and family life). Note both the victim and perpetrator may seek to rely on this right.

→ Can a claim of discrimination be made under article 14?

→ The impact of a rights-based approach to criminal law.

→ The impact of a rights-based approach to civil law.

Diagram plan

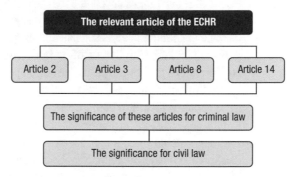

A printable version of this diagram is available from www.pearsoned.co.uk/lawexpressqa

Answer

This essay will examine the potential relevance of the European Convention on Human Rights to legal issues around domestic violence. It will look at the potential relevance of four key articles and then consider in practical terms how those discussions would affect the law. Human rights in this area have been used in the past to restrict the law's application, by emphasising the right to private life of the parties. However, it will be argued in this essay that human rights in fact require the law to intervene to protect victims of domestic violence.[1]

[1]Here the introduction sets out clearly how the question is going to be tackled.

Article 2 requires the state to protect citizens' right to life and article 3 protects the right to protection from torture or inhuman or degrading treatment. Inhuman treatment in article 3 includes actual bodily harm or intense mental suffering (**Ireland v UK** (1978) 2 EHRR 25). Degrading treatment includes conduct which humiliates, debases or diminishes dignity (**Valasinas v Lithuania** (2001) 12 BHRC 266). In deciding whether conduct is degrading the intention of the abuser and the effect of the conduct on the victim can be taken into account (**Price v UK** (1988) 55 D & R 198).[2] With both articles 2 and 3 the state is required to ensure that not only do the state or state officers not kill or torture citizens, but that citizens' rights under those articles are not infringed by other people (**A v UK** [1998] 3 FCR 597). This is clearly significant in the context of cases of domestic violence. Many cases of domestic violence will involve conduct which is captured by article 3 and, in particularly serious

[2]Notice that the definition of torture and inhuman or degrading treatment is broader than just physical harm.

cases, article 2 will be involved. Under the case law developed by the European and national courts if the state is aware that an individual's rights under articles 2 or 3 are in danger of being breached then the state must take reasonable and effective action (**Z v UK** [2001] 2 FCR 246; **Van Colle v CC of Hertfordshire** [2008] UKHL 50). These obligations are particularly strong in cases where the victim is vulnerable: i.e. they are a child or a victim of domestic violence (**Opuz v Turkey** [2009] ECHR 33401). This does not mean that the state must protect all victims of serious domestic violence.[3] First, the state only has an obligation in cases where the state is aware of the danger to individuals. Second, the state only has an obligation to take reasonable measures. That said, one might think it rare that it would be reasonable to do nothing in a case where it was known a victim was suffering domestic violence. It should also be noted that article 3 is an absolute right and so its breach cannot be justified by references to other rights or interests.

[3]Be careful not to exaggerate the obligations under articles 2 and 3.

Article 8 protects the right to respect for private and family life. This includes physical and psychological integrity (**Pretty v UK** (2002) 12 EHRC 149). If, therefore a case of domestic abuse was not sufficiently serious to raise article 3 issues, it will nevertheless involve article 8. Like articles 2 and 3 the obligation on the state extends to protecting an individual from infringements of their article 8 rights by other people. However, unlike articles 2 and 3, an interference of an article 8 right can be justified. Article 8 paragraph 2 explains that an interference can be justified if necessary, for example, to protect the rights of others.[4] This might suggest that although a victim of domestic violence might seek to rely on article 8 in order to obtain protection from violence, a state may be justified in not interfering by referring to the property rights of the abuser. Choudhry and Herring (2006a), however, have argued that in cases of domestic violence where there is a clash between the rights of the abuser and the victim, the victim's rights should win out.[5] This is because they argue that an abuser can be said to forfeit their property rights if they are using them to carry out abuse, or that in comparing the importance to the individuals of the rights involved, the rights of the victim of abuse should carry more weight.

[4]Never forget that article 8 is not an absolute right and whenever you discuss it you need to consider whether a breach can be justified.

[5]It is good to refer to academic articles where possible.

Article 14 protects individuals from discrimination in respect of their convention rights. This might be relevant if it were accepted that the failure to tackle domestic violence impacted disproportionately on

[6]Remember with
discrimination that
discrimination can be
justified, but only if there
is very good objective
justification. It is extremely
rare for sex discrimination to
be justified.

[6]Remember with
discrimination that
discrimination can be
justified, but only if there
is very good objective
justification. It is extremely
rare for sex discrimination to
be justified.

women. It seems from the statistics that women are far more often
the victims of domestic violence than men. A failure by the state to
offer adequate protection from domestic violence is, therefore, likely
to particularly harm women. This could be said to amount to sex
discrimination.[6]

Turning now to analyse the application of the points just made and
thinking first about the response of the criminal law. Where the police
are aware that a victim is suffering domestic violence then they have
a duty to take reasonable steps to protect the victim under articles 2
or 3 in especially grave cases and under article 8 in less grave cases.
The police must take reasonable steps to protect the victim. This will
nearly always mean that arrest is appropriate and often prosecution.
This may be so even if the victim does not want an arrest or prosecution because under articles 2 and 3 a breach of the obligation to
protect cannot be justified, even by the wishes of the victim. In **Opuz
v Turkey** the applicant repeatedly told the police that she and her
mother were being abused by her husband, and then later withdrew
the complaint. The police failed to investigate adequately or prosecute
the case.[7] It was held that they had breached their obligations to the
women under articles 2 and 3 after the mother was killed and the
woman seriously injured by the man. Interestingly the court thought
the fact that the allegations were withdrawn should have alerted the
police to the fact that there may have been threats from the man and
that therefore it was a particularly serious case.[8]

[7]This is a really important
case on this topic and is
worth knowing well.

[8]This is interesting because
it might be thought that if
the victim does not want the
police to intervene they do not
have to. This case alerts the
state authorities to the fact
that withdrawal of complaints
or requests not to assist might
well indicate that the victim is
under further pressure.

In relation to occupation orders a similar point can be made. If the
level of violence is sufficiently serious to involve articles 2 or 3 then
an occupation order will nearly always be appropriate, indeed it may
be required if necessary to protect the victim. Even in cases where
the harm is less grave, it may still be argued that the rights of the
victim should trump those of the abuser and so the state should
have an obligation to take reasonable steps to protect the victim
(Choudhry and Herring (2006a)). That will often involve making an
occupation order. It should also be born in mind that domestic violence often harms children, even if they are not directly involved. So
any rights of the adults may be justifiably infringed if necessary to
protect the interests of children.[9] It might also be argued that the
state has an interest in combating domestic violence as part of the
campaign to achieve gender equality. So the interests of the state
may outweigh any of the abuser (see Madden Dempsey (2009)).

[9]Don't forget the interests
of children when discussing
issues around domestic
violence.

This essay has shown that the advent of the Human Rights Act 1998 means that the state now has obligations to protect victims of domestic violence. No longer can these 'domestics' be regarded as private business. Indeed the state is in many cases obliged to take reasonable steps to protect victims.

 Make your answer stand out

■ Choudhry and Herring (2006a) 'Domestic Violence and the Human Rights Act 1998: A New Means of Legal Intervention' *Public Law* 752 is a very helpful discussion of the issues in this essay.

■ Read *Opuz* v *Turkey* [2009] ECHR 33401 to acquire a good understanding of how the European Court on Human Rights tackles domestic violence cases.

! Don't be tempted to...

■ Exaggerate the obligations imposed on the state under the European Convention. Note the obligation only arises where the state is aware or ought to be aware of the violence and it would be reasonable to intervene.

■ Assume that article 8 is an unqualified right which cannot be justifiably infringed.

❓ Question 5

Francesca met Tom at a night club and they went out together for a couple of weeks. Since she ended the relationship Tom has sent Francesca several texts and gifts. She has also seen him loitering on the street outside her flat. She has become concerned that he is becoming obsessed with her. This has made her ill and she has missed several weeks of work. She is also worried about her flatmate, Toya, who suffers from a mental illness and says she hears voices. Toya once called Francesca a devil and threw a book at her. Discuss the orders that a court could make.

Answer plan

➜ Can Francesca obtain a non-molestation injunction against Tom?

➜ Can Francesca get an order under the Protection from Harassment Act 1997 against Tom?

➜ Can Francesca get an order against Toya?

Diagram plan

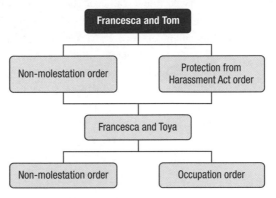

A printable version of this diagram is available from www.pearsoned.co.uk/lawexpressqa

Answer

[1]Always remember to discuss all the sources of remedies.

[2]Refer to the statutory source of definitions where appropriate.

First, we will consider the remedies that Francesca might claim against Tom. She could either seek a non-molestation order under the Family Law Act 1996 or seek an order under the Protection from Harassment Act 1997.[1]

In order to obtain a non-molestation injunction Francesca will need to show that she is an associated person in respect to Tom as defined in section 62 Family Law Act 1996.[2] As they are not cohabiting, she will have to claim that they fall under the category of having had an intimate personal relationship with each other which is or was of a significant duration. The court would need to determine whether they had an intimate personal relationship. We are yet to have any case law on this category but it is likely to require some kind of sexual relationship. The difficulty in her case is whether a relationship of a few weeks is of 'significant duration'. District Judge Hill has suggested that a relationship of several years would be. That must be right, but a relationship of several weeks may not be sufficient to be of significant duration. Perhaps Francesca's best argument is to rely on **G v F (Non-Molestation Order: Jurisdiction)** [2000] 2 FCR 36 where Wall J suggested that if it was unclear whether the relationships fell within the list of an associated person it should be treated as if it did. Indeed he suggested that unless it was clear that a couple were not associated

[3] It is difficult to say very much about when the court will make a non-molestation order: it is left to a court as a matter of discretion. What you can do is to state the basic principle the court will apply and list some of the factors the courts will consider.

[4] This is an important point so show the examiner that you are aware that a single act of harassing conduct, however bad, cannot infringe section 1 of the Act.

[5] Always discuss the possible defences to the wrong in section 3. The most significant is the defence that the defendant was acting reasonably.

[6] Don't forget the availability of damages under the Protection from Harassment Act 1997. That can make the Act more attractive than the Family Law Act 1996.

[7] Here you are highlighting that you know that a breach of section 1 of the 1997 Act can amount to both a civil wrong and a criminal offence. This will impress the examiner.

[8] They are not cohabitants unless they are living together as spouses or civil partners.

it would be presumed that they were. If this approach is followed then Francesca and Tom could be associated persons and a non-molestation order could be made against Tom under section 42(5) of the Family Law Act 1996. The court would need to consider whether it should make an order having regard to all the circumstances, 'including the need the secure the health, safety and wellbeing of the applicant...' There is little to guide the courts here, but if the court thought that the order would protect Francesca from further molestation it is likely to make the order.[3] The terms of the order could refer to specific kinds of molesting order such as sending her unwanted texts (s. 42(6) Family Law Act 1996).

An alternative remedy for Francesca would be under the Protection from Harassment Act 1997. There is no need to show that the parties are associated in order to obtain a remedy under this Act. It therefore may prove a better option for Francesca. She would need to show that Tom had pursued a course of conduct against her which amounted to harassment and which he knew or ought to know amounted to harassment (s. 1 Protection from Harassment Act 1997). A course of conduct involves conduct on at least two occasions.[4] Here the sending of texts and presents involve at least two pieces of conduct, but are they harassing? If the court thought that the presents and texts were a normal part of 'courtship' then they may not amount to harassment (**R v King**). However, if the number sent went beyond 'reasonable behaviour' (s. 3(3) Protection from Harassment Act 1997)) then it could fall within the scope of the Act (**R v King** 20 June 2000).[5] If it is shown that the behaviour was harassing and that Tom ought to have known that, the court can make an order prohibiting further conduct. Further under section 3(2) damages can be awarded for any financial loss or psychological harm (**Singh v Bhakar** [2006] FL 1026).[6] Francesca has lost income from work and so an award might well be made. A breach of the Act can also amount to a criminal offence and Francesca could inform the police and ask for a prosecution to be brought.[7]

Considering next the position of Francesca and Toya. Francesca has a good case for arguing that they are associated people for the purposes of the Family Law Act 1996, section 62. Included within the list of associated people are those who live 'in the same household, otherwise than merely by reason of one of them being the other's employee, tenant, lodger or boarder'.[8] If they are flatmates that would suggest that they are both tenants and one is not a tenant of the other. If might be different if either of them owns the property and is letting it to the other. In that case they may not be associated people and the 1997 Protection from Harassment Act would need to be used. In the case of the Family Law Act 1996 an order is likely to be available if the court thinks it will offer protection. It seems from **G v G** [2000] 2 FLR 36 that an order can be made even if the conduct is unintentional. So the fact that conduct may be the result of a mental illness will not stop the court making an order.[9] There may, however, be a problem if the Protection from Harassment Act 1997 is relied upon because it seems there is only one piece of conduct and so there is no course of conduct. Therefore no orders can be made under that Act. A non-molestation order cannot be used to remove Toya from the flat. For that Francesca will need an occupation order.

[9]This is a good point to make because it shows the examiner that you realise that domestic violence is about protection from abuse, rather than punishment.

An occupation order could also be sought to remove Toya from the flat. Assuming Francesca is entitled to occupy the flat by virtue of a lease she can rely on section 33 of the Protection from Harassment Act 1997. The court would need to consider the significant harm test under section 33. If the court were persuaded that the harm Francesca would suffer if an order was not made was greater than the harm Toya would suffer if the order was made then the court must make an occupation order. The problem for Francesca is that if Toya is regarded as a vulnerable person it may be decided that removing her from the flat will cause her more harm than it would to remove Francesca from the flat. Although the conduct of the parties is one factor to consider under section 33(6) it is not the only factor and Toya's needs may be such that a court will not want to remove her from the house. In any event the court will consider how soon any lease is coming to an end and if Francesca will not have to wait long until the lease ends they may be reluctant to make an order. It should be added that **G v G** makes it clear that there is no need to show that any conduct was intentional and so Toya's conduct can be taken into account, even though it is unintentional.

All in all, it seems likely that a court will be willing to make an order against Tom under the Protection from Harassment Act 1997 and this could include a claim for damages. The court may well be willing to make a non-molestation order against Toya, but an occupation order is unlikely.

Make your answer stand out

- Consider the Protection from Harassment Act 1997 as well as the Family Law Act 1996.
- Explain the differences between the remedies that the different orders have.
- Remember the financial orders that can be made under the Protection from Harassment Act 1997.
- Go into more detail about how the significant harm test in section 33 of the Protection from Harassment Act 1997 works.

! Don't be tempted to...

- Assume that conduct is the key factor in occupation order cases. It is the harm the parties may suffer which is important.
- Make general statements about when the orders are available, without applying them to the facts of the problem question.

Divorce and dissolution

4

How this topic may come up in exams

This topic can come up as either an essay question or a problem question. Fortunately the law on divorce and dissolution of civil partnerships is virtually the same, except for the fact that adultery is not a fact upon which a petition for dissolution can be based. So watch out for that difference.

Problem questions are likely to require a good knowledge of the case law defining the different facts of divorce or dissolution. Essay questions often focus on reform. You need to be aware of the problems with the current law. It is also important to know of the proposed reforms in the Family Law Act 1996, which were never implemented. What those reforms were and why they failed can provide some useful tools to discuss the role of divorce law and how any reform might operate.

Don't forget to emphasise that this is an area where divorce law 'on the books' is rather different from divorce law 'in the real world'. The Special Procedure means that if a divorce is undefended it faces minimal judicial scrutiny. The days of lengthy court hearings requiring proof of adultery are long gone.

■ Attack the question

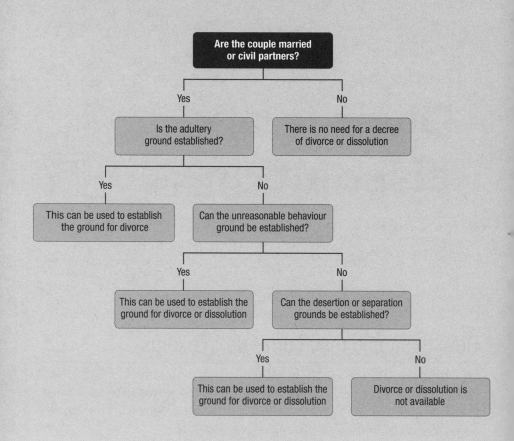

❓ Question 1

Tricia and Simon have been married for just eight months. Tricia has discovered that Simon has been seeing a former girlfriend, Ulrika. She had been willing to overlook this, but she feels he has not been attentive enough to her. She describes him as 'emotionally cold, distant and rather geekish'. They still live together, but Tricia now wants a divorce. Advise her on whether in law she is entitled to one.

Answer plan

→ Discuss when a petition for divorce can be presented.

→ Set out the ground for divorce.

→ Explain the facts that need to be proved to establish the ground for divorce.

→ Consider whether Tricia can rely on the adultery fact.

→ Can Tricia use the fact of unreasonable behaviour?

→ Explore the possibility of relying on the two- or five-year separation ground.

Diagram plan

A printable version of this diagram is available from www.pearsoned.co.uk/lawexpressqa

Answer

[1] Remember always to apply the legal principle to the facts of the problem you are dealing with.

A divorce petition can only be presented one year from the date of the marriage (s. 3(1) Matrimonial Causes Act 1973) and so Tricia is going to need to wait an extra three months before starting proceedings.[1] It is possible to seek an annulment of a marriage at any time, but there is no evidence in this case that the grounds for annulment are made out.

[2]There is normally no need to learn bits of statute off by heart, but it is worth learning this one.

[3]It is useful to set out clearly in any problem question on divorce how the ground for divorce must be shown.

[4]Again, keep statements about the law focused on the facts of the case.

[5]A common error students make is to say that adultery is the ground for divorce. Don't make that mistake.

[6]This situation of a cold spouse is a common one in divorce problem questions and so it is worth knowing the case law. Notice that the answer uses two contrasting cases to demonstrate the legal issues raised.

The ground for divorce is 'that the marriage has broken down irretrievably'.[2] That ground can only be proved if the petitioner is able to satisfy one of the five 'facts'. It was emphasised in **Buffery v Buffery** [1988] FCR 465 it is not enough just to show the marriage has broken down irretrievably, one of the facts must be shown. Once one of the facts are shown the courts should grant a decree unless it is persuaded that 'on all the evidence' the marriage has not broken down irretrievably.[3]

So which fact might Tricia rely on? Should she claim that 'the respondent [Simon] has committed adultery and the petitioner [Tricia] finds it intolerable to live with the respondent'.[4] She will have difficulties in proving this. Adultery in the law is limited to sexual intercourse between a spouse and someone to whom they are not married. So Tricia would need to show that Simon has had sexual intercourse with Ulrika, merely 'seeing her' would not be enough to amount to adultery, nor even sexual activity short of sexual intercourse. Even if she could show that adultery had taken place she would need to show she finds it intolerable to live with Simon.[5] As the Court of Appeal in **Cleary v Cleary** [1974] 1 All ER 498 has made clear it is not necessary to show that she finds it intolerable to live with him because of the adultery. In **Roper v Roper** [1972] 1 WLR 1314 it was even suggested that if a husband had committed adultery a wife could divorce him even if the reason she found it intolerable to live with him was because of the way he blew his nose. So, perhaps the courts would accept the rather vague objections that Tricia has. However, the fact that she is still living with him will be a major obstacle.

Tricia may seek alternatives to rely on the ground that 'the respondent [Simon] has behaved in such a way that the petitioner [Tricia] cannot reasonably be expected to live with the respondent'. She will face several difficulties. One is that her objections seem primarily to concern things he does not do, rather than positive acts of behaviour. In **Katz v Katz** [1972] 3 All ER 219 the Court of Appeal held that behaviour had to be more than a state of affairs and needed to be conduct. In **Smith v Smith** [1975] 2 All ER 19, it was suggested that a comatose spouse could not be divorced because they would not be behaving. So it seems that Tricia is going to have to point to positive acts from Simon, rather than simply his failure to display affection.[6] Tricia will also need to show that Simon's behaviour has meant it is not reasonable to expect him to live with her. In **O'Neill v O'Neill** [1975] 3 All ER 289 the Court of Appeal has explained that the test is objective, not subjective. This means that it is not a matter of whether Tricia thinks she can reasonably live with Simon, but rather whether a reasonable person thinks that Tricia could reasonably be expected to live with him. The fact that they are still living together would probably indicate that she could be expected to live with him, but there have been cases where the courts have accepted that the ground is made out, even though the parties are still living in the same house (**Bradley v Bradley** [1973] 3 All ER 750), but these tend to be cases where the parties have nowhere else to live.[7]

[7]Here we have a position where the case law does not give a clear answer and so you need to set out the law we do know and make a sensible prediction as to how the law may develop.

If Tricia is not able to rely on the adultery or behaviour fact then she will have to rely on the two- or five-year separation fact. She will, however, need to have lived separately from Simon for two years (if he consents to the granting of the petition) or five years, if he does not.

[8]Sometimes the problem question does not include all the facts and your answer must deal with alternative possibilities. So in this answer we have considered both the position if Simon opposes the petition and if he does not.

This answer has assumed that Simon is going to defend the petition. If he is happy for the divorce to go ahead and does not defend it, then under the special procedure there will be no need for the facts of the petition to be proved and Tricia is likely to obtain the divorce without difficulty.[8]

 Make your answer stand out

- Use plenty of examples of unreasonable behaviour from the case law. A good discussion of the case law can be found in Harris-Short and Miles (2007) *Family Law* ch. 5, Oxford: OUP.
- Discuss in more detail the special procedure that can be used if the petition is not defended.
- Analyse in more detail the court's approach to living apart. See Lowe and Douglas (2006) *Family Law* 271–2, Oxford: OUP.

> ## ! Don't be tempted to...
>
> ■ Confuse the facts and grounds of divorce. So, saying 'adultery is a ground for divorce' is inaccurate. Irretrievable breakdown is the ground for divorce, and the adultery fact is a fact which can prove the ground for divorce.
>
> ■ Over-simplify the facts of divorce. Students sometimes talk about 'adultery' being a fact, whereas intolerability must also be shown. It is all right to talk about the 'adultery fact' as a shorthand, as long as you make it clear in your answer that there is more to this than just adultery.

◤ Question 2

What, if anything, is wrong with the current law on divorce?

Answer plan

→ Use the Law Commission Report's summary of the problems with the current law.

→ Discuss whether the law on divorce is confusing.

→ Consider whether the facts for proving divorce are discriminatory.

→ Some say the current law distorts bargaining positions. Is that a fair complaint?

→ Does the current law create unnecessary hostility?

→ Explore whether the current law does enough to save marriages.

→ Would it be fair to say the current law makes things worse for the children?

Diagram plan

A printable version of this diagram is available from www.pearsoned.co.uk/lawexpressqa

Answer

In this essay we shall use the analysis of the Law Commission Report 192 as the basis for our discussion.[1] It provides a thorough review of the current law and lists what are generally agreed to be main criticisms of the current law. Despite the difficulties with the law highlighted in that report the attempt to reform the law in the 1996 Family Law Act failed, in that it was never implemented. It seems following this the appetite for reform is limited.

First, there is the claim that the current law is confusing and misleading. There is a variety of ways in which this objection can be made. It may be suggested that it is difficult for people to understand that although the ground for divorce is 'irretrievable breakdown' (s. 1 Matrimonial Causes Act 1973), that can only be proved by one of the five facts. Indeed you can get the odd position that a couple can show their marriage has irretrievably broken down but because they cannot show the existence of one of the facts (**Buffery v Buffery** [1988] FCR 465). Another concern is that because the parties can only list one of the five factors, the parties may be required to rely on a matter which in fact did not really cause the breakdown. For example, the petition may rest on the fact of the husband's adultery, but the real cause of the breakdown may be that the parties have fallen out of love. Yet another potential source of confusion is the fact that although the statute appears to suggest that the parties must prove the facts stated in the petition, as a result of the Special Procedure, there is no need to prove the facts if the petition is undefended. It is true, as Mears (1991) points out, that with all these points a solicitor can guide a client through the complexity, but that does not really justify having a confusing law.[2] And it is no help for a party which is seeking to get divorced without the help of a lawyer.

A second complaint mentioned by the Law Commission is that the law is 'discriminatory and unjust'. The focus here tends to be on the two years separation grounds. The argument is that this ground can be relied upon if the parties are able to afford separate accommodation, but cannot be used by those who are less well off. This means that it is easier for wealthier couples to divorce than less well-off couples. Mears says that the law only disadvantages those who cannot prove that the relationship has broken down and doing

[3]It is worth emphasising that most couples rely on the fault-based fact. This shows the examiner that you are aware of the importance of understanding how the law works in practice.

[4]This point is always worth bearing in mind when criticising the law. There may be problems with the current system, but would it be any better under a different one?

[5]The examiner will be pleased you have shown that you are thinking critically about the arguments that are presented. Just because an argument is commonly made don't assume it is a good one. Think whether there are any possible objections to it.

so is not unfair. The real issue is whether two years' separation as evidence of relationship breakdown is necessary or appropriate. This issue is probably not a significant one in practice because most couples are able to rely on a fault-based fact and so do not need to rely on separation.[3]

The next complaint that the law distorts the bargaining power of the parties is that if one party wants a divorce and the other does not, then the one who does not can delay the proceedings significantly. They could defend the divorce petition or require the other party to rely on one of separation grounds. The concern is that they could offer not to defend a divorce petition in return for say, a more advantageous financial settlement. This is a genuine concern, but it would exist in any system for divorce, unless we simply require one party to lodge a request for a divorce which would then be granted.[4]

A fourth concern, and perhaps the most commonly made objection, is that the current law creates bitterness. It requires the parties to dredge up past issues and to put them in the public arena. Creating such embarrassment and hostility is counterproductive. It seems particularly objectionable that if a couple are both happy to divorce, they still need to produce an allegation of fault. Indeed it is hard to think of a system for divorce which would encourage more bitterness than the current one. On the other hand there are those who say that if we do not require the allegation of fault we are failing to recognise the wrongs people do that cause marital breakdown. If one party is clearly responsible for the breakdown of the marriage, should the law not state that? In response it might be questioned whether it is the job of the law to allocate blame in this area. A further point that could be made is that a couple divorcing are very likely to feel bitter towards each other. Assuming we can have a divorce law where there will be no bitterness is unrealistic.[5]

A fifth concern is that the current law does not do anything to encourage reconciliation. Section 6 of the Matrimonial Causes Act 1973 does require solicitors to discuss the possibility of reconciliation and, if appropriate, provide the names of organisations that can help. This provision does not seem to mean much in practice. The Family Law Act 1996 proposed changing the law to encourage couples to spend time thinking carefully about divorce and to offer free marriage guidance services. One of the lessons from the failure of the proposed reforms was that very few marriages can be saved by

[6]It is a good idea to use lessons from the Family Law Act 1996 where possible.

the time a petition for divorce is lodged. Marriage saving, if it is to be done, needs to be used much earlier than the time of the petition.[6]

A final concern is that the law makes things worse for children. In a way this repeats some of the points above. Encouraging the allegation of fault and the bitterness that can result can work against the interests of children. It is noticeable that the interests of children seem to be lost in the debates around divorce reform. It is interesting that the 1996 Act suggested that couples with children who wished to divorce should have a longer waiting period than those without. Whether making couples with children wait longer for their divorce helps or harms children is a matter for debate. There is a contrast here with family law generally which places the welfare of the child as the paramount consideration.[7]

[7]The examiner always likes it when you make comparisons with other areas of family law.

✓ Make your answer stand out

- Consider critically the complaints made about the current law. Don't assume they are valid. See Day Sclater and Piper (1999) *Undercurrents of Divorce*, Aldershot: Ashgate, for discussion of the complaints about the current law.
- Show a good awareness of how the law operates in practice with the special procedure. Eekelaar (1991) *Regulating Divorce*, Oxford: Claredon Press, provides a good discussion of how the law works.
- Discuss the lessons learned from the Family Law Act 1996 in more detail. See Eekelaar (1999) 'Family Law: Keeping us on Message' *Child and Family Law Quarterly* 387 for a helpful discussion.

! Don't be tempted to...

- Have unrealistic expectations of what the law on divorce can do.
- Focus only on the issues surrounding fault.

? Question 3

Adam and Mary have been married for ten years. Adam now wants a divorce and seeks your advice. He accepts that Mary has been the perfect wife and he cannot fault her. It is simply that they have fallen out of love. For the past two years they have had separate bedrooms and although they exchange a few pleasantries they barely talk to each other. Adam is a vicar and lives in a large vicarage, which is owned by the Church. Adam and Mary have no money and a disabled son. Mary has said that, although she accepts the marriage is over, if she has to move out of the vicarage she will have nowhere for herself or her son to live.

Answer plan

→ Explain clearly the ground for divorce.

→ Can Adam rely on any of the facts establishing the ground?

→ Consider especially whether he can rely on the two- or five-year separation.

→ Discuss whether the grave financial or other hardship defence applies.

Diagram plan

A printable version of this diagram is available from www.pearsoned.co.uk/lawexpressqa

Answer

The ground for divorce is that the marriage has irretrievably broken down (s. 1, Matrimonial Causes Act 1973).[1] It is only possible to show that the ground is made out if one of the five facts in section 1(2) are made out.[2] In this case Adam accepts that his wife has behaved perfectly and so he cannot focus on the fault-based facts (the adultery and unreasonable behaviour grounds).[3] So, he will only be able to rely on the facts based on separation. These are that 'the parties have lived apart for a continuous period' of at least two years if Mary consents to the granting of the divorce; or five years if she does not.

[1] It is good to start the answer to a problem question on divorce by setting out the basic structure of the law.

[2] Note also that reference is made to the specific statutory provisions. The examiner will want to see that.

[3] There is no point going into the detail on these because they are clearly not relevant to this problem.

The first issue to address is whether Adam and Mary can be said to have been living apart. This involves physical and mental aspects. There must be physical separation and an intention to live separately. As regards the physical issue, typically this will involve the parties living in different houses, but the courts have accepted that a couple can be treated as living apart even if they are in the same house. After **Santos v Santos** [1972] Fam 27 and **Mouncer v Mouncer** [1972] 1 All ER 289, the courts are willing to accept that although living in the same place a couple may not have a communality of life and so are treated as living apart. The court will consider questions such as whether they are eating together (**Hopes v Hopes** [1948] 2 All ER 920); whether they sleep in the same room (**Mouncer v Mouncer**); whether one spouse cleaned for other or provided services (e.g. laundry) (**Mouncer v Mouncer**).[4] It seems from the facts of Adam and Mary's case the court will look at the details of their life to determine if they have managed to effectively live separately under the one roof.[5]

[4] It is important to list some of the practical issues that the court will take into account.

[5] It's not possible to state categorically whether or not the court will regard them as living separately. From the limited facts provided all you can do is set out the kind of factors the courts will take into account.

The mental aspect of separation is that at least one of the parties recognises that the marriage is over. So a couple who simply start to live separately but do not regard the marriage as over would not be living apart for the purposes of the Matrimonial Causes Act 1973 (**Santos v Santos**). We would need more evidence of Adam and Mary's state of mind, but it may well be that the marriage has been regarded by Adam as over for two years.[6]

[6] Candidates often forget to include the mental aspect when discussing separation so the examiner will be pleased to see it here.

It must be emphasised that even if Adam is able to show that the parties have lived apart for two years Mary will need to consent to the divorce if he is to rely on that ground. If she does not he will need to show that they have lived apart for five years.[7] He will need to ensure that there is only very limited interaction between them while they are sharing the vicarage.

[7] Remember that once five years have passed there is no need for there to be consent to the divorce. This is a point the examiner will want you to emphasise.

Even if Adam is able to establish the ground for divorce, Mary may seek to rely on section 5 of the Matrimonial Causes Act 1973. This allows for the court to decline to grant a divorce, even in cases where the ground is established, if doing so would cause financial or other hardship and that it would in all the circumstances be wrong to dissolve the marriage. In this case Mary will argue that the divorce will mean she must leave the vicarage and there will be nowhere for her and the child to live. Normally the courts can deal with financial hardship following divorce by making a financial order, but in this case as they have no money that is not a possibility. Adam may argue that state housing will be available and although less desirable than the vicarage, their position will not be 'grave'. The courts have certainly required the hardship to be very severe before being willing to use section 5 (**Archer v Archer** [1999] 2 FCR 158). A more technical argument may be that the housing problem will not result from the divorce, but rather the breakdown from the relationship.[8] The wording of section 5 appears to state that it is the divorce which causes the hardship. Adam may make the point that being divorced will not, in fact, put her in a worse position than she is at the moment. However, that may be too technical a point for the courts. That said the courts have been very reluctant to use section 5 (**Archer v Archer**). It may be that Mary will be able to find local authority housing or alternative housing. Or indeed that Adam can find somewhere else to live. If, therefore, the ground for divorce has been made out it is unlikely that section 5 will be used to bar the divorce.

[8]The examiner will be pleased to see you making this point because it shows you have been looking at the wording of the section carefully and trying to think of arguments that may not apply.

 Make your answer stand out

- Discuss section 5 in detail and especially the requirement that the hardship must flow from the divorce. More detail on the case law can be found in Harris-Short and Miles (2007) *Family Law* ch. 5, Oxford: OUP.
- Consider carefully the case law on what living apart involves: see Lowe and Douglas (2006) *Family Law*, 271–2, Oxford: OUP.

! Don't be tempted to...

- Assume that you cannot live apart if you share the same house.
- Forget about section 5.

Question 4

Should divorce and dissolution be fault based?

Answer plan

➜ Explain the terms fault-based and no-fault-based divorce.
➜ Consider whether there are psychological arguments in favour of a fault-based system.
➜ Does fault-based divorce promote justice or support marriage?
➜ Discuss whether fault-based divorce creates problems with couples trapped in loveless marriages.
➜ Examine the argument that divorce should be seen as a private matter.
➜ Some say that the courts cannot allocate blame for divorce, is that a fair point?
➜ Analyse the claim that fault-based divorce encourages bitterness.

Diagram plan

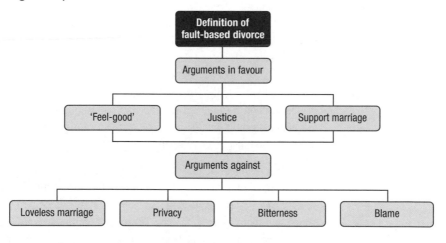

A printable version of this diagram is available from www.pearsoned.co.uk/lawexpressqa

Answer

Before discussing whether the law should move to a no-fault system, it is helpful to consider what exactly a no-fault system is. It is generally understood to be a divorce system which requires the parties to allege and prove something blameworthy about the

[1]Make sure you discuss the possible versions of a no-fault system. This shows you are thinking carefully about the wording in the question.

other party (such as adultery or unreasonable behaviour). A no-fault system could involve proof of a matter which did not indicate blame (e.g. that the marriage had irretrievably broken down) or not require the proof of any matter (e.g. a system which just requires the parties to lodge a form).[1]

[2]Although the question is about what the law should be, you can use the current law as a basis for the discussion.

The current law under the Matrimonial Causes Act 1973 is a bit of a mixture of a no-fault and fault based system.[2] It is no-fault in the sense that the ground for divorce is irretrievable breakdown. However, it is fault-based in that the only way one can prove that is by relying on one of the facts, some of which include fault-based factors, such as those referring to adultery or unreasonable behaviour. It would be possible under English law to have a no-fault-based divorce if one relied on the two- or five-year facts, but most divorces rely on the fault-based facts.

Those who support fault-based grounds for divorce make three main points. First, it is said that the making of allegations and blame is an inevitable part of marriage. Indeed a survey by Davis and Murch (1988) found that those divorcing wanted more fault, rather than less fault in their proceedings.[3] At least they wanted the chance to tell a court all the terrible things that their spouse had done to them. They did not seem so keen on their spouse doing the same in return! It has even been suggested that allowing the parties to let off steam in the divorce proceedings, may be cathartic. Even if there is any merit in this, it must be doubted whether the courts and legal process are the best way of providing an opportunity for the parties to let off steam. There must be cheaper and less public venues.

[3]Where possible refer to academic studies to back up your claim.

[4]It is good to mention some of the leading figures in the debates.

[5]Notice that the point here is that maybe there should be blame at the end of a marriage but it is not for the courts to allocate the blame.

Perhaps a better argument is that law needs to uphold the moral foundations of marriage. Where one party breaks a fundamental vow of marriage (e.g. by committing adultery) that needs to be acknowledged and recognised by the law. Baroness Young has complained that divorce is taken less seriously than a breach of contract.[4] That, however, assumes that the breach of the marriage vow is a legal issue. It might be thought that a breach of a marriage vow is a social matter or even a religious one. It is for the friends of the couple or members of their community to determine what moral blame attaches, but it is not for the courts.[5] Even if it were an appropriate job for the courts it would take a long costly hearing to truly determine who, if anyone, was to blame for the ending of a marriage.

This leads to a third argument that having a fault-based divorce system helps to uphold marriage. In part this repeats the argument just made that the law needs to show that breach of a marriage obligation is taken seriously. However, some economists (such as Rasmusen) argue that there needs to be a disincentive to prevent people ending marriages without blame. Although this seems to imagine people are rational about ending relationships and think through the issues logically. That may be questioned.[6]

[6]The examiner will be impressed to see you bringing in a brief reference to economists in a law essay.

Turning to the arguments against a fault-based system. First, it means that if there is a couple who have not behaved badly to each other but have just fallen out of love, they must remain married. Is it to anyone's benefit to keep couples married to each other if they no longer wish to be. Indeed, even the Archbishop of Canterbury in the debates leading up to the 1973 Matrimonial Causes Act thought that the existence of 'empty shell' marriages undermined the notion of marriage.[7]

[7]The examiner will like to see this reference to the history behind the legislation.

Second, divorce may be seen as a private matter. If a couple have decided that the marriage is over, is it not best to regard this as a private matter and allow them to end it. Demanding that they prove allegations of fault suggests a rather paternalistic attitude towards them. Supporters of fault-based divorce would argue that the law on divorce is not just a private matter because it impacts on the status of marriage.

Third, requiring parties to make allegations of fault against each other seems designed to increase bitterness. Surely we do not want the parties trying to dredge up past rows. We would rather they focus on what will make a good future for their children.

Finally, there is the real difficulty in knowing who is at fault at the end of a marriage. It can be very difficult to determine the facts. Even if we know the facts it can be difficult to determine who is to blame.

To conclude it is argued the case for moving towards a no-fault system is very strong. That said it must be admitted that among the general public there does not seem to be a strong campaign to reform the law. Most people seem to be able to use the system to get the divorce they want. So, yes, we should move to a no-fault system, but perhaps it is not the highest priority of reform in family law.[8]

[8]The conclusion brings together the main themes of the essay well.

Make your answer stand out

- Consider what the aims of the law on divorce should be. A good discussion can be found in Hasson (2003) 'Divorce Law and the Family Law Act 1996' *International Journal of Law, Policy and the Family* 338.
- Consider further the validity of the economic arguments for fault-based divorce. Rasmusen (2002) 'An economic approach to adultery law' in A. Dnes and R. Rowthorn (eds) *The Law and Economics of Marriage and Divorce*, Cambridge: CUP, provides a useful discussion.
- Discuss who is in the best position to allocate blame, if that must be done.

! **Don't be tempted to...**

- Assume there is only one kind of no-fault divorce system.
- Only the law has a role to play in divorce.

Question 5

Critically consider what the aims of the law on divorce should be.

Answer plan

→ To what extent should the law on divorce have a role in supporting marriage?

→ Consider whether the divorce law should be seeking to save marriages.

→ Discuss whether the divorce law can reduce bitterness between the parties.

→ Should the reduction of costs play a role in debates over divorce?

→ Analyse whether concerns over domestic violence should affect the law on divorce.

→ How important is it that couples who wish to re-marry should be free to do so?

→ Debate how the law on divorce can deal with the emotional issues.

Diagram plan

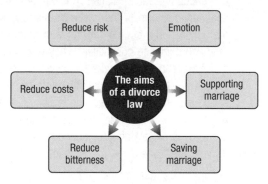

A printable version of this diagram is available from www.pearsoned.co.uk/lawexpressqa

Answer

This essay will consider some of the aims for divorce law which have been proposed. It is noticeable that while there have been many calls for reform of the divorce law among academics, it is not an issue which has captured the public imagination. Further there is little agreement on how the law should be reformed. A major source of the disagreement is a lack of consensus on what the aims of a divorce law should be.[1]

To some a primary aim of the law on divorce should be to uphold marriage. It might be argued that the law on divorce sends a message about how we are to understand marriage. If divorce were to be allowed very easily that might suggest that the law does not regard marriage as anything particularly important. Similarly if a marriage could only be brought to an end after a serious wrong had been shown that might suggest the law recognised marriage as an important institution, which should not lightly be set aside. Ruth Deech (2009) has argued that the liberalisation of the divorce laws has led to an increase in the number of divorces.[2] It is argued that this aim is not very realistic. It is hard to imagine that a couple think about the law on divorce when their marriage gets into trouble. True, a very harsh divorce law might mean there would be fewer divorces, but it would not mean there would be less marital breakdown. What makes a marriage valuable is how it is understood by the parties and how it is regarded in the society, the legal rules on divorce must play only a tiny, if any, impact on those.[3]

[1] This paragraph tells the examiner what are going to be the main themes of the essay.

[2] It is good to refer to leading commentators on the debates where possible.

[3] The examiner will like you putting the arguments on either side of this issue.

A second argument is that the law on divorce should be used to try and encourage reconciliation. This was a major theme in the now abandoned reform of the law in the Family Law Act 1996. Under that legislation a couple seeking a divorce would be offered free marriage guidance counselling. They were also required to attend an information meeting where they would be told about the harms that divorce causes and would therefore be encouraged to consider saving their marriage. One of the lessons of the failure of the 1996 Act reforms is that seeking to save a marriage when a couple seek a divorce is acting too late. Indeed often the reason for seeking a divorce is that one of the parties wants to remarry.[4]

[4]Here the 1996 Act has been used as a good example to back up the point being made.

Thirdly, it is sometimes said that divorce law should seek to reduce the bitterness between the parties, but perhaps it is more realistic to say the law should not increase the bitterness. The Law Commission accepted that the current law tends to increase, rather than decease the bitterness. It does this by requiring couples to make allegations against each other if they are not willing to wait for two years. Supporters of the current law may say that the parties will feel bitter towards each other, whatever the law says. The filling in of forms is unlikely to make matters any worse. However, in reply it might be pointed out that we are talking about public court documents. To require parties to list their grievances in a public way may be said to exacerbate any ill-will between the parties.[5] Tied to this principle is the idea that the law should promote a continuing relationship between the spouses. It might be argued that there is little the law can do in this area. That said supporters of mediation argue that encouraging mediation might be a way for encouraging a good relationship between the parties.

[5]Here the essay has tried to acknowledge that there are arguments on both sides of this debate.

Fourth, the divorce procedure should be cheap for the state and for the parties it is claimed. The current system involves considerable legal aid expenditure or private costs for clients. A system which simply involved the filling in of a simple form to end a marriage would be much cheaper. This might be a slight red herring. While unnecessary costs are always undesirable, the real question is whether the costs are necessary or not. It is true that divorce could be procedural and cheap, but the issue then is whether that would mean divorce would be seen as too easy.[6]

[6]It is easy in academic discussions to forget the issue of costs, but it is a crucial one in practice and so the examiner will be pleased to see your awareness of it.

Fifth, the divorce law should do what it can to limit the risk of violence. The breakdown of a relationship can herald domestic violence. It is said that delaying the divorce process or making it last

[7]It is good here to link in the issue of divorce, with other topics on the syllabus, in this case domestic violence.

a long time can create a danger of domestic violence. This was a particular concern with the Family Law Act 1996 proposals under which couples with children would need to wait a year-and-a-half before being able to divorce.[7]

Finally, it might be thought that the law should help the parties deal with the emotional turmoil involved. Martin Richards has criticised the law for failing to take seriously the emotions that rage through people on divorce. Shelley Day Sclater has criticised the Family Law Act 1996 for assuming that everyone wanted to be 'decent' and 'sit down and talk through the issues with their spouse' and that that failed to accord with the reality of people's emotions on marital breakdown.[8] This is true, but it leaves open the question of whether the law is best placed to oversee emotional support for the parties. Counselling and other psychological support services could operate independently of the law.

[8]It is good to refer here to the work of these sociologists and psychologists to show a wide range of knowledge.

To conclude, there is little agreement over what should be the aims of a divorce law. Perhaps the lessons of the Family Law Act 1996 is that we should have modest expectations. There is not much the law can do to heal past wrongs and perhaps the most we can hope for is that the law does not make things worse. And finally, there is no avoiding the issue of costs. A simple no-fault divorce system would be cheap to operate.

✓ Make your answer stand out

- Consider the lessons to be learned from the Family Law Act 1996. See Reece (2003) *Divorcing Responsibly*, Oxford: Hart, for an excellent discussion.
- Remember that the law is not the only player on divorce. See Day Sclater (1999) *Divorce: A Psychological Study*, Aldershot: Dartmouth, for a helpful look at the psychological issues.
- You could look further at the interests of children on divorce. Richards (1994) 'Divorcing children: Roles for parents and the state' in M. Maclean and J. Kurczewski (eds) *Families, Politics and the Law: Perspectives for East and West Europe*, Oxford: Claredon Press, for a helpful discussion.

! Don't be tempted to...

- Exaggerate the importance of the law.
- Restrict discussion to only legal issues.

Financial issues on separation

How this topic may come up in exams

Financial issues on separation are common themes for exam topics. A fundamental distinction is drawn between couples who are married or civil partners; and cohabitants. In the case of the former the Matrimonial Causes Act 1973 contains provisions allowing the court a broad discretion to distribute the couple's property. While in the latter the court must rely on property law to determine who owns what property. An essay question may well focus on the theoretical issues behind the division of property, while problem questions will raise questions involving an application of the Matrimonial Causes Act 1973 or the application of property law to cohabitants. As this is a very discretionary-based system it can be difficult to predict with certainty what the results of the application might be.

Attack the question

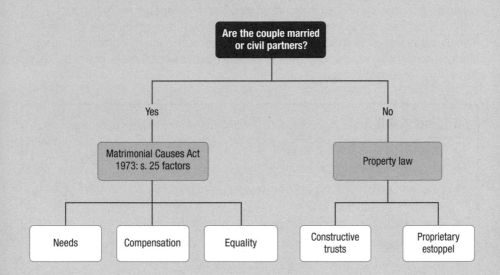

❓ Question 1

Margaret and Hugh separated, having been married for five years. They have two children. When they got married they were both high flying lawyers. Shortly afterwards Margaret became pregnant and gave up her career to care for the children. She did not return to work during the marriage. Hugh's career has taken off during the marriage and he earns £1.5 million a year. They have a house valued at £1 million (which was bought using Margaret's money) and savings of £1 million. They separated three months ago. After they separated Margaret bought a lottery ticket and won £2 million. Discuss what financial orders the court might make for spousal support.

Answer plan

→ Explain the approach of section 25 Matrimonial Causes Act 1973.

→ Set out the basics of the courts' approach after *White* and *Miller*.

→ Consider how the needs principle; the equality principle and the compensation principle apply to this case.

→ Discuss what the courts have said about assets acquired before a marriage.

→ Explore the attitude of the courts to assets acquired after separation.

→ What has been the courts' approach to family homes?

Diagram plan

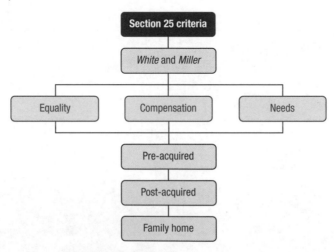

A printable version of this diagram is available from www.pearsoned.co.uk/lawexpressqa

Answer

The starting point for tackling this question is section 25 of the Matrimonial Causes Act 1973. This sets out the factors that the court will apply when considering what orders to make on divorce. The first consideration must be the welfare of any child of the marriage (s. 25(1) Matrimonial Causes Act 1973). However, we are asked to focus on spousal support and so it will be assumed that an agreement has been reached over the level of child support.[1]

The House of Lords in the leading decisions of **White v White** [2001] AC 596 and **Miller v Miller** [2006] UKHL 24 has provided some guidance on how the courts will apply the discretion under section 25. Their lordships stated there that the key principle governing the law in this area is that the result reached must be fair. They explained that there were three principles underpinning the courts' understanding of fairness: sharing, compensation and needs.[2]

It is necessary to apply those principles to this case. The requirement of needs is unlikely to be a significant factor in this case because there are easily sufficient assets to meet the needs of the parties.[3] Needs in this context is to be interpreted liberally as reasonable needs, bearing in mind the lifestyle the couple enjoyed during the marriage (**J v J** [2009] EWHC 2654 (Fam)). In this case any reasonable order is likely to meet the needs of the parties.

The requirement of sharing requires that there be an equal division of the assets the parties have at the time of the hearing (**J v J**) between the parties unless there is a good reason not to divide them equally (**White**). There are several issues which could be relied upon here as reasons to depart from equality.[4] First, it might be argued that the fact Margaret brought money into the marriage should be a factor to be taken into account. In **Miller** the House of Lords suggested that such an argument would be particularly powerful in the case of short marriages. In Margaret and Hugh's case, five years would be regarded as a short marriage. It is arguable, therefore, that Margaret will be given the one million pounds she brought into the marriage and it will not be divided between them. However, in **Miller** Baroness Hale indicated that the family home would always be regarded as family property and therefore suitable for equal division, even if bought with assets that existed prior to the marriage. It seems, therefore that the Court is likely to regard the one million pounds that Margaret brought into the marriage as family property to be divided equally because it was used to purchase the family house.

Second, Hugh might want to claim that his financial contribution to the marriage was significant and so justifies a departure from equality. In **White v White** the House of Lords made it clear that a financial contribution and non-financial contribution (e.g. child rearing) would be regarded as equal. However, the courts have subsequently accepted (**Charman v Charman**) that if the money-maker can show that his or her contribution was exceptional then it might be that a departure from equality is justified to order to recognise that. However in **Charman** the Court of Appeal indicated that there would need to be an exceptional case for this to be so. Just being a highly successful business person is unlikely to be sufficient. Therefore Hugh's argument is unlikely to succeed.[5]

[5]It is important to point out that *Charman* indicated that the exceptional contribution of the money-maker will only very rarely be a justification for departing from equality, therefore be clear in your conclusion that it is unlikely to apply to Hugh.

Third, Margaret will argue that the money she acquired as a result of the lottery win will not be divided between them. In **J v J** Charles J accepted that even assets acquired after the marriage was broken down could be available for distribution. However, he accepted that it would be a good reason to depart from equality that an asset was acquired after the marriage, unless it could be shown that the acquisition was the product of work done during the marriage. In this case that is not so and Margaret seems likely to retain the proceeds from the lottery.[6]

[6]The issue of whether post-marriage assets can be divided equally is a highly topical one. Keep your eyes out for any recent cases on this and use them to support your argument. This will show the examiner that you are up to date.

From the reasoning so far it seems likely that Margaret can retain her £2 million lottery winnings and that there will be an equal division of the £1 million pounds from the house and £1 million savings. However, there is still the compensation issue. In **McFarlane v McFarlane** [2006] 2 FCR 213, where the couple separated after a lengthy marriage, an equal division of the £3 million assets was held insufficient to compensate Mrs McFarlane for the fact that during the marriage she had given up her potentially lucrative career to care for children. A similar argument could be made by Margaret in this case. She could point out that a division of the family assets of a million pounds each would not be fair. In particular she could point out that as Hugh would be earning £1.5 million per annum it would not take long before he had acquired significantly more than her. There are, however, two differences between Margaret's case and McFarlane.[7] First, her marriage is much shorter. Second, her lottery win has meant she has significant assets. In reply to the first, she

[7]It is a good idea in problem questions to set out the differences between the case you are looking at and the leading cases the courts have already decided.

might argue that although the marriage is shorter the impact it has had on her earning potential is still significant. It may be important for the court to determine how easily she can return to work and how far behind where she would have been in the career ladder. In relation to the second point she might reply that she should be entitled to compensation for the losses caused by the marriage whether she has assets from elsewhere or not. If Margaret succeeds the court might award a periodic payments order for perhaps five years. In **McFarlane** the award was for £250,000 and the court may be tempted to make a similar award in this case.[8] A court may well be persuaded that after five years of payments the impact on her earning potential caused by the marriage will be minimal.

[8]While you are not expected by the examiner to produce exact sums that would be awarded, you can give some indication of the kinds of figures that might be used. Referring to figures used in the decided cases is a good way of doing that.

In conclusion, it is likely that Margaret will be able to retain her lottery winnings, but the other assets will be divided equally between the couple. Margaret may also be able to claim a periodic payments order of £250,000 per year, for up to five years.

✓ Make your answer stand out

- Compare and contrast this case with those of *Miller* and *McFarlane*. You could analyse these decisions in more detail. Look at Cooke (2007) 'Miller/McFarlane: law in search of a definition' *Child and Family Law Quarterly* 98 for a helpful discussion.
- Consider in more detail the circumstances in which a departure from the equality division may be appropriate. See Miles (2008) 'Making sense of need, compensation and equal sharing after Miller; McFarlane' *Child and Family Law Quarterly* 378.
- Consider further the case law on assets acquired after divorce. See the discussion in Herring (2010a) 'Money, money, money' *New Law Journal* 300.

! Don't be tempted to...

- Assume there is always an equal division of assets.
- Argue that it will be easy for a high earner to claim they have made an exceptional contribution.

? **Question 2**

Tom and Barbara have lived together for ten years. They have never married and have no children. Sadly, their relationship has come to an end. They live in a large house which they bought when their relationship started, using Barbara's savings and a mortgage. The house was put in Barbara's name. The property was in need of considerable repair and Tom has spent many long evenings over the years updating it. Barbara and Tom have always kept their own separate bank accounts. The arrangement they came to was that Barbara would pay the mortgage from her account and Tom would pay the general household expenses from his account. They say they never discussed ownership of the house, save one evening early in the relationship when Barbara bought Tom a 'welcome to our home' mug for his birthday present. Barbara at one point said 'I owe you' after a week when Tom had been working particularly hard on the house. Apart from the house they have no other assets of value. Discuss how the court will deal with their financial position.

Answer plan

→ Explain the courts' approach to unmarried couples.

→ Assess who has legal ownership, considering in whose name the legal title is registered.

→ Consider whether there is a resulting trust, focusing on the contributions to the purchase price.

→ Discuss whether there is a constructive trust, looking at the financial and non-financial contributions that the parties have made.

→ Examine whether there is a claim for a proprietary estoppel based on a promise or reassurance of a property interest.

Diagram plan

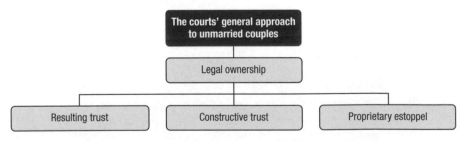

A printable version of this diagram is available from www.pearsoned.co.uk/lawexpressqa

Answer

[1]If you have an unmarried couple who have children then you can also consider whether an order under the Children Act 1989 Sch 1 will be made, as well as any claim for child support under the Child Support Act 1995.

[2]Make it clear from the start that the court's jurisdiction in this area is limited and quite different from cases where there is a divorce or dissolution.

[3]This is always the place to start with unmarried couples.

[4]It will be very rare that a resulting trust is useful in the context of a cohabiting couple. Whenever a resulting trust arises a constructive trust will arise as well and that will provide a more effective remedy. Nevertheless resulting trusts should still be discussed briefly to show the examiner you are aware of all the possible legal claims.

[5]This is an important point: we are looking for an actual conversation and not an unspoken assumption.

When a childless couple[1] who are not spouses or civil partners separate the court only has the power to declare who owns what. It does not have the power to redistribute property, as it does with spouse or civil partners. In this case, therefore, the court can simply declare ownership of the property and, if appropriate, make an order under Trusts of Land and Appointment of Trustees Act 1996.[2]

The starting point is to determine legal ownership.[3] This depends in whose name the property is registered at the Land Registry. In this case that will be Barbara. The only way that Tom can establish an interest in the property would be in equity. Express trusts of land can only be made in writing (s. 53(1)(b) Law of Property Act 1925). There is no evidence of that and so Tom will need to rely on an implied trust: a resulting trust, a constructive trust or a proprietary estoppel.

For a resulting trust Tom will need to show that he has made a financial contribution to the purchase of the house. As it seems he has made neither a financial contribution to the purchase price nor to any of the mortgage instalments he cannot claim a resulting trust (**Huntingford v Hobbs** [1993] 1 FCR 45).[4]

For a constructive trust the traditional position is as set out in **Lloyds Bank v Rosset.** It must be shown that there was a common intention to share ownership of the house and that the claimant has relied on the common intention to his or her detriment. Lord Bridge suggested two ways of finding a common intention.

The first was that there had been an express agreement reached between the parties. This requires more than a mutual belief, there must be a conversation (**Fowler v Barron** [2008] EWCA Civ 733).[5] In this case the 'welcome to our home' mug might be relied upon as evidence that there was a conversation in which they agreed to share ownership. In **Hyett v Stanley** ([2003] 3 FCR 253) the Court of Appeal accepted that circumstantial evidence could prove that such a conversation took place even if the parties could not remember it. The mug might lead the court to assume the parties were used to talking about 'our home'. However, the courts require proof of an agreement to share ownership, not just occupation (**G v G** [2005] EWHC 1560) and it may be that the mug does not do this. The other comment 'I owe you' is also probably insufficient as it is not a clear statement that ownership will be shared. In **James v Thomas** ([2007] 3 FCR 696) it was held the statement 'You will be well provided for' was not sufficient for a constructive trust.[6] And Barbara's statement seems just as vague as that one.

If the court decides there is insufficient evidence of an express agreement to share, it may be willing to infer one. Lord Bridge in **Rossett** suggested that only a direct contribution to the purchase price or a mortgage instalment would be sufficient. More recently in **Lightfoot v Lightfoot-Brown** [2005] EWCA 201 Arden LJ suggested a slightly broader approach that payments that were 'referable to the acquisition to the house' may be sufficient to lead to an inference of sharing of ownership. Tom might argue that although he did not make a direct contribution to the purchase price or to the mortgage the fact he paid for all of the other bills enabled Barbara to buy the house. This argument may succeed. Some of the most recent cases have shown a more liberal approach to inferring an agreement. In **Stack v Dowden** [2007] UKHL 17 Baroness Hale suggested that the hurdle for a constructive trust in **Rosset** had been set 'rather too high'. It may well be that in cases like Tom's the courts will now be willing to infer an agreement even in the absence of a direct contribution to the purchase price (**Le Foe v Le Foe** [2002] 1 FCR 107).[7]

[7]This is a difficult issue to write on in the exam because it seems the attitude of the courts is changing, although we have not had a clear statement to the effect that the *Rosset* criteria has been abandoned.

It is also necessary to show that there has been reliance on this common intention (**Chan Pui Chun v Ho** [2003] 1 FCR 520). This would be shown in this case by the work that Tom has done on the property.

[8]It is terribly difficult to know for sure how a court would determine shares in a case like this. You might well decide the court would decide that Barbara would get more than 50 per cent. There is no clearly wrong or right answer. What the examiner is looking for is that you are able to suggest a reasonable figure. As long as you can explain why you choose it you will not be penalised if the examiner would have given a different proportion.

If a constructive trust is found then the issue is what shares the parties have. Following **Stack v Dowden** this is done by determining the intentions of the parties (and not by what is fair). The court will try and ascertain their intention by looking at all of the facts including how they arranged their finances, who paid for outgoings, how the purchase was financed. In this case the fact that the property has been financed by Barbara would be taken into account. As would the fact they had kept their finances separate (suggesting there was not an assumption that 'everything would be shared'). On the other hand the fact that Tom paid for the outgoings and that he did an enormous amount of the work would be considered. An important factor may be the length of the relationship. It is likely a 50:50 share would be ordered here, but that is not beyond doubt.[8]

A final claim Tom may make is based on a proprietary estoppel. He would need to show that Barbara had led him to believe he was going to have an interest in the property and had acted to his detriment in reliance on that and that it would be conscionable in all the circumstances that he receive an interest (**Gillet v Holt** [2000] 2 FCR 705). In this case his primary difficulty is finding the assurance that there will be a share in the property. The courts are reluctant to rely on general unspoken assumptions in this context (**Gillet v Holt**). The statement 'I owe you' might not be a sufficiently clear assurance that the property will be his (**Lissimore v Downing** [2003] 2 FLR 308), although it must be admitted the courts have not been consistent in this and in some cases the courts have been willing to rely on vague statements (**Bibby v Stirling** (1998) 76 P&CR 36). If he did succeed he would be awarded the sum that was conscionable in all the circumstances, bearing in mind what he was promised and the extent of his detriment (**Gillet v Holt**). It seems that Tom's strongest claim is likely to rest on a claim based on a constructive trust rather than a proprietary estoppel.

 Make your answer stand out

■ Use as detailed a knowledge as possible of the current law. Gardner (2008) 'Family property today' *Law Quarterly Review* 422 provides a very useful analysis of the current law.

■ Show the examiner that you are aware of the uncertainties surrounding the current law: see Hayward (2009) 'Family values in the home' *Child and Family Law Quarterly* 242.

■ There has been considerable debate over the significance of *Stack* v *Dowden*, and you could disucss that further. See George (2008) '*Stack* v *Dowden* – Do As We Say, Not As We Do?' *The Journal of Social Welfare and Family Law* 49.

! Don't be tempted to...

■ Assume the law has not changed since *Rossett*. Explore some of the recent developments (e.g. *Stack* v *Dowden*).

■ Argue that vague beliefs or assumptions can found the basis for constructive trusts or proprietary estoppels.

Question 3

Three years ago Alan and Tom entered a civil partnership, although they had lived together for ten years prior to that. Unfortunately the relationship has come to an end and they have agreed to a dissolution. They have both worked during the relationship, earning similarly large salaries. They have £500,000 jointly owned assets, most of which are the result of an inheritance Tom gained before he met Alan. Unknown to Tom, Alan has been setting aside a small sum each week to create a fund which he uses to invest in the stock exchange. He has had considerable success and his current holding is worth £1 million. During the relationship Alan was repeatedly violent to Tom and was unfaithful to him. When they first got together they signed a contract stating that in the event of the breakdown of their relationship they would divide their assets equally.

Answer plan

→ Compare dissolution and divorce: will Alan and Tom have the same rights as a divorcing married couple?

→ Analyse to what extent the *White* v *White* and *Miller/McFarlane* principles apply in this case.

→ Consider whether this will be treated as a 'long' or a 'short' civil partnership.

→ Which assets will be treated as 'matrimonial assets'?

→ Discuss the relevance of conduct to this case.

→ Describe the courts' likely approach to the contract.

Diagram plan

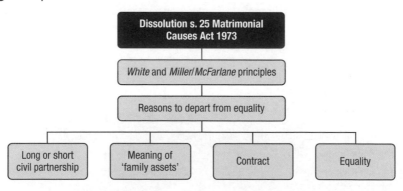

A printable version of this diagram is available from www.pearsoned.co.uk/lawexpressqa

Answer

The principles governing the division of property following a dissolution of a civil partnership are the same as those governing the division of property following divorce. The factors in section 25 of the Matrimonial Causes Act 1973 should all be considered.[1] Although there are no reported cases yet on financial orders on dissolution, it is generally assumed that the courts will use the same principles that are used on divorce.

The starting point in this case will be to achieve a fair result (**White v White** [2001] 1 AC 596). This will require the court to consider the principles of needs; sharing and compensation (**Miller v Miller**; **McFarlane v McFarlane** [2006] 2 FCR 213).[2]

Looking first at need, the court will want to ensure that the reasonable needs of the parties are met. This will involve looking at the future needs. As both parties have a good salary, it is likely that their needs will be met. It is unlikely, therefore, that needs will play a central role in this case.[3]

Next there is the principle of equal sharing. The starting point is that all the assets of the couple will be divided equally, but that need not be done if there is a good case not to. Tom may argue that the money representing his inheritance should not be shared. In the case of a long relationship the courts typically divide all of the couple's assets, but in a shorter relationship only the family assets (those acquired during the marriage) will be divided. It is generally accepted that in the case of a marriage the court will look at the length of the whole of the relationship, and not just the length of the actual marriage (**GW v RW** [2003] EWHC 611). Presumably the court will take the same approach to civil partnership.[4] If so that would mean we are dealing with a thirteen-year relationship. It is difficult to know whether this would be regarded as a lengthy relationship or not. Relationships under ten years are generally regarded as short (**Miller v Miller**), while a relationship of over twenty years would be long (**White v White**). It may be that between ten and twenty years is a hybrid status where some of the non-marital assets would be shared but not all (see the arguments of John Eekelaar (2006b)). So a court, in relation to this argument may see a case for dividing the sum representing the inheritance in 75%/25% division.[5]

Alan may want to argue that his stock fund should not be divided equally. One argument he may want to make is the one just

[1] Set out the key statutory provision early in the essay.

[2] It is good to set out these guiding principles early on in the essay as it provides the essay with a clear structure.

[3] Once you have concluded that an issue is not really relevant for the case, there is no need to discuss the issue further. Focus on those points which will be of significance.

[4] While it is generally assumed that the principles for divorce will be the same as those for civil partnership, we cannot be sure as there is no case saying that.

[5] Make it clear there is no case saying this, it is just a suggestion as to how the law might develop.

discussed, which is that if it is a short relationship, only the assets acquired during the marriage are divided. If he loses that argument the fund will be divided. If, however, it is accepted that it is a short relationship then there is an issue over whether or not this is a 'family asset' which should be divided. In **Miller**, Baroness Hale and Lord Nicholls differed on quite what 'family assets' were. Lord Nicholls seemed to regard all acquisitions during a marriage to be 'family assets'. However, Baroness Hale, who was in the majority on this issue, held that there might be some income which the other party could not be said to have contributed towards. Alan might argue that his share holding falls within this category because Tom did not know about it and so could not be said to have helped in its creation. The courts are still struggling to interpret the differences between the approaches of Baroness Hale and Lord Nicholls. **S v S** [2006] EWHC 2793 seemed to take a rather narrow interpretation of Baroness Hale's approach and limited it to cases where income did not relate to any activity during the marriage.[6] If that is followed then Alan's argument may fail.

[6]The examiner will be impressed with a good knowledge of the dispute between Baroness Hale and Lord Nicholls.

Another factor that the courts will consider is Alan's conduct. However, the courts have made it clear that the conduct of the parties will be taken into account only exceptionally (**S v S** [2006] EWHC 2793). It must be conduct that it would be inequitable to disregard (section 25(2)(g) Matrimonial Causes Act 1973). The courts are most likely to take into account conduct if it has caused a financial loss to one of the parties. In this case where no financial loss has resulted the court is unlikely to take it into account, however reprehensible the conduct may be (**Miller v Miller**). The kinds of cases where conduct might be considered is where a party has wasted money through gambling or wantonly destroyed property.[7]

[7]Again this is an issue which should be discussed because it is raised by the facts given in the problem question, but you can conclude that it will be an issue which will affect the order the court will make.

All of the arguments made to date could be overshadowed by the contract signed by the parties at the start of their relationship. In **Radmacher v Granatino** [2010] UKSC 42 the Supreme Court made it clear that courts will attach more weight to contracts than they had in the past. It was not suggested that pre-marriage (or presumably pre-civil partnership) contracts should be regarded as binding, but rather the courts should give effect to them, unless they would be clearly unfair. The courts will also need to be persuaded that the circumstances in which the contract was signed were reasonably fair. If one party had forced another to sign a contract or there was fraud no weight would be attached to it.[8] If that

[8]Don't forget that contracts only carry weight if they were negotiated in a free way and there was no fairness in their creation.

[9]Show the examiner you have a good knowledge of this important recent case.

approach were followed here the assets may well be divided equally in accordance with the terms of the contract. It would be hard to see why that should not be regarded as outside the bounds of what might be seen as fair.[9]

Make your answer stand out

- Having considered the differences between Baroness Hale and Lord Nicholls in *Miller* use recent case law if available to support the points you make.
- Discuss further the relevance of the length of the relationship, see Eekelaar (2006b) 'Property and Financial Settlements on Divorce' *Family Law* **36**, 754.
- You could analyse further the law's approach to pre-nuptial contracts. See George, Harris and Herring (2009) 'Pre-Nuptial Agreements: For Better or For Worse?' *Family Law* 934.

! Don't be tempted to...

- Assume that the courts will automatically give effect to 'pre-nups'.
- Exaggerate the weight the courts will place on conduct.
- Assume that civil partnerships will be treated differently from marriages.

 # Question 4

Why should the courts make any financial orders between spouses in the event of a divorce?

Answer plan

→ Discuss the theory that financial orders are necessary to meet the basic needs of the children.

→ Consider whether financial orders can be explained as a form of damages for breach of contract.

→ Examine the argument that financial orders are equivalent to the divisions of assets of a business partnership.

→ Explain the role of equality in the development of the law.

→ To what extent can financial orders on divorce compensate spouses for losses incurred as a result of the marriage?

→ Should the law in this area take into account the interests of the state?

Diagram plan

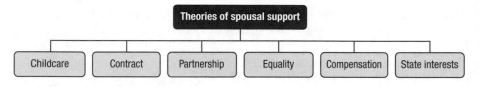

A printable version of this diagram is available from www.pearsoned.co.uk/lawexpressqa

Answer

[1]This sets out the basic structure of the essay and helps the examiner understand how you will approach the essay.

While there is widespread agreement that at the end of a marriage a court may need to redistribute assets between the spouses, there is less agreement on why this should be so. This essay will look at some of the theories which have been promoted and consider what might justify a redistribution of property in the event of a divorce.[1]

The essay question asks us to focus on financial orders between spouses, rather than child support. However, one theory in favour of spousal support is that it can be seen as part of child support. If it is accepted (as most but not all commentators do) that a parent should be legally obliged to support their children, then this must involve supporting someone to look after the children. If that is to be the spouse, then support of a spouse is involved. It is no good providing food for a child if there is no one to prepare it. Further, if the spouse who is looking after the children is in dire poverty this will have an impact upon the quality of care offered to the children. Hence, it can be argued that some degree of spousal support can be justified as an aspect of childcare. However, that may simply be enough to enable the spouse to live and be able to meet the needs of the child. In the case of a rich couple a spouse may seek more than that.[2]

[2]Recognise the limits of the approach. In this case it might justify a subsistence level of support, but no more.

A second theory is based on contract. In essence this regards divorce as a breach of the marriage contract and that financial orders on divorce are damages for breach of the contract. It might even be argued that a marriage is a promise to support each other for life and divorce should provide, as far as possible, damages for a breach of that obligation. This theory has few supporters nowadays, rightly so. It might be questioned whether marriage should be regarded as a guarantee to support for life. That might go against the idea that after divorce spouses should be encouraged to be self-sufficient. Also the

3Again show you are
considering both the
strengths and weaknesses
of the theories.

4It is always good in essays
on theory to refer to cases
where the theory has
been applied. It shows the
examiner that you can move
from the abstract to the
concrete.

5Never forget that in most
cases the needs of the
children take up most of
the assets. The reported
cases tend to involve
better-off couples.

6The examiner will be keen
to see you are aware of
the way that the law may
impact differently on men
and women.

idea of divorce as breach of contract does not sit comfortably with the no-fault divorce. Despite these points in some of the cases involving very rich couples some weight does seem to be attached to the idea that a spouse should continue in the lifestyle to which she has become accustomed for the rest of her life.[3]

A more popular view is the third, based on partnership. The argument there is that marriage should be regarded as a partnership. Each spouse might contribute to the partnership in a different way, but the fruits of the partnership should be shared. A flavour of this approach can be found in **White v White** [2001] 1 AC 596 itself with the importance attached to the fact that childcaring can be as equal a contribution to a marriage as money earning.[4] There are, however, difficulties with the partnership approach. It might be said to involve little more than a reworking of the contract argument. The assets of a business partnership are only equally owned if that is what the parties have agreed. Further, the partnership approach does not readily explain how assets that were acquired before or after the marriage should be open to redistribution. Perhaps most problematic is the fact that it does not explain why in many less well-off couples the assets end up with the children and their primary carer and are not divided equally (see Eekelaar (2000)).[5]

A fourth theory that has some support is to emphasise the principle of equality (see Parkinson (2005)). If equality is seen as the essence of marriage it might be argued that the court should ensure that the benefits and disadvantages of a marriage are shared equally. If one party has made gains from the marriage and the other losses the law can appropriately intervene to ensure there is equality. Perhaps we can see an aspect of this in the **McFarlane v McFarlane** decision where their lordships acknowledge that Mr McFarlane's career had flourished during the marriage, whereas Mrs MacFarlane's had greatly suffered. Orders were made to try and equalise the benefits and disadvantages of the marriage. Typically it is men who gain financially through the marriage and women who lose out, although that is no longer always the case.[6] One issue for those seeking to promote equality is to consider whether the courts are simply trying to ensure that there is equality at the day of divorce, or whether the courts are trying to ensure there is equality in the future. Those who emphasise the latter point out that the disadvantages of marriage can last for some time into the future.

Some of the themes just discussed also appear in an approach which focuses on compensation (see Murray (2008)). The focus on this approach is that where a spouse has suffered a financial loss during the marriage they should be compensated by the other party, where that loss flows from a decision reached by the couple as to how they should distribute their roles. So if a husband and wife agree that the wife should give up work to care for the children he should compensate her for the loss of income and earning capacity she suffers as a result of that decision.

[7] It is good to refer to specific commentators where possible.

Finally, some commentators (see Herring (2005)) have argued that there are important state interests that affect how property on divorce should be distributed.[7] The state has interests in ensuring that spouses are not left dependent on the state following divorce if their partner is wealthy enough to support them. The state might also want to use financial orders on divorce to encourage (or discourage) childcare; to attempt to uphold (or not uphold) the stability of marriage; or to combat economic disadvantages between men and women.[8] To develop the thinking on just one of these issues, if we had a legal system which had no way of redistributing property on divorce that would be a strong disincentive for a working woman to give up employment to care for children. By contrast the current system can be seen as offering some protection to women who do that, and so encourage it as an option.

[8] It is easy to assume that the only interests are those of the divorcing couple. The interests of the state and others are also important and recognising this will gain extra marks.

As can be seen from this discussion there is some merit in most of these theories. Given the complexities of family life and the broad range of issues raised, perhaps it is not surprising that there is no single theory which can explain the current law. It seems best understood as a mixture of theories recognising the partnership involved in marriage; seeking to ensure there is an equal division of the benefits and disadvantages of marriage; and ensuring that the state interests in not disincentivising parental care of children is protected.[9]

[9] This paragraph provides a neat summary of the issues that have been discussed.

Make your answer stand out

■ You could expand the discussion on the nature of equality in this context. See Eekelaar (2000) 'Post-divorce financial obligations' in S. Katz, J. Eekelaar and M. Maclean, *Cross Currents*, Oxford: OUP.

■ The interests of the state could be discussed further. See Herring (2005) 'Why financial orders on divorce should be unfair' *International Journal of Law Policy and the Family* 218.

■ There could be more discussion of whether the law should be more predictable or whether discretion is beneficial. See Miles (2005) 'Principle or pragmatism in ancillary relief' *International Journal of Law, Policy and the Family* 242.

■ More could be made of feminist approaches to this issue. See O'Donovan (2005) 'Flirting with academic categorisations' *Child and Family Law Quarterly* 415.

! **Don't be tempted to...**

■ Make the discussion too abstract.

■ Assume that one theory alone can explain the law.

📝 Question 5

Is the current law dealing with property disputes of cohabitants satisfactory?

Answer plan

→ Start with a summary of the current law.

→ Explain that express agreements are central to the law on constructive trusts.

→ Discuss the reluctance of the courts to infer agreements.

→ Consider the argument that the law reflects gender bias.

→ Many lawyers have complained of uncertainty in the current law. Is this a fair criticism?

→ Analyse different possibilities for reform of the law.

Diagram plan

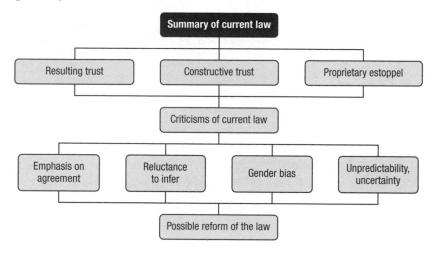

Summary of current law

Resulting trust | Constructive trust | Proprietary estoppel

Criticisms of current law

Emphasis on agreement | Reluctance to infer | Gender bias | Unpredictability, uncertainty

Possible reform of the law

A printable version of this diagram is available from www.pearsoned.co.uk/lawexpressqa

Answer

[1]Make it clear right at the start how differently married and unmarried couples are treated.

When a couple who are married or civil partners separate the court has wide powers to make period payments orders or to redistribute property.[1] These are not available for cohabiting couples. For cohabiting couples all the court can do is to declare who owns what. To do this the courts turn to the law of property which requires them to consider first who is the legal owner and then who is the owner in equity. Sometimes this is unproblematic. If when they purchased the property a couple bought the property in joint names and have made it clear that they intend to own the property equally there are few problems. However, all too often the property is only in the name of one of the parties. Then the courts need to turn to the law on resulting trusts, constructive trusts and proprietary estoppel. These rules were designed to deal with property disputes and they are not therefore designed to deal with disputes with the language of fairness that family lawyers are familiar with.[2]

[2]This is an important point to make in this essay: many of the difficulties in the cases result from the fact that the law being used is not really designed to deal with cases of this kind. This shows the examiner you are able to take an historical perspective of the issue.

[3]Remember to keep focused on the question asked.

As the focus of this essay is on the problems with the current law, what the law actually is will only be briefly summarised.[3] A resulting trust arises from a direct contribution to the purchase price for a property. This creates a rebuttable presumption that the property is to be shared proportionally in accordance with the amounts the couple have contributed. According to the House of Lords in **Lloyds Bank v Rossett** a constructive trust can be found if there is an express agreement to share ownership of the house and actions in reliance of that agreement. An agreement can be inferred from a direct contribution to the purchase price or a mortgage instalment. Some of the later cases (e.g. **Le Foe v Le Foe** [2002] 1 FCR 107, **Stack v Dowden** [2007] UKHL 17) have suggested that the courts may be more willing than in the past to infer an agreement to share ownership. If the courts do find a constructive trust they will consider all of the facts of the case in an attempt to determine the shares in which the parties intended to hold the property. A proprietary estoppel can be claimed where the applicant can show that the owner led him to believe he was going to have or did have an interest in the property and had acted to his detriment in relying on that and that it would be conscionable in all the circumstances that he receive an interest (**Gillet v Holt** [2000] FCR 705).[4]

[4]Here we have summarised in one sentence the central elements of a proprietary estoppel. It is worth in revision learning such brief summaries so that you can use them in the exams.

[5]The question asked you whether the current law was satisfactory and you are making it clear to the reader here that you are aware of a number of unsatisfactory elements which you will discuss in the essay.

The current law has been roundly condemned. There are five objections in particular.[5] The first is that for both proprietary estoppel and for constructive trusts there must be an explicit promise or agreement that the ownership of the property will be shared. However, this is unrealistic. Many couples do not discuss the ownership of property: they have more interesting things to discuss! Maybe the courts assume all cohabitants are trained lawyers! Even if they have discussed it, it is highly unlikely that years later there can be an accurate recall of precisely who said what to whom over that candle-lit dinner.

Second, it has been complained that the law is too strict in being willing to infer an agreement to share ownership of the property. The focus in **Rossett** and in the law on resulting trusts to direct financial contributions privileges those who earn and disadvantages those whose childcare commitments mean they are not able to make a financial contribution to the property (see Olsen (1998)).

A third, and linked point, is that it is said that the current law enforces gender bias. The emphasis on financial contributions as already mentioned works against the interests of those involved in childcare, who are most likely to be women. It has also been argued that the emphasis on an express agreement works in favour of the more assertive and articulate partner which in reported cases is often the man. In **Burns v Burns** [1984] Ch 317 although a woman had lived with a man for nearly 20 years and regarded

[6]It is a good idea in this essay to give a practical example of where the law produced an unfair result.

[7]It is good to show the examiner that you are able to think about the difficulties lawyers in the real world face with cases of this kind.

[8]Don't feel embarrassed about pointing out flaws with the law. The examiner does not want you to assume that the law is perfect!
Of course, you need to back up your complaints with good evidence and coherent objections.

[9]You have not been asked specifically to address reform, which is why this paragraph is fairly short. But part of criticising a law must include a suggestion as to how it could be better.

[10]In any question on cohabitation it is a good idea to discuss the Law Commission Proposals.

herself as his wife, she was not entitled to any share in the property because she never discussed ownership of the house with him.[6]

A fourth objection is that it can be extremely difficult to predict how a particular case will be decided. Will the evidence of the imperfectly remembered conversation be sufficient to found a constructive trust? What weight will the court give the different factors that can be taken into account in deciding what shares each party has under a constructive trust (**Stack v Dowden**)? Lawyers in practice complain how difficult it is to advise clients on the likely outcome of these cases (see Law Commission Report 278).[7]

A final objection is that the law itself is uncertain. As already mentioned, although Baroness Hale in **Stack v Dowden** indicated that the courts would nowadays be more flexible in inferring constructive trusts than they had been in the past, it is still far from clear what kind of evidence will be accepted. Further, it is still unclear what weight is to be given to the different factors mentioned in **Stack v Dowden** used to determine the shares under a constructive trust. The law appears to lack a coherent basis.[8]

Turning briefly to consider how the law could be reformed.[9] One option is to grant cohabiting couples the same remedies on separation that spouses or civil partners have. However, that would be controversial because it would be said to undermine the special status of marriage. The Law Commission have proposed a system under which cohabiting couples could receive some financial redistribution of property, but not so the same extent as a married couple. Under the Law Commission proposals if an applicant could prove that either the other party has gained an economic benefit during the marriage or that she has suffered an economic disadvantage as a result of the relationship, then the court can make an order ensuring a fair sharing of those gains or losses. However, the court could not make ongoing periodic payment orders. The focus would be on the unfairness during the time of the relationship and not with any needs the parties may have in the future. These proposals would give the law a greater degree of certainty. However, there is no sign that the government is due to implement them in the near future.[10]

✓ **Make your answer stand out**

■ Read the Law Commission Report 278 for a detailed discussion of the problems with the current law and some solutions.

■ A comparison with how other jurisdictions deal with the issues surrounding cohabitants might be helpful: see Bailey-Harris (1998) 'Dividing the assets on breakdown of relationships outside marriage: challenges for reformers' in R. Bailey-Harris (ed.) *Dividing the Assets on Family Breakdown*, Bristol: Jordans.

■ Consider whether there are good reasons why cohabitants should be treated differently from married couples. See Glennon (2008) 'Obligations between adult partners: Moving from form to function?' *International Journal of Law Policy and the Family* 22.

■ A feminist analysis of the case law on cohabitants would be helpful: see Wong (2004) 'Cohabitation and the Law Commission's Project' *Journal of Social Welfare and Family Law* 265.

❗ **Don't be tempted to...**

■ Get too bogged down in the detail of the current law.

■ Get sidetracked into considering whether marriage and cohabitation should be treated in the same way in all areas of family law.

Parenthood

How this topic may come up in exams

This issue is highly topical. It used to be easy to know who was a child's mother or father. No longer! It is now common for children to have a number of adults who play a parental role in a child's life. Further with advances in forms of assisted reproduction it can no longer be assumed that children have one genetic mother and one genetic father. This has made the question of who a child's mother and father are much more complex, but also much more interesting!

The law on ascertaining parenthood is confusing and it is important you learn the provisions carefully. It is also crucial to keep in mind that in family law there is a fundamental distinction between being a parent and having parental responsibility. Always make it clear whether you are discussing who is a parent or who has parental responsibility. At a theoretical level there is a deep divide between those who think that it is social parenthood ('the doing of parenting') which should be emphasised and those who think that it is the genetic link which is key. That debate is a major theme in essays.

■ Attack the question

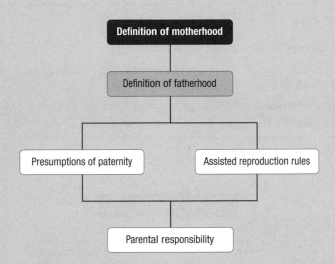

Question 1

Who is the mother and father of a child in the eyes of the law? What principles does the law use to allocate parenthood?

Answer plan

→ Provide the legal definition of the mother and the father.

→ Explain the differences between social and genetic parenthood and consider whether the law follows either one in its allocation of parentage.

→ Set out the different ways that a person can have rights and responsibilities in relation to parenthood in the law.

Diagram plan

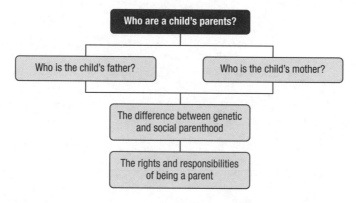

A printable version of this diagram is available from www.pearsoned.co.uk/lawexpressqa

Answer

[1] Be as precise as you can in referring to statutory provisions, for example give the year of the statute and the number of the appropriate section.

It is much easier to define a mother than it is to define a father. Section 33 Human Fertilisation and Embryology Act 2008 defines a mother as the woman who has carried the child.[1] She need not be the genetic mother. It is, therefore, the gestational, rather than genetic link, which makes a woman the mother. There is one exception to that and that is under the Human Fertilisation and Embryology Act 2008, where a civil partner of a woman receiving treatment at a licensed clinic will be treated as a parent (although rather oddly not, technically the mother) of a child (s. 42 HFE Act

2008) and similarly an unmarried female partner of the woman can be treated as the parent if she satisfies the 'agreed female parenthood conditions' (s. 44 HFE Act 2008). The 'agreed female parenthood conditions' contain a number of different criteria, but most significantly require that both the mother and her partner agree that the partner will be the parent of the child.[2]

A father of a child is normally the man who is genetically related to the child.[3] In **Leeds Teaching Hospital v A** [2003] EWCA 259, Butler Sloss P held that in the absence of some particular statutory provision or a legal presumption to the contrary the fall back position of the law is that the genetic father is the legal father. There are, however, two important exceptions to this. The first is where there is a legal presumption of paternity which has not been rebutted. The second is where there is a statutory provision saying otherwise.

There is a legal presumption of fatherhood in the following circumstances: a man who is married to a woman at the time of the birth is presumed to be the father of the child (this is known as the pate rest presumption); a man who is registered as the father of a child on the birth certificate is presumed to be the father; maybe a man who has entered into a parental agreement with the mother will be presumed to be the father; or where the facts of the case are such that the paternity can be inferred (e.g. if the man spent the night with the woman nine months before the birth). These presumptions can be rebutted under section 26 Family Law Reform Act 1969 if it is shown that on the balance of probabilities some other man was the genetic father of the child. This is normally done by the performance of DNA tests.[4] If these are done and the true genetic father is established he will be the father in the eyes of the law and the presumption will cease to be relevant.

The second exception to the rule that the genetic father is the legal father is where a statutory provision says otherwise. Under the Human Fertilisation and Embryology Acts of 1990 and 2008 a sperm donor, donating sperm to a licensed clinic will not be a father of the child (s. 41 HFE Act 2008). Further, the Act provides that a husband of a woman who gives birth following treatment at a licensed clinic will be treated as the father (s. 35 HFE Act 2008). Also a man who complies with the 'agreed fatherhood conditions', which include that the mother has given notice that she consents to the man being regarded as the father of a child (s. 37 HFE Act 2008).

[2]There is probably not time to go into all of the detail of these conditions and so it is sensible to focus on the most significant ones.

[3]In discussions of paternity it is useful to set out this general principle, before looking at the exceptions to it.

[4]The crucial point that the examiner will be looking for is that you are aware that the man will be presumed to be the father, even if he is not, in fact, the genetic father, unless steps are taken to rebutt that presumption.

[5]Don't forget to mention adoption and surrogacy when considering parenthood. This shows the examiner that you are maintaining a broad perspective on the subject and not dividing it up into little boxes.

It should also be noted that the Adoption and Children Act 2002 provides that following an adoption the birth parents of a child will cease to be parents, while the adopters will become the parents in the eyes of the law. The same is true following the making of a Parental Order under section 54 Human Fertilisation and Embryology Act 2008 in a case of surrogacy.[5]

Having summarised the law, we are now in a position to determine the principles of allocation of parenthood. There is a major division among commentators between those who argue that social parenthood (doing the day-to-day tasks of looking after a child) is what should make a person a parent (e.g. Masson (2006)) and those who think that the genetic link is what is crucial to parenthood (e.g. Bainham (2008a)).[6] It should be added at this point that there is some flexibility in the law given by the fact that it is possible to give parental responsibility to those who are involved in the day-to-day care of a child without granting them parenthood. Bainham (2008a) argues that parenthood should attach to the genetic link, while social parents should be given parenthood.[7] However, supporters of social parenthood argue that a person who has a genetic link with a child, but plays no active role in the child's life does not deserve any formal link with the child.

[6]It is good to refer to academic commentators and articles here.

[7]It is helpful to refer to specific academics who are involved in the debates.

Looking at the current law, by granting motherhood to the social link established through gestation, rather than the genetic link, it seems that motherhood is based on social parenthood. Fatherhood, by contrast, is more complex. It seems that basically genetics is at the heart of fatherhood. However, where that would produce a result which is totally at odds with social parenthoods the law can depart from the principle. Hence, a sperm donor will not be treated as a father. It might even be said that a married man will be treated as the father on the basis that he is likely to be involved as the social father. However, the fact that in recent cases (e.g. **Re H and A** [2002] 2 FCR 469) the courts have shown a willingness to order DNA tests to determine the validity of the presumption indicates that the biological truth is more important than ensuring the social father is regarded as the legal father. Perhaps the best summary is that the current law on fatherhood is a rather uneasy mixture of emphasising social parenthood and genetic parenthood.[8]

[8]The examiner will be pleased to see you use the theoretical debate over the importance of the genetic or social parent to consider the current law.

✓ Make your answer stand out

■ Make detailed reference to the Human Fertilisation and Embryology Act 2008. McCandlass and Sheldon (2010) 'The Human Fertilisation and Embryology Act 2008 and the tenacity of the sexual family' *Modern Law Review* 175 provides some useful discussion.

■ Go into more detail on the differences between genetic and social parenthood. See Masson (2006) 'Parenting by being; parenting by doing – In search of principles for founding families' in J. Spencer and A. Du Bois-Pedain *Freedom and Responsibility in Reproductive Choice*, Oxford: Hart.

■ Feminist analysis of allocation of parenthood would be useful: see Jones (2010) 'The identification of "parents" and "siblings"' in J. Wallbank, S. Choudhry and J. Herring (eds) *Rights, Gender and Family Law*, Abingdon: Routledge.

■ Not much of the writing is sympathetic of claims for the importance of genetic links but Bainham (2008a) 'Arguments over parentage' *Cambridge Law Journal* 322 is an exception and is well worth reading.

! Don't be tempted to...

■ Confuse parental responsibility and parenthood. The essay title has asked you about parenthood not parental responsibility.

■ Forget that in most cases children are born through normal sexual intercourse and assisted reproduction cases are fairly rare.

 # Question 2

Should all parents automatically be given parental responsibility?

Answer plan

→ Set out who has parental responsibility in the law.

→ Explain what parental responsibility means.

→ Discuss whether the allocation of parental responsibility should reflect who actually does the work of caring for the child.

→ Should fears over misuse of parental responsibility be a factor in deciding who should be given it?

→ Do fathers have a right to parental responsibility?

→ Consider how important it is that the law is certain.

Diagram plan

A printable version of this diagram is available from www.pearsoned.co.uk/lawexpressqa

Answer

Before addressing the question of who should get parental responsibility it is important to determine who gets parental responsibility under the current law and what parental responsibility actually means. One of the difficulties in dealing with this question is that it is far from clear what parental responsibility is and so, not surprisingly, there is considerable debate over who should get it.[1]

[1]Here you are setting out the main issues to be discussed in this introduction.

All mothers automatically get parental responsibility (s. 4 Children Act 1989). A father will have parental responsibility if:

■ He is married to the mother.

■ He is registered as the father on the child's birth certificate.

■ He enters a parental responsibility agreement with the mother.

■ He obtains a parental responsibility order from the court.

■ He is granted a residence order.

■ He has adopted the child or is appointed guardian.[2]

[2]It can be useful in an essay to use a bullet point list like this to present the material clearly. But remember the essay should generally be in regular paragraphs.

As this list shows not all fathers automatically get parental responsibility. One way of understanding the law is that a father needs to be vetted and approved by either the mother or the court before obtaining parental responsibility. Someone who is not a parent can acquire parental responsibility if they are appointed guardian or granted a residence order or emergency protection order (s. 5 Children Act 1989).[3]

[3]Even though you have not been asked about what the law is but what it should be, it is still useful to start with a summary of what the current legal position is.

One of the difficulties in discussing who should get parental responsibility is that it is far from clear what parental responsibility means.

[4]You could write a whole essay on what parental responsibility means, but that is not what you have been asked about so stick to the topic of the essay.

Section 3 of the Children Act 1989 explains that parental responsibility means all of the rights and duties which by law a parent has in relation to a child. However, this leaves unanswered what those are. As the focus of this essay is on who should get parental responsibility it is enough to state parental responsibility involves having the ability to make legally effective decisions about a child's upbringing.[4]

[5]Where possible refer to studies to back up your claims.

[6]This is an important point to make: most fathers do not need parental responsibility.

Turning now to the central themes in the debates over the allocation of parental responsibility, one key question is the significance of parental responsibility in practice. It is perfectly possible to live as a parent without having parental responsibility. Indeed in the study by Pickford of unmarried fathers the vast majority were amazed to learn they did not have parental responsibility.[5] That indicates that they had never needed to use it, otherwise they would have realised they did not have it! Given that it is legitimate to ask 'why should a father need parental responsibility',[6] there are two reasons. First, it might be said to be a symbolic matter. Having parental responsibility is a legal acknowledgement that you are legally the child's father and have the associated rights. The second is that there may be cases, albeit rare, where the father would need to have parental responsibility: if the mother was away and the child needed medical treatment, for example, or where he disagrees with the mother. These points are central to our discussion: a father does not generally need parental responsibility, unless he needs to make a decision independently of the mother. It follows from that that we might only want to give parental responsibility to a father who knows the child well enough to be able to make decisions for her. Fathers who do not see their children do not realise they should not have the ability to make decisions for children (see Deech (2009)). Wallbank (2009) has argued that parental responsibility should follow those who are engaged in the day-to-day work of caring for children. As mothers undertake the vast majority of childcare work the law is right to reflect that. Indeed unmarried fathers who are not registered on the birth certificate are unlikely to be engaged in day-to-day care of the child. They therefore, do not need parental responsibility and, if they do not know the child well, might exercise it inappropriately.[7]

[7]This paragraph has conveyed a good number of points in a short space, referring to academic experts in the area. Try and develop a concise way of writing so that you can get across many points briefly.

Another issue is fear over misuse. If all fathers were automatically granted parental responsibility it would have to be acknowledged that some inappropriate fathers might get parental responsibility, for example rapist fathers, or fathers who had engaged in domestic violence. It might be said in response that a father intent on harming the mother or child would do so whether or not he had parental responsibility. This should not therefore be used as a reason for denying good fathers parental responsibility. In **Re S (A Minor)(Parental Responsibility)** [1995] 3 FCR 225 the Court of Appeal was not convinced by fears over misuse, pointing out that in such cases the court could make orders to remove or restrict the parental responsibility. In response, however, it might be said that in extreme cases that might be too late (if, for example, the father has used parental responsibility to remove a child from a school). The correct question to ask is whether the fears of misuse are sufficiently grave to justify depriving fathers who might deserve parental responsibility from having it. As under the current law only those unmarried fathers who are not registered on the birth certificate or have not entered a parental responsibility agreement with the mother will not have parental responsibility. It might be argued that, given the statistics on domestic violence and child abuse, a fair number of them will pose a risk to the child or mother; but relatively few will be involved significantly in a child's life, that the risk of abuse outweighs the unfairness to the 'legitimate' fathers.[8]

[8]You might not agree with this. It is a matter of opinion. The examiner won't mind which view you take on controversial issues as long as you are able to present good arguments in favour of your view and set out the reasons for them.

Some claim that the current law improperly infringes on the rights of fathers. It might be said that the law is discriminatory on the basis of discrimination: it assumes all mothers should have parental responsibility, but not all fathers. One response is to refer to the fact that all mothers have, through the pregnancy and birth, shown commitment to the child, which fathers do not. It might also be said to be discriminatory on the basis of marital status on the basis that married fathers are deemed to be appropriate where unmarried fathers are not. In **B v UK** [2000] 1 FCR 289 both of these arguments were rejected by the European Court of Human Rights on the basis that while unmarried fathers covered a wide range of fathers, from the utterly committed to the utterly uncommitted, with married fathers nearly all were committed. An argument not considered in detail by the court was whether it might be said that a child is discriminated against on the basis of the marital status of her parents, if her father is not given parental responsibility.[9] The European Court has generally take a strong line against discrimination against illegitimate children and so that argument may have a greater chance of success than one based on the rights of the fathers.[10]

[9]This is a good point to make. It is easy in human rights arguments just to think about the rights of parents. The rights of children are important too!

[10]It is always good to bring in arguments based on the ECHR and the Human Rights Act. They are particularly relevant in this question.

A final issue concerns certainty over who has parental responsibility. Under the current law it is possible for a parent to produce a document to show that he or she has parental responsibility, by producing the birth certificate, a marriage certificate, a parental responsibility order or agreement the person can show they have parental responsibility. However, if all fathers automatically had parental responsibility a genetic link alone would generate parental responsibility. This would make it much harder for third parties such as schools or hospitals who need to know whether or not a particular individual has parental responsibility.

[11]It is wise to recognise that in relation to controversial issues there are good points on both sides of the argument.

As we have seen in this discussion there are strong arguments to be made on both sides of the question.[11] After the extension of parental responsibility to fathers registered on the birth certificate in the Adoption and Children Act 2002, it is submitted that the number of fully involved fathers who lack parental responsibility is small. The benefit of the current law is that it offers protection against the misuse of parental responsibility and promotes certainty in respect of proving who has parental responsibility. It should also be remembered that if a father wants parental responsibility all he needs to do is apply to the court for a parental responsibility order and the court can determine whether or not he should have it. While it must be admitted that a negative message is sent about fathers through the allocation of parental responsibility, the practical concerns outweigh the concerns about the symbolism.

✓ Make your answer stand out

- You could discuss further what parental responsibility means: see Eekelaar (1991a) 'Parental responsibility: State of nature or nature of the state' *Journal of Social Welfare and Family Law* 37 and Reece (2009) 'The degradation of parental responsibility' in R. Probert, S. Gilmore and J. Herring (eds) *Responsible Parents and Parental Responsibility*, Oxford: Hart.

- There is an interesting discussion of the difference between the terminology parentage, parenthood and parental responsibility in Bainham (2006) 'The rights and obligations associated with the birth of a child' in J. Spencer and A. du Bois-Pedain (eds) *Freedom and Responsibility in Reproductive Choice*, Oxford: Hart. See also Diduck (2007) 'If only we can find the appropriate terms to use the issue will be solved: law, identity and parenthood' *Child and Family Law Quarterly* 458.

- You could consider the proposed reforms in the Welfare Reform Act 2009 to try and pressurise mothers into providing the names of fathers when they register births. The potential impact of this on parental responsibility is discussed in Wallbank (2009) '"Bodies in the Shadows" Joint Birth Registration, parental responsibility and social class' *Child and Family Law Quarterly* 21, 267.

! **Don't be tempted to...**

■ Assume all fathers have parental responsibility.

■ Assume all mothers are perfect.

? Question 3

Veronica is happily married to Peter. One evening at a works party she got drunk and had sex with Simon. Nine months later she gave birth to a daughter, Sue. Peter is happy to assume that Sue is his. Initially Simon was uninterested in Sue, however four years later when he suffered an injury at work which rendered him infertile, he brought proceedings requesting a DNA test to determine Sue's paternity. Peter belongs to a small religious group, the leaders of which have instructed him to leave Veronica if it transpires that Sue is not his child, even though he has undertaken an equal amount of childcare with Sue. Veronica opposes Simon's application because she fears it will destroy her marriage.

Discuss whether the court is likely to order DNA tests.

Answer plan

→ Consider the arguments that will be used in favour of ordering DNA tests.

→ Assess what arguments will be used against carrying out tests.

→ Explore whether the Human Rights Act 1998 will add anything to the discussion.

Diagram plan

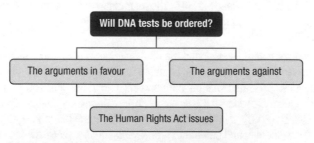

A printable version of this diagram is available from www.pearsoned.co.uk/lawexpressqa

Answer

[1] It is important to show an awareness of the different views that the courts have taken. Don't feel embarrassed about saying that decisions contradict each other.

[2] Notice this is one of the rare situations in family law where the interests of the child are not paramount. This shows that you are looking at this issue in the broader context of child law, which the examiner will like.

[3] You are showing the examiner that you have read the case and are aware of the arguments that influenced the judge in this case.

[4] It is important to show the examiner that you are aware of the history of the case law. In this case you are mentioning J v C to show that even though Re H and A was after Re F, the courts still seem sometimes to rely on the kind of reasoning used in Re F.

Where there is a dispute over the paternity of a child section 21 Family Law Reform Act 1969 allows the court to order biological tests. The courts have not been consistent in their approach towards ordering tests.[1] The welfare of the child is not the paramount consideration, but rather the House of Lords in **S v S, W v Official Solicitor** [1972] AC 24 explained that tests would be ordered unless that would be against the interests of the child.[2]

In recent years the courts have generally ordered tests in cases of these kinds. The courts tend to assume that it is better for a child to know the truth than to be raised in a deception (**Re D** [2006] EWHC 3545). In **Re H and A** [2002] 2 FCR 469 Ward LJ recognised that children had a right to know the truth about their parentage and referred to article 7 of the UN Convention on the Rights of the Child. In that case the argument in favour of tests was very strong because it was widely known that there were question marks over the paternity of the child and there was no way the child would not be aware of the issues at some point. Ward LJ believed it was better for the child to know the truth now, than have the truth suddenly discovered later in life.[3]

The arguments against would focus on **Re F** [1993] Fam 314. In that case a married woman had an affair. As in Sue's case the husband was willing to assume that the child was his, but threatened to leave if it transpired the child was not. In fact this case may be stronger because Peter's religious beliefs might be evidence that it is more likely he will go through with his threats than it was in **Re F**. The Court of Appeal in **Re F** emphasised that the welfare of the child, while not paramount, was a very important consideration. The court, when considering the child's welfare, placed greater weight on the stability of the family unit than knowledge about the truth of paternity. More recently, in **J v C** [2006] EWHC 551 tests were again not ordered.[4] The mother assured the court that the child would be told the truth when he was older, but at this stage discovering the truth would cause grave disruption. It was better for the child at this stage not to know the truth. Again a similar point might be made in relation to Sue. That said, in **J v C** the father was uninterested in having contact. It may, therefore, be in Sue's case the court would consider whether it would benefit Sue if she were to have contact with Simon. If not, that might be an argument against doing tests.

[5]The examiner will want you to bring in a human rights angle where possible.

[6]The examiner will want to be reassured that you realise that with article 8 rights, it can always be argued that a breach of them is justified under article 8(2).

[7]Note in this problem question it is difficult to be certain what a court will order. What you have done is given to the examiner a list of the factors to be taken into account and set out the key question the judge will ask.

The court might look at the case from the perspective of the Human Rights Act.[5] In **Mikulic v Croatia** [2002] 1 FCR 720 the court accepted that a child had a right to know her biological parenthood as part of her right to respect for private life under article 8. The court held that the state needed to ensure that this right was protected. However, the court did accept that there could be good reasons to interfere with that right under article 8(2) if necessary to protect the child's welfare (**Yousef v The Netherlands** [2002] 3 FCR 577).[6] Notably the European Court has seen these cases as involving the rights of the child, rather than the rights of the father to establish his paternity. The European Court of Human Rights would, then, start from the point of view that the child has a right to know the truth, but would see the burden of proving that the tests would cause such harm that they should not be done on those not wanting them.

It is difficult to predict how the courts would resolve this dispute. It seems following **Re H and A** that there is a preference for establishing the truth. However, it is clear from **J v C** that that is not an absolute preference and significant harm to the child will justify not ordering tests. If the court is satisfied that Sue is being well looked after by Veronica and Peter and that carrying out tests could cause Sue serious harm if it led to the breakdown of the family they may be satisfied that tests should not be ordered.[7]

 Make your answer stand out

- Look at the case law on both sides of the argument and explore the uncertainty over the law's approach. Interestingly one of the leading commentators on this issue has changed her mind on the correct approach to take. Compare Fortin (1996) 'Re F: the gooseberry bush approach' *Modern Law Review* 296 with Fortin (2009b) 'Children's Right to Know Their Origins – Too Far, Too Fast?' *Child and Family Law Quarterly* 336.

- Look in more detail at the case law of the European Court of Human Rights on this. See Choudhry and Herring (2010) *European Human Rights and Family Law* ch. 5, Oxford: Hart.

- You could look further at the arguments over why blood ties should be important. See Lind (2008) 'Responsible fathers: paternity, the blood tie and family responsibility' in J. Bridgeman, H. Keating and C. Lind (eds) *Responsibility, Law and the Family*, London: Ashgate.

> **! Don't be tempted to...**
>
> - Focus too much on the 'father's rights'. The court will emphasise the interests of children.
> - Assume that *Re H and A* represents the law. There have been several cases since then.

? Question 4

Suni became pregnant after a short relationship with Colin. Suni later married Wu and gave birth to baby Alberta and Wu was registered as her father. Colin has sent cards and presents for Alberta and he sometimes sends money to Suni for her upkeep. Alberta is now three and Colin wants to play a more active role in Alberta's life. Suni has agreed that Colin can see Alberta for a few hours twice a year. However, Colin wants parental responsibility, which Suni opposes. Suni is worried that Colin, who has strong religious views, will use parental responsibility to interfere in the way she is raising Alberta. Advise Colin on whether a court is likely to grant him parental responsibility.

Answer plan

→ Consider whether the current levels of contact between Colin and Alberta argue in favour or against Colin getting parental responsibility.

→ Discuss how the courts will deal with Suni's concerns over misuse.

→ What weight will be attached to Colin's level of commitment to Alberta?

→ Explain the different understandings of parental responsibility and how they may affect whether it will be granted to Colin.

→ What significance, if any, will be attached to Suni's possible reaction to the granting of parental responsibility?

Diagram plan

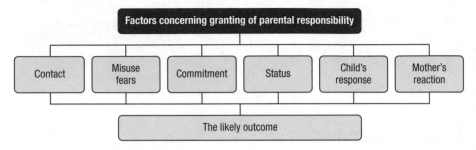

A printable version of this diagram is available from www.pearsoned.co.uk/lawexpressqa

Answer

[1]The problem question implies that Colin is the father, but does not say so explicitly. But this is a crucial issue so it is worth starting with that. If you think there is an ambiguity in the problem question it is better to be up front with the examiner with that.

[2]It may seem obvious that the welfare principle applies, but it still needs explaining. Don't be embarrassed about saying the obvious. If you don't say it the examiner may worry that you are ignoring it.

[3]The examiner will like the fact you are specifically addressing how this criterion is likely to be used in Colin's case.

It will be assumed in answering this question that it has been established that Colin is the father of a child, because if he is not he can only obtain parental responsibility if he is awarded a residence order, which seems very unlikely.[1] It will also be assumed that it has not been possible to persuade Suni to agree to enter a parental responsibility agreement. In that case Colin will need to apply to the courts for a parental responsibility order under section 4 Children Act 1989. Section 1 of the Children Act 1989 applies and therefore the court's paramount consideration will be whether making the order will promote the welfare of the child.[2] There is no presumption in favour of awarding parental responsibility (**Re H (Parental Responsibility)** [1998] 2 FCR 89). The case law suggests the following factors will be considered.

The court will look at the quality of the relationship between Colin and Alberta, and in particular the extent to which contact has taken place (**Re S (A Minor)(Parental Responsibility)** [1995] 3 FCR 225). This does not mean that a parental responsibility order will not be made if there has not been contact, but where there has been regular contact there will need to be very good reasons not to award parental responsibility. In **Re J (Parental Responsibility)** [2002] 3 FCR 433 a father failed in an attempt to get parental responsibility after he was described by the court as 'almost a stranger' to the child. Colin's application appears weak in this regard.[3] He has kept contact through cards, but he cannot claim to have established a relationship with Alberta. If you can show this was due to Suni's attitude, rather than a lack of care on his part the court may attach less weight to this factor.

The court will consider the reasons why Colin wants parental responsibility and whether there are concerns that he will misuse it. Generally the courts are not willing to place much weight on vague fears of misuse (**Re S (A Minor)(Parental Responsibility)**). In this case the main issue seems to be a concern that Colin will interfere in Suni's upbringing of the child. The court is likely to take the view (as it did in **Re S**) that if a father misused his parental responsibility then the court would remove it. It is worth noting that the courts have said that the mother should consult with the father with parental responsibility over important issues concerning the child's upbringing (**Re J**). So there is scope for arguments over how Alberta should be raised. In **Re D** [2006] EWHC 2 a father was given parental responsibility but then prohibited in interfering in medical or schooling issues. A court could make such a restriction on parental responsibility if there were concrete fears concerning Colin's misuse. On a more positive note the court would want to know why Colin was applying for the order and what benefits his having parental responsibility would accrue to Alberta.

Another factor the court will consider is whether or not he has shown commitment to Alberta (**Re H (Parental Responsibility)**). In this case Colin can emphasise the fact he has kept in touch over the past three years by cards and has offered some financial support. Suni might respond by arguing that he has only made some contributions to Alberta's upkeep and has not made a full contribution. Regular financial support has been accepted in some cases as an argument in favour of granting parental responsibility (**Re S (A Minor)**). However, it seems not to be a hugely important factor.[4]

[4]When in a problem question like this you are listing factors the court will take into account, try to give an indication about which issues will be given particular weight.

In **Re S (A Minor)** it was suggested that parental responsibility gave an unmarried father a status and confirmed that he is the father. It referred to parental responsibility as 'a stamp of approval' demonstrating the court's approval of his commitment. The Court of Appeal seemed to see the value of parental responsibility as essentially being symbolic. If that case were followed then only if Colin had acted in a highly inappropriate way would he be denied parental responsibility. The court's approach has been criticised with Helen Reece (2009) referring to the 'degradation of parental responsibility'.[5] It must be admitted that there are other cases

[5]This is a useful phrase to remember and bring into essays concerning parental responsibility.

where the practical importance of parental responsibility is mentioned (**M v M** [1999] 2 FLR 737).

Another factor mentioned in **Re S (A Minor)** was that the child would be disturbed if she later found out that her father was denied parental responsibility and it would create a very negative image of him in her mind. This argument has not been well received by academics (e.g. Herring (2009a)) on the basis that teenagers are unlikely to care too much about legal proceedings, perhaps years ago, as opposed to their actual experience of what their father has done in their life.[6]

[6]Don't feel embarrassed about saying you think the argument that a judge has used was a weak one.

A final factor the court will consider is the reaction of the mother to the order. Generally the courts are not willing to attach much weight to the upset granting the order will cause the mother (**D v S**) unless it can be shown that Suni is so upset that her ability to be a good parent will be affected.

In summary, Colin is likely to emphasise **Re S (A Minor)** and argue that he is a committed father and therefore deserves the stamp of approval offered by a parental responsibility order. In response, Suni is likely to emphasise the lack of contact between Colin and Alberta and argue there is no real relationship between them. Although the result cannot be predicted with certainty, the statistics indicate that parental responsibility orders are rarely refused and so a court is likely to make a parental responsibility order.[7]

[7]This summary brings together well the key issues the courts will be taking into account, which the examiner will like to see.

 Make your answer stand out

- Consider in more detail the relevant cases. See Reece (2009) 'The degradation of parental responsibility' in R. Probert, S. Gilmore and J. Herring (eds) *Responsible Parents and Parental Responsibility*, Oxford: Hart.

- You could put the arguments over parental responsibility in the context of wider disputes over the position of fathers in family law. See Gilmore (2003) 'Parental responsibility and the unmarried father – a new dimension to the debate' *Child and Family Law Quarterly* 15.

- The essay could also refer to some of the arguments that could be made based on the Human Rights Act 1998. See Choudhry and Herring (2010) *European Human Rights and Family Law*, ch. 5, Oxford: Hart.

Don't be tempted to...

■ Assume that only those who are going to play a role in the life of the child will get parental responsibility.

■ Focus on the rights of the adults, rather than the interests of the child.

Question 5

Do children in English law have a right to know their genetic origins? Should they?

Answer plan

→ Clarify what is meant by a right to know and what are genetic origins.

→ Consider the position of children born following sexual intercourse.

→ Discuss when the courts will use DNA tests to see if presumptions are rebutted.

→ Explain the extent to which a right to know is acknowledged in the law on assisted reproduction.

→ Do those who are adopted have a right to know their birth families?

→ Assess the significance of the Human Rights Act in this area.

→ Set out the different policy issues that can arise.

Diagram plan

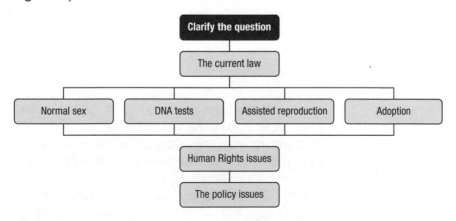

A printable version of this diagram is available from www.pearsoned.co.uk/lawexpressqa

Answer

[1]It is always good to put just a bit of historical context when answering a question.

[2]Examiners like it when you explore the ambiguities behind a question before discussing it.

[3]It is important in this topic to discuss not only the right to know, but also the right not to know. This shows the examiner that you are thinking 'out of the box'. Always try turning questions on their head (i.e. asking the opposite of what is asked) to see if that gives you an interesting angle on them.

[4]Never forget the gender issues. Is what is being said equally true for men or women, for mothers and fathers? The examiner will be keen to see an awareness of gender issues.

It is only fairly recently that it has been possible to ascertain a child's genetic identity with any degree of certainty through DNA tests.[1] Before they were available no doubt children assumed that the people they were raised by were their parents. The technology has caused considerable debate among family lawyers over the extent to which children have a right to know their genetic origins. It is important to be clear that there are quite a number of issues that are hidden behind the one question.[2] First, there is the question of whether this is a right children have or whether it is a right that someone has when they become an adult. Second, there is the question of what information a person has a right to: just medical information; or does it include the right to know the name of one's parents; or even the right to meet them? Third, there is the question over the right *not* to know.[3] A child might be given information which they would rather not have known. These are issues we shall return to later in this essay. Before that, we need to look further at the current law.

When children are born as a result of normal sexual intercourse there is little attempt to ascertain their genetic origins. DNA tests are not automatically carried out on babies so that an attempt can be made to determine who their parents are. A mother is required to register the birth of the child. She can register the birth, but is not required to name the father. The Welfare Reform Act 2009, when it comes into force, will allow fathers to register and is designed to encourage a mother to name the father. However, there is no effective punishment if she does not or cannot. There is, therefore, little attempt in relation to normal sexual intercourse to ensure a child can know who her father is. By contrast, the obligation on mothers to register the birth means that children will know who their gestational mothers are.[4]

In cases of normal sexual intercourse where a man is not registered as the father (or the wrong man is) the law relies on the genetic father bringing an application to court, seeking an order under the Family Law Act 1986 that tests be performed. Although the case law is not entirely consistent most of the recent cases have preferred ordering tests (**Re H and A** [2002] 2 FCR 469; **Re T** [2001] 3 FCR 577). The courts in those cases have emphasised that it is important for children to know the truth about genetic origins. This has meant that unless there are strong arguments to the contrary (e.g. **Re F** [1993] Fam 314) the court will order tests. This case law might be read as suggesting that the courts recognise a child's right to know the truth about their genetic origins (as stated in **Re T**). However, it is important to realise that the question of DNA tests only arises where a father wants to establish that he is the father. It would, therefore, be accurate to say that the law is giving effect to a father's rights to establish his paternity, rather than the child's right to know her genetic origins.[5]

Following the Human Fertilisation and Embryology Authority (Disclosure of Donor Information) Regulations 2004 a child born as a result of donor's gametes can discover the donor's name, date of birth, town of birth, and any statement made by the donors. Following the Human Fertilisation and Embryology Act 2008 there is now a register of all gamete donors. A child, once she has reached the age of 16 is entitled to find out the information on the register. This might appear to be a strong statement giving effect to children's rights to know their genetic origins, indeed that was the basis upon which the regulations were justified. However, the right is far less protected than might appear. That is because there is no obligation on parents to inform their children that they have been born using donated gametes. The studies (e.g. Maclean and Maclean (1996)) indicate very few parents in such cases do inform their children. Of course, if a child has no idea she was born using donated gametes she will not know she could look on the register. Without such a legal obligation it seems the law is only paying lip service to the alleged right to know genetic origins.

In relation to adopted children section 79 of the Adoption and Children Act 2002 requires the Registrar General of Births to keep records so as to enable a person to discover details of their birth certificate, which will include details of the child's mother, but not necessarily father. There is also an adoption contact register that enables an adopted person to seek to make contact with their birth families. Unlike assisted reproduction, most adopted children do know they are adopted and so their right to access this information is reasonably well protected.[6]

So, despite the rhetoric, it is suggested that the law does little to protect the alleged right to know one's genetic origins. Through the birth registration system, and the Adoption and Children Act 2002 access to information about one's gestational mother is readily obtained, but the law does relatively little to protect rights for a child who wishes to discover their genetic origins.

The English courts, perhaps surprisingly, have played relatively little attention to the case law on the issue from the European Court of Human Rights. **Mikulik v Croatia** [2002] 1 FCR 720 recognised that a child had a right to know her biological parentage as part of her right to private life in article 8 of the Convention. Three points are interesting about that conclusion. First, it is noticeable that this is seen as an aspect of private life, rather than family life. The importance of that is the court thought the information was of value to an individual, even if there was no actual relationship between them and their genetic parent. Second, the court saw this as the child's right, rather than a parent having a right to establish their paternity. Third, because the right is part of article 8, an interference can be justified under paragraph two. In **Yousef v The Netherlands** [2002] 3 FCR 577 it was accepted that if the child would be harmed by the information that might justify interfering with her right know her genetic origins.[7]

[7]It is always useful to bring in the human rights dimension in this issue.

Should the law protect a right to genetic origins? Those in favour make a number of points. First, Eekelaar (2006a) has argued that information about one's genetic origins is a basic good and that no one would wish to be brought up deceived about their genetic origins. Second, it has been argued that children who have not been able to find out about their genetic origins (e.g. adopted children) suffer psychological harm in being denied access to the information. Third O'Donovan argues that there may be medical reasons why a child needs to know their genetic origins.[8] However, that last point would not lead to children having a right to know the names of their genetic parents, only certain key medical information.

[8]Don't forget there may be very concrete practical reasons why knowing genetic origins is important.

What arguments could be made against the alleged right? Some commentators are willing to accept that there are arguments in favour of allowing access to the information they are commonly outweighed by other considerations such as maintaining stability of the family in which the child is being raised; or not discouraging sperm donation. For example, in the assisted reproduction context, we need to weigh up the benefits of providing the knowledge of the genetic origins with the impact that will have on the parents raising the child; rates of sperm donation; and the confusion the child may feel when informed of their origins (see Price and Cook (1995)). Those who make such an argument might also argue that far more important than any genetic links a child has with other adults, is the day-to-day social care of the child, and this should be emphasised. The genetic truth should not be disclosed at the cost of harming the social care of the child (see Fortin (2009b)).

As we have seen the law does allow access to information about genetic origins, but it does not seem to regard it as an especially strong right. That it is suggested is correct. Knowledge about genetic origins can have benefits but these need to be weighed carefully against all of the possible disadvantages that a child can suffer if the truth is revealed. Genetic origins may be important, but they are not the only thing that is important to a child.[9]

[9]Here the conclusion brings together the main issues that have been discussed in the essay.

 Make your answer stand out

- Explore the various meaning of a right to know genetic origins. See Fortin (2009b) 'Children's Right to Know Their Origins – Too Far, Too Fast?' *Child and Family Law Quarterly* 336 for a useful discussion of how a 'right to know' can have a variety of meanings.
- One of the problems with acknowledging the right to know in the context of sperm donation has been the resulting shortage of sperm donors. That issue could be explored further and is discussed in Turkmendag, Dingwall and Murphy (2008) 'The removal of donor anonymity in the UK: The silencing of claims by would-be parents' (2008) *International Journal of Law, Policy and the Family* 283.
- Refer to a broad range of academic writings. Consider O'Donovan (1988) 'A right to know one's parentage' *International Journal of Law, Policy and the Family* 27 and Bainham (2008b) 'What is the point of birth registration?' *Child and Family Law Quarterly* 449.

! Don't be tempted to...

- Assume that the law is the same in relation to mothers and fathers.
- Confuse the issues of who is a parent and the right to know genetic origins. You could give a daughter the right to know who her genetic father is, without making him the father.

Children's rights

7

How this topic may come up in exams

This is a highly topical issue and is a popular theme with examiners. An essay question may ask you generally about children's rights. These essays are likely to ask you to consider whether the law should acknowledge children's rights. You will need to be able to discuss some of the theoretical literature. A major theme is the extent to which children should have autonomy rights even where their decision will cause them some harm. Alternatively the essay could ask you about children's rights in a particular area of the law, such as medical decisions or representation in court.

Problem questions are likely to involve situations where a child wishes to do something which her parent, or someone else, thinks is harmful or unwise. It may be you will need to consider the law on disputes over children, which is discussed in Chapter 8.

▨ Attack the question

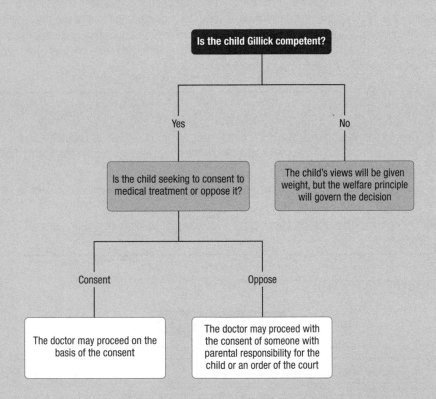

❓ Question 1

Sam, aged 14, is seriously ill and needs a blood transfusion. Without it he has an 80 per cent chance of dying. He and his parents refuse to consent because they belong to a religious group that believes that blood transfusions are sinful. He has been assessed by a psychiatrist as highly intelligent and mature. During their discussions Sam's parents have asked his doctor to perform cosmetic surgery on his nose. Sam opposes any such surgery, but his parents are very keen. Advise Sam's doctors on whether they can lawfully give Sam the blood transfusion or perform the surgery on his nose.

Answer plan

→ Start by considering whether Sam is Gillick competent. Determine his understanding of the medical and family issues. Consider too whether his religious upbringing affects the assessment of his capacity.

→ On the issue of the blood transfusion explain the effect in law of Sam and his parents' refusal.

→ On the issue of cosmetic surgery, discuss the effect of his consent and his parents' refusal.

Diagram plan

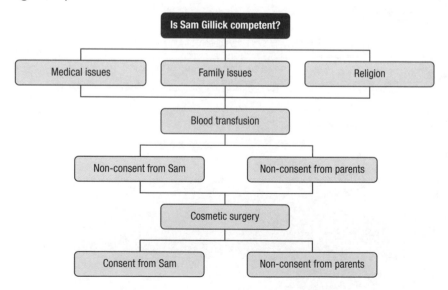

A printable version of this diagram is available from www.pearsoned.co.uk/lawexpressqa

Answer

[1]It is always sensible to start a problem question involving children's rights by considering whether the child is Gillick competent.

[2]The examiner will want you to make clear that even if a child is not Gillick competent his or her views can still be considered as one factor in deciding what is in the child's interest.

[3]This is an important point: discuss the understanding of both the medical and family issues when considering Gillick competence.

[4]The examiner will not want to see you making a crude assumption that religious children are not capable of making their own decisions.

[5]We have to move on to the next stage of the problem and so it is appropriate to make an assumption of this kind.

To deal with this issue we must first determine whether Sam is Gillick competent[1] because if he is not his views will carry very little weight save as one of the factors in deciding what will be in his interest.[2] The House of Lords in **Gillick** [1986] AC 402 held that even a child under the age of 16 could be competent to consent to medical treatment if he or she had sufficient understanding of the issues. First it is necessary to consider whether Sam understood the medical issues involved. As the Court of Appeal emphasised in **Re R** [1992] 2 FCR 229, a child would need to understand the proposed treatment, the consequences of the treatment, and the consequences of not giving the treatment. For example, in **Re L** [2005] 1 FCR 421, the child was found not competent because L did not understand exactly what would happen to her if the treatment was not provided. In this case, Sam is described as highly intelligent and he may, therefore, be able to show that he understands the medical issues around both the blood transfusion and the cosmetic surgery.

The House of Lords in **Gillick** emphasised that to be competent not only must a child understand the medical issues, he or she must also understand the moral and family issues involved.[3] In **Re E** [1992] 2 FCR 219 a child was found not to be competent because he did not appreciate how upset his parents would be if he were to die. In this case Sam would need to show he appreciated the impact his death would have on his parents. In relation to the cosmetic surgery he would need to show he was aware of the potential impact on his family life if he were to oppose the treatment his parents wished him to have.

A final issue on competence is his religion. The courts have been concerned about the competence of children with strong religious views. In **Re L** the court noted that he had spent his life within the Jehovah's Witness community and felt he had only a limited experience of the world. This contributed them to finding him not competent. **Re S** [1994] 1 FCR 607 took a similar line in relation to a child of strong religious views. These cases have been criticised by some commentators. Certainly it should not be assumed that because a child is religious he or she is therefore lacking capacity.[4]

We will assume that the courts are willing to find Sam competent.[5] If we consider the first issue, the doctors are not permitted to carry out the operation if the competent child and those with parental

[6]It might seem obvious and even repetitive to say that the interests of the children prevail, but the examiner will not mind the emphasis on this crucial point.

responsibility withhold consent, unless they get a court order (**Glass v UK** [2004] 1 FCR 553). So in this case if the doctors wish to perform the transfusion they will need an order of the court declaring the transfusion lawful. The court will decide whether or not to authorise the transfusion judged on what is in the best interests of the child (**Re A (Conjoined Twins)** [2000] 3 FCR 577. Weight will be placed on the views of the child (**Re MM** [2000] 1 FLR 224) and of the parents (**Re T** [1993] 1 FCR 973) but at the end of the day the best-interests test will prevail.[6] In this case it is hard to see how the court will avoid finding that it is in Sam's best interests to have the transfusion and will authorise it.

[7]The examiner will be watching out to see if you have got this point. Don't make the assumption that a child or parent can get any treatment they want.

Turning next to the issue of the cosmetic surgery. In **Gillick** the House of Lords confirmed that a competent child could give effective consent to receive medical treatment. However, in subsequent cases (especially **Re R** and **Re W** [1992] 2 FCR 785) it was explained that this did not mean the child had the right to refuse treatment. If a competent child refuses to consent, the child can still be given treatment if the parents with parental responsibility consent. However, there is an important caveat on this and that is the doctor should only give the treatment if he or she is convinced it is in the best interests of the patient (**Gillick**).[7] So the doctor will need to be persuaded that the operation will be in Sam's best interests, particularly bearing in mind that Sam himself objects to it. Unless there is some very strong reason why the operation is needed it is submitted that it is unlikely to be in his best interests. The doctor could bring the matter to court and seek an order confirming the legality of the operation. Forcing an operation on a competent child without his consent could well infringe his rights under article 3 of

[8]It is always helpful to bring in ECHR issues.

the European Convention on Human Rights.[8] It is therefore most unlikely the court will authorise the cosmetic surgery in this case.

✓ Make your answer stand out

- Discuss in more detail the cases where a child will be Gillick competent. See Harris-Short and Miles (2007) *Family Law* ch. 8, Oxford: OUP, for a helpful discussion.

- Discuss the Human Rights Act issues that arise. See Choudhry and Herring (2010) *European Human Rights and Family Law* ch. 6, Oxford: Hart.

- You could explore in more detail the judgments in *Gillick*. There is a detailed analysis in Gilmore (2009) 'The limits of parental responsibility' in R. Probert, S. Gilmore and J. Herring *Responsible Parents and Parental Responsibility*, Oxford: Hart.

! Don't be tempted to...

- Assume that because a child has capacity to consent she has capacity to refuse treatment.
- Argue that because a child lacks capacity to make a decision on one issue he or she lacks the capacity to make any decision.

🔖 Question 2

Assess the arguments that are used against acknowledging children's rights.

Answer plan

→ Consider which jurisprudential theory of rights can be used in relation to children.

→ Discuss whether the misuse of children's rights is an argument against giving children rights.

→ Examine the argument that children cannot have rights because they are dependent on their parents.

→ Is there a clash between the idea that children have rights and that children need protection?

→ Should we be more concerned with enforcing adult obligations towards children than granting children rights?

→ Explore the difficulties there are in enforcing children's rights.

Diagram plan

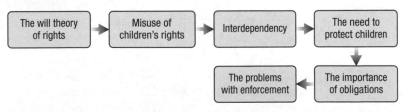

A printable version of this diagram is available from www.pearsoned.co.uk/lawexpressqa

Answer

Much has been written on the importance of recognising that children have rights and there has been great debate on which rights children should have. This all assumes that children should have rights. That assumption may seem obvious: children should have human rights because they are human. But in fact there have been a number of commentators who have questioned the assumption of the benefits of recognising human rights and their arguments will be examined in this essay.[1]

First, some writers from the perspective of jurisprudence have argued in favour of the 'will theory of rights'. This argues that rights can only exist where a person can choose whether or not to exercise those rights. Rights which are enforced without your permission cannot be seen properly as rights. Supporters of such a line argue that children who cannot choose whether or not to enforce their rights, should not be seen as having them. Supporters of children's rights argue that if one adopts a rival version of rights called the interest theory, which protects the interests of children it does not require that they have capacity. Alternatively one could adopt the will theory but argue that someone other than the child (e.g. the parents) can decide whether or not to enforce the rights.[2]

A second concern is that children's rights can be misused to pursue the interests of adults, rather than children. Indeed it is not difficult to find examples of how children's rights have been used in a way to undermine the interests of women, and perhaps even children themselves. For example, it has been suggested by Smart and Neale that talk of children's rights in the contact context have been used to promote the interests of fathers rather than children and as a way of overcoming arguments based on women's interests.[3] This is an important concern. However, it should not be regarded as a 'knock out' blow against children's rights, but rather emphasises how important it is that children's rights be treated with care. We must ensure that claims brought using children's rights are indeed seeking to promote the interests of children, rather than adults.[4]

A third claim is that children are dependent on their parents. This means that it is not possible to separate out the interests and rights of children and parents. Their rights and interests are so intertwined that to talk of children's rights is misleading. A rather different claim is

[1] It is helpful in an essay to set out some of the main themes that will be dealt with.

[2] It would be possible to write a whole essay on the jurisprudential issues. However, this is a family law exam so keep this discussion fairly brief.

[3] The examiner will want to see you giving a practical example of how rights have been misused.

[4] The examiner will be pleased to see you considering whether this is an argument to put in the balance or whether it is an argument which is a 'knock out' blow against other arguments.

that rights are based on individualistic values which do not work well in family life which is based on mutuality (see Sevenhuijsen (1997)). Indeed some commentators (e.g. Smart (1989)) have promoted an ethic of care which places weight on relationships and caring, rather than an ethic of justice which prioritises rights. It is submitted that these arguments have much force, but it is a criticism that can be made of rights generally. Adults, like children, live in a network of relationships which makes talk of rights problematic. If we are to retain a legal system that uses rights, children should be allowed to use them, just as adults are. It may be, therefore, that we need to use rights in a sensitive and careful way to ensure they protect relationships and do not undermine them (see Herring and Taylor (2006)).[5]

[5]This discussion will score well in an exam because it shows that you are aware that rights can be used in a variety of ways and there are different forms of rights-based arguments.

A fourth concern is that we need to protect children, not risk their welfare by giving them rights. This argument is particularly motivated by the concern that letting children make decisions for themselves can lead to them being taken advantage of by adults. We need to focus on protecting children from harm, rather than giving them freedom. This concern overlooks the points that human rights can be used to protect children. For example, in **Z v UK** [2001] 2 FCR 246 the European Court of Human Rights held that children have a right to be protected from abuse at the hands of their parents.[6] It also assumes that a rights based approach would allow children to make decisions which would cause them serious harm. Jane Fortin, a leading advocate of children's rights, has argued that we should never use a model of children's rights which would lead to children's rights being exercised in a way which harmed children.[7] That said, other models of children's rights would allow children autonomy rights which would cause them harm. The point is, however, that whether children's rights will or will not risk their welfare depends on which version of children's rights you adopt.

[6]It is helpful here to give a precise argument.

[7]Where possible refer to leading commentators, rather than just saying 'some people say...'.

Onora O'Neill (2002) has argued that we should not focus on children's rights, but rather on the obligations that adults have towards children.[8] However, there is no reason why these are necessarily inconsistent. Indeed one reason why we might say that adults have obligations, is because children have rights. Certainly O'Neill makes a good point that in focusing on the rights of children we should not lose sight of the corresponding obligations that adults have.

[8]Referring to the writing of a philosopher will suggest to the examiner that you have been reading widely.

A final concern over children's rights is over enforcement. Children do not have access to courts and so it may be difficult to ensure that their rights are protected. This is a genuine concern, but should not lead us to abandon children's rights. There are ways around this difficulty. Parents or others can bring claims on behalf of children. The children's ombudsman could be empowered to bring proceedings on behalf of children.

To summarise the opponents of children's rights raise some valid concerns. However, their objections should not cause us to abandon children's rights. Rather we should be careful in how they are used and we should make sure there is proper enforcement. The arguments show that although much good can be done with children's rights, much harm can be done too.[9]

[9]This provides a useful summary of the key issues raised in the essay.

 Make your answer stand out

- Consider some of the different theories of rights: see for example the writing on relational autonomy: Herring (2010b) 'Relational autonomy and family law' in J. Wallbank, S. Choudhry and J. Herring (eds) *Rights, Gender and Family Law*, Abingdon: Routledge.
- Read Onora O'Neill's (2002) article ('Children's rights and children's lives' *International Journal of Law Policy and the Family* 24) so that you can discuss her objections in detail.
- Consider whether an ethic of care may be a more effective way of promoting children's interests: See Choudhry, Herring and Wallbank (2010) 'Welfare, rights, care and gender in family law' in J. Wallbank, S. Choudhry and J. Herring (eds) *Rights, Gender and Family Law*, Abingdon: Routledge.
- It is well worth referring to M. Freeman (2007) 'Why it remains important to take children's rights seriously' *International Journal of Children's Rights* 5 as a powerful call for recognising children's rights.

! Don't be tempted to...

- Spend too long on the jurisprudential issues.
- Assume there are no problems with talk of children's rights.
- Keep the discussion too theoretical and avoid actual cases.

Question 3

Should children's autonomy rights be respected?

> ## Answer plan
>
> → Child liberation.
>
> → Paternalism.
>
> → Eekelaar's (2006a) model: basic, developmental and autonomy interests.

Diagram plan

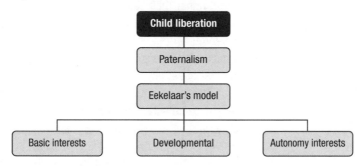

A printable version of this diagram is available from www.pearsoned.co.uk/lawexpressqa

Answer

[1]It is a good idea to discuss the key words in the essay at the start, in this case the issue of autonomy.

[2]There are lots of theories of children's rights and it is sensible to limit yourself to discuss three. Make it clear to the examiner that you realise there are more issues that could be discussed.

Before answering this question it is necessary to explain the notion of autonomy.[1] Autonomy is in essence the right to be able to make decisions for yourself. To be able to forge one's own vision of the 'good life' (see Raz (1986)). Of course autonomy is limited: you have no right to make decisions which will cause harm to other people. But it is generally seen as an essential aspect of autonomy that one can make decisions which cause the person harm or which might be regarded as foolish by others. John Eekelaar (2006a) sees the 'right to make mistakes' as an essential part of autonomy. In this answer I will consider three possible answers to the question: child liberation; paternalism; and the model promoted by John Eekelaar (2006a).[2]

According to child liberationists, such as Holt (1975) and Farson (1978), children should be given the same rights that adults have. They view modern understanding of childhood as a form of slavery whereby children are assumed incompetent and lacking rights so that adults can exercise power over them. Holt and Farson take their argument to its logical conclusion arguing for children having the rights to vote, work and engage in sexual relations in the same way as adults. For them, children should have the same autonomy rights as any adult. And they should be able to exercise these rights in foolish or harmful ways, just as adults do.[3]

[3]The examiner will be watching to see if you appreciate that most supporters of autonomy believe that an autonomous decision should be respected, even if other people would think it a foolish one.

There are plenty of critics of such an approach. It is argued that allowing children the same freedoms as adults will not lead to their liberation, but rather their abuse and entrapment. Children simply lack the physical and mental maturity, experience of life and ability to weigh arguments to be able to make competent decisions. Such a response may readily be responded to by child liberationists by arguing that autonomy rights should only be given to competent people. Their point is simply that we should not assume that children lack capacity and that adults have it. Each person should be assessed on their capacity, not their age. This argument is an attractive one. The difficulty with it is practicality. In many walks of life we need to rely on generalisations. Take the selling of alcohol. We could test every person who wants to buy alcohol to see if they understand the issues concerning it and consider its potential effects physically upon them. However, that would be time consuming and raise privacy issues. Instead we use the age of 18 as a rough guideline: above that age we assume you are competent and below the age not. This will work harshly on some precocious teenagers, but it works as a general rule. In short we sacrifice fairness to some teenagers, in the name of having an efficient scheme. This is justifiable as precocious teenagers will not need to wait too long until they reach the appropriate age.[4]

[4]There is a good discussion here of the benefits and disadvantages of using age as a proxy for competence.

At the other extreme there is paternalism. This view is that children's autonomy should not be respected: we should be protecting children from harm, rather than allowing them to make harmful decisions. A paternalist need not deny all relevance of autonomy, he or she might be willing to allow a child to make decisions over something which will not be harmful. Jane Fortin (2006) has come close to this, while arguing in favour of children's rights, she argues

[5]Fortin's approach to children's rights is influential and an examiner will be pleased to see reference to it.

[6]John Eekelaar's approach to children's rights has proved very influential and examiners will want you to discuss it.

[7]Don't be afraid in an essay to come out clearly in favour of one approach. The examiner will prefer you to be clear about your views than mark an essay with a vague, inconclusive summary.

that rights should never be used in a way which harms children.[5] This kind of view is not acceptable to those who regard the right to make mistakes as essential to the notion of autonomy. If you are allowed to make decisions for yourself as long as you do not make decisions we don't agree with is hardly respecting a person's ability to make decisions for him- or herself.

A more modest version of children's rights is that promoted by John Eekelaar (2006a).[6] He starts by detailing three kinds of interests: basic, developmental and autonomy. Basic interests relate to the basic interests that a child needs in order to live and survive: food, shelter and emotional support. Developmental interests are the things that a child needs to develop as a person. They might include education, social interaction. Finally there are autonomy interests which allow the child to make decisions for him or herself. Eekelaar argues that children's autonomy interests should be respected unless they infringe their basic or developmental interests. This would mean that children would generally be able to make decisions for themselves, but not if doing so would cause them serious harm. Eekelaar explains his model in this way. He sees our ideal as producing a system which will mean that come the age of 18 a child has maximum autonomy: being able to decide how they wish to lead their life. He describes it as promoting 'dynamic self-determination'. That requires two things. First, that decisions are not taken during childhood which significantly restrict the range of life choices open to a child. That is why a decision cannot be taken which harms a child's basic or developmental interest. Second, that children are able to practise making decisions so that when they reach adulthood they have learned that skill. That is why it is important to respect children's autonomy decisions.

Eekelaar's model is an attractive one and neatly fits as a middle course between the more extreme paternalistic or liberationist models. It recognises the importance of allowing children to make decisions for themselves, but also the need to protect children from serious harm. It provides the best model for the law to rely on.[7]

Make your answer stand out

- Have a look at Herring (2009a) *Family Law* 4th edn, Harlow: Pearson, at 441–2 where I list some possible concerns about Eekelaar's (2006a) model. Do you find any of them convincing?

- Read Fortin's (2006) article on children's rights ('Accommodating Children's Rights in a Post Human Rights Era' *Modern Law Review* 299. Is it possible to develop an approach to children's rights which will never lead to their harm?

- Archard (2004) *Children, Rights and Childhood*, London: Routledge, provides a very useful discussion of the use of age as a guide for capacity. You could use that to bring in some further arguments.

- Consider further how children's autonomy can be balanced against the interests of parents. See Herring (2010b) 'Relational autonomy and family law' in J. Wallbank, S. Choudhry and J. Herring (eds) *Rights, Gender and Family Law*, Abingdon: Routledge.

! **Don't be tempted to...**

- Try and cover every possible theory on children's rights.

- Assume that children's rights theories will allow a child to make any decision he or she likes.

 Question 4

Does the Human Rights Act offer a good way of protecting children's rights?

Answer plan

→ Summarise the general approach of the ECHR to children.

→ Discuss the decision in *Nielsen* v *Denmark*.

→ Assess the decision in *R(Begum)* v *Denbigh High School*.

→ Consider how the courts have used human rights arguments in cases involving corporal punishment.

Diagram plan

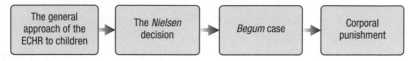

The general approach of the ECHR to children → The *Nielsen* decision → *Begum* case → Corporal punishment

A printable version of this diagram is available from www.pearsoned.co.uk/lawexpressqa

[1]If you are going to be using a phrase repeatedly in a question it is permissible to use an abbreviation like this. Just let the examiner know by putting the phrase in full the first time, with its initials in brackets afterwards, as we have done in this essay.

[2]It is important that you show the examiner that you are aware that children's interests can be claimed directly as rights, or be used as a reason to justify an interference with the rights of adults.

[3]The examiner will like to see this questioning of *Nielsen*. Many academics suspect that it does not represent the current attitude of the court.

Answer

The European Convention on Human Rights (ECHR)[1] was written with adults primarily in mind. Indeed children are not specifically mentioned in the convention. Further the case law in the ECHR on children's rights is rather limited. Although there are plenty of cases where it has been held that the interests of children justify an interference in the rights of adults (e.g. **Hokkanen v Finland** [1995] 2 FCR 320).[2] Despite these points it will be argued that the Human Rights Act (HRA) 1998 does hold promise as a vehicle for giving effect to children's rights.

Although the ECHR does not mention children, the European Court of Human Rights (ECtHR) in **Nielsen v Denmark** (1989) 11 EHRR 175 has confirmed that whenever the ECHR uses the word 'everyone' that includes children. So children can claim all the same rights that adults can under the ECHR. However, it is clear that the ECtHR does not think that children should have the same rights as adults. In **Nielsen v Denmark** a child aged 12 was detained in a hospital with his mother's agreement. He sought to be released, and argued that his rights under article 5 of the ECHR were being breached. The European Commission held that when children are aged 12 their rights are exercised on their behalf by their parents. As the child's mother had agreed to his detention the boy could not seek to exercise his own rights. That decision seems therefore to be a rather restrictive understanding of children's rights: they have rights, but they are to be exercised by parents. However, two points should be made about the *Nielsen* decision. One is that the case was only heard by the Commission and not the ECtHR. Second it was decided in 1989 and attitudes towards children have been changing. So it is possible that in the future the ECtHR will take a different line.[3] Nevertheless it is not surprising that Andrew

141

Bainham (1998) has complained of the 'pitifully inadequate' response of the ECHR to children's rights.

The points made so far should not lead us to conclude that the HRA does not offer children's rights advocates any ammunition. I will take two examples. First, the decision in **R (Begum) v Denbigh High School** [2006] 1 FCR 613. In that case Shabina Begum wanted to wear a jilbab to school, in accordance with her religious beliefs. The school uniform policy did not permit her to and she brought legal proceedings. The House of Lords accepted that she had a right to manifest her religion under article 9, just like any adult did. However, the majority found that there was no interference in her human rights because there were other schools nearby she could attend that would have allowed her to wear the jilbab. Although she lost the case, it shows that the courts were, in principle, willing to protect children's rights. Indeed subsequently in **R (Watkins-Singh) v Aberdare Girls' High School** [2008] 2 FCR 203 the court found in favour of a girl who objected to a uniform policy that did not allow her to wear a kara (a bracelet) in accordance with Sikh religion.[4]

[4]It is good to contrast these two cases brought by children challenging the legality of uniform policy. This shows the examiner you know a good range of case law and also brings out the issue well.

Another area of law where the rights of children have been protected is in the area of corporal punishment. In **A v UK** [1998] 3 FCR 597 the ECtHR found England's law on corporal punishment contravened the ECHR.[5] It allowed parents to inflict punishment that could infringe a child's right to protection from torture and inhuman or degrading punishment. As a result section 58 of the Children Act 2004 was passed to make it clear that lawful chastisement could not be permitted if it involved causing actual bodily harm. Children's rights advocates still seek to have corporal punishment outlawed altogether, but the HRA has proved a useful vehicle in improving the law to date.

[5]This is a good case to use because you can use it to show the examiner that the government can be required to act in a positive way to protect children's rights.

In conclusion, although the ECtHR has only played a rather limited role in progressing children's rights, there are signs in the English courts that the HRA can be used by children to improve their legal standing.[6]

[6]The conclusion is moderate: it shows the examiner you realise that so far the impact of the HRA has been limited, but you believe that in the future it could become more significant.

✓ Make your answer stand out

- Consider a little further why the *Begum* case and the *Watkins-Singh* case were decided differently. You could also have a look at *R (Playfoot)* v *Millais School* [2007] 3 FCR 754. See Harris (2009) 'Playing Catch-up in the Schoolyard? Children and Young People's "Voice" and Education Rights in the UK' *International Journal of Law, Policy and the Family* 73.

- Fortin (2006) 'Accommodating Children's Rights in a Post Human Rights Era' *Modern Law Review* 299 provides a useful discussion of how the courts looked at chidlren's rights. You could rely on this article to bring out some more ways in which the HRA could be used.

- You could provide more detail on the approach of the ECHR: see Choudhry and Herring (2010) *European Human Rights and Family Law* ch. 6, Oxford: Hart.

! Don't be tempted to...

- Exaggerate the extent to which the HRA has currently been used to protect children's rights.

- Only consider ECtHR cases, there are, in fact, more UK cases than European cases to discuss.

? Question 5

Brian, aged 14, has fallen out with his parents. He seeks a court order that he be allowed to stay out until 11pm; that his parents prepare him only vegetarian food; and that he be allowed to go on holiday with his uncle and aunt to Greece. His parents oppose the application.

Answer plan

→ Leave of the court.

→ Maturity of the child.

→ Seriousness of the issue.

→ Whether court intervention necessary.

→ Human Rights Act claims.

Diagram plan

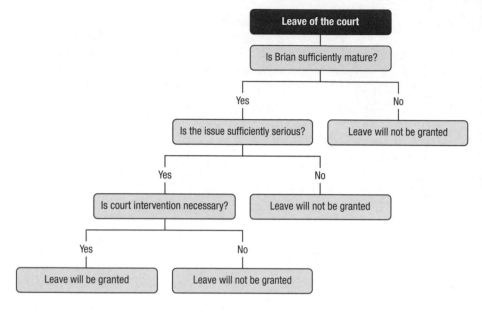

```
                          ┌──────────────────────────┐
                          │     Leave of the court    │
                          └──────────────────────────┘
                                       │
                          ┌──────────────────────────┐
                          │ Is Brian sufficiently mature? │
                          └──────────────────────────┘
                          Yes                        No
            ┌──────────────────────────┐  ┌──────────────────────────┐
            │ Is the issue sufficiently serious? │  │ Leave will not be granted │
            └──────────────────────────┘  └──────────────────────────┘
            Yes                        No
   ┌──────────────────────────┐  ┌──────────────────────────┐
   │ Is court intervention necessary? │  │ Leave will not be granted │
   └──────────────────────────┘  └──────────────────────────┘
   Yes                        No
┌──────────────────────────┐  ┌──────────────────────────┐
│ Leave will be granted     │  │ Leave will not be granted │
└──────────────────────────┘  └──────────────────────────┘
```

A printable version of this diagram is available from www.pearsoned.co.uk/lawexpressqa

[1]Refer as precisely as possible to the key statutory provisions.

[2]The examiner will be pleased to see you setting out the jurisdiction the court has for making these orders. This may seem obvious, but it is an important part of the legal analysis.

[3]This is a problem question where you will not be able to give a definitive answer. What the examiner will expect is for you to list the factors that a judge will take into account.

[4]The examiner will be pleased to see you being precise here, rather than just saying 'Brian must be mature'.

Answer

One of the significant changes in the Children Act 1989 was that it enabled children to bring proceedings in their own name under rule 9.2A of the Family Proceedings Rules 1999, SI 1999/3491.[1] The kinds of orders Brian is seeking will be specific issue orders and so should be sought under section 8 of the Children Act 1989.[2] As he is under 18 he will need the leave of the court to bring the proceedings.

In deciding whether to grant leave the court will consider a number of factors.[3] One is Brian's maturity. The court will focus on his maturity rather than his age (**Re S (A Minor)(Independent Representation)** [1993] 2 FCR 1). The child will need to be able to instruct the solicitor in the proceedings. This will mean they will need to be able to follow what is happening and give directions to their lawyers. This will require intelligence and emotional maturity (**Re N (Contact: Minor Seeking Leave to Defend and Removal of Guardian)** [2003] Fam Law 461). We do not know enough about Brian to assess this issue.[4]

The court will also consider the seriousness of the issue. In **Re C (A Minor)(Leave to Seek Section 8 Order)** [1994] 1 FLR 26 a 14 year-old girl wanted an order allowing her to go on holiday to Bulgaria with her friend's family, against the wishes of her parents. Johnson J refused to grant leave claiming that the issue was too trivial to be resolvable by the courts. This case is likely to be a major problem for Brian. The issues he is concerned with seem as trivial or more so than those in **Re C**.[5] It should be remembered that **Re C** was a first instance decision and Brian may seek to challenge it. He may point out that adults are permitted to bring disputes on issues which may seem trivial such as children's surnames or whether parents should be nude in front of children etc. So it may be argued that the triviality criterion should not be used.

[5] It is a good idea to use a decided case and then consider whether the problem question is like or unlike that case.

Another issue raised in **Re C (A Minor)(Leave to Seek Section 8 Order)** [1994] 1 FLR 26 is whether it is the kind of issue the family should be left to resolve themselves. As stated in that case the courts are reluctant to resolve the minutiae of family life and prefer people to resolve these issues themselves. This seems a powerful argument against intervening in the staying-out time issue and the dietary dispute. In relation to the latter it would require the court to order parents to act in a particular way, which they are generally reluctant to do.[6]

[6] This shows a good appreciation of general judicial attitudes. Judges don't like getting involved in the intimate details of family life.

It may be that Brian's best argument is to claim that the case law in this area needs to be re-examined in the light of the Human Rights Act 1998.[7] Under article 6 the right of access to the courts is guaranteed. Further in **Mabon v Mabon** [2005] EWCA Civ 634 the Court of Appeal held that article 8 entitles children to representation in cases involving disputes between parents.[8] It seems a small step from that to arguing that children should have the right to bring proceedings in their own name.

[7] It is always good to refer to HRA arguments.

[8] You will need to make it clear to the examiner that you are not saying this case is exactly the same as the *Mabon* case, but they are analogous.

In conclusion, the current case law suggests that Brian is not likely to be granted leave. However, arguments based on the Human Rights Act 1998 may mean that Brian will be able to persuade the courts to take a new approach. The court may still be persuaded that theses are trivial issues and in relation to the dietary question will be concerned about forcing a parent to act in a particular way.[9]

[9] This conclusion brings together well the key factors that the court will consider.

✓ **Make your answer stand out**

■ It would be good to put this issue in the context of wider debates over how children are represented in court. See Fortin (2007) 'Children's Representation through the looking glass' *Family Law* 500.

■ You could discuss in more detail some of the human rights issues that could be raised. These are discussed in Lyon (2007) 'Children's participation and the promotion of their rights' *Journal of Social Welfare and Family Law* 99.

■ The examiner would be impressed if you referred to some studies of how children are represented in court. Have a look at Lowe and Murch (2001) 'Children's participation rights in the family justice system' *Child and Family Law Quarterly* 137.

❗ **Don't be tempted to...**

■ Confuse cases where children seek to be represented in cases between adults, with cases where they wish to instigate their own litigation.

■ Assume that children have a right to bring litigation.

Disputes over children

How this topic may come up in exams

This is a popular topic for problem questions. You may find overlaps here with Chapter 7 on children's rights, if the question involves a child who has particular views. Be clear as to what orders are available and have a good knowledge of the case law. Remember that in this area the welfare principle is paramount. So in each case the judge will determine what is best for the particular child in this particular family. What you need to do in answering the problem question is highlight the issues which will concern the court and what general approaches the courts tend to adopt.

Essay questions can also appear. Particularly popular are essay questions on contact. This is a controversial issue, with fathers' rights groups complaining that the law favours mothers, while women's groups complain that the courts do not take concerns about domestic violence seriously enough. It is worth looking at the material in Chapter 3 on domestic violence for this issue.

■ Attack the question

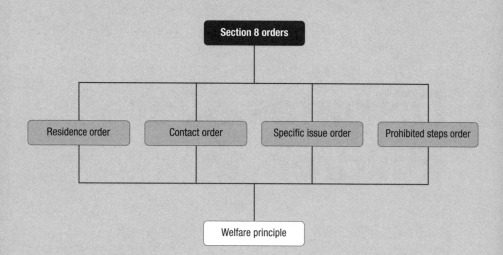

❓ Question 1

Tim Jones and Shavi Shah had a son, who they registered with the name Jack Jones. They have since separated and Jack lives with Shavi but sees Tom weekly. Shavi has remarried and her new husband (Ahmad Shah) wants to change Jack's name to Jack Shah. They have been calling him Jack Shah for nearly a year when Tim finds out. He seeks an order that Jack be known by the surname Jones. Shavi argues against the order stating that Ahmad is only willing to fully act as Jack's father if Jack has his name and that the name Shah will make it easier for him to fit into the community he lives in. Tim also seeks an order that Jack be raised as a Christian. He claims that that was the agreement between Shavi and him. Shavi and Ahmad want to raise him without religious belief. Discuss what orders the court is likely to make.

Answer plan

→ Discuss how the courts deal with disputes over names.

→ Consider the arguments the courts will use in determining what is in Jack's welfare. In particular what weight will be attached to his registered name; cultural factors; his step-father's wishes; and the lapse in time since the change of name.

→ Consider how the court will apply the welfare principle in relation to the dispute over religion.

Diagram plan

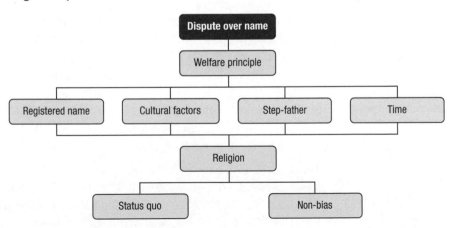

A printable version of this diagram is available from www.pearsoned.co.uk/lawexpressqa

Answer

In the two main issues at hand: the name change and the religion; the starting point is the welfare principle. The court will make the order that will best promote the welfare of the child. The interests of the parents will not come into play, but rather it is simply a matter of what is best for the child (**Re B** [2009] UKSC 4).[1]

[1]It is always worth starting problem questions with this clear statement of principle.

Looking first at the names issue. It is helpful, first, to summarise the law on names. Parents are required to register a birth within 42 days and to state the surname by which it is intended that the child be known (Registration of Births and Deaths Regulations 1987, reg 9).[2] But a person's actual name is the name that the person is generally known by (**Re T (Otherwise H)** [1962] 3 All ER 970). There is no difficulty normally if the parents are in agreement. They can change the child's surname simply by ensuring the child is generally known by a different name. The position is, however, different where the parents have separated. Then, under section 13 of the Children Act 1989, if there is a residence order in force no one can cause the child to be known by a new surname without the written consent of every person with parental responsibility. Perhaps surprisingly the courts have said that even where a residence order is not in place then there should be a consultation with each parent with parental responsibility (**Dawson v Wearmouth** [1999] 1 FCR 625). There is even a suggestion in **Re PC** [1997] 3 FCR 544 that even if only one parent has parental responsibility they should still consult before changing a name. We are not told in this case whether there is a residence order or not or who has parental responsibility, but it seems that that does not matter.[3] Tim should have been consulted. But, one of the surprising things about the case law is that there appears to be no punishment for this failure to consult. If the matter is brought to court the judge will decide the names issue based on what is in the best interests of the child.

[2]It is good to make precise reference to the statutory provision, where possible.

[3]Here is an example of a problem question where the examiner has not given you all the information you need to answer the question. Usually you have then to give alternative answers depending on the missing fact.

[4]Notice that, as is typical for problem questions in this chapter, it is not possible to give a definitive answer. Rather you can list the factors the court will pay especial attention to when determining what will promote the child's welfare.

The factors that will be taken into account in this case include the following.[4] First, it has been suggested that the presumption is that a child should keep the registered name (**Re C (Change of Surname)** [1999] 1 FCR 318). This can be seen as part of the general principle that the courts prefer not to change the current arrangements for a child if they are working well (emphasised recently by the Supreme Court in **Re B** [2009] UKSC 4). It can also be seen as a way of

[5]Although this is a problem
question you should refer to
the writings of academics,
especially when they provide
useful guidance on how the
law will be interpreted.

discouraging disputes over surnames (see the writing on this issue of
Mary Hayes (1999)).[5] However, the courts have made it clear that the
registered name is only one factor they will take into account. Another
factor relevant here is the fact that Jack has been known by the
surname Shah for the past year. To change his name back again to
Jones, may cause him embarrassment and difficulty (**Re C (Change
of Surname)** [1999] 1 FCR 318). The courts have emphasised that
it is not desirable for children to keep changing names. There is a
further point here and that is the courts have recognised (e.g. **Re B
(Change of Surname)** [1996] 2 FCR 304) that there is a limit to
the extent to which the court can affect the name a child is known
by from day-to-day. Therefore what the courts have tended to do
is make orders about the surname the child is known by in formal
documents (**Dawson v Wearmouth**). Yet another issue here is the
role the name might play in the relationship between the parents. It
seems that if the name Shah is not used then it will affect Ahmad's
relationship with Jack, but Tim might claim that the loss of name will
affect his relationship. The House of Lords in **Dawson v Wearmouth**
made it clear that the issue of names is not one of parental rights.
It was a matter of child welfare. However, they have accepted that
change of name is more likely to be authorised if the child no longer
sees the father with the original name (**Re S (Change of Surname**
[1999] 1 FCR 304). The court is likely to be sceptical of claims that a
name will affect significantly the relationship with a child, but if they
are persuaded it will that will be a factor to consider in the welfare

[6]This paragraph has shown a
good summary of the factors
that the courts will take into
account and gives examples
of how these have been used
in the case law.

analysis. The court will also take into account the cultural significance
of surnames (**Re S (Change of Names: Cultural Factors)** [2001]
3 FCR 648). If it could be shown that a child will have difficulties with
a particular name in the community in which they are living then this
will be a factor.[6]

[7]It is well worth mentioning
this compromise approach
to disputes over names.
Baroness Hale promoted it
when she was in the Court of
Appeal and she now sits in
the Supreme Court.

It is difficult to predict how all these different factors may be
weighed. One approach which may appeal to the court is that
promoted in **Re R (A Child)** [2003] 1 FCR 481 of using a double-
barrelled surname (e.g Jones-Shah).[7] This has received judicial (**Re
R (A Child)**) and academic support (see Herring (2009d)), but may
not satisfy either party. Another solution is to say that Jack can be
known as Shah generally, but on official documents as Jones.

Turning to the religious issues, although at one time the courts
had a clear preference for children being raised in the Church of

[8]The examiner will like this brief historical point because it shows you have a broad view of the subject.

[9]It is useful to refer to the HRA issues.

England (**Shelley v Westbrook** (1817) Jac 266).[8] However, especially following the Human Rights Act 1998, the courts are careful not to show any preferences between religions (**Hoffman v Austria** [1994] 1 FCR 193).[9] The more difficult cases are those where a child has an established religious belief (**Re T** [1993] 2 FCR 973), but that is not an issue here. The courts have rejected a claim that a child should at birth be seen as belonging to a particular religion (**Re S (Change of Name: Cultural Factors)** [2001] 3 FCR 648. The most likely outcome in this case is to match that in **Re J (Specific Issue Orders: Muslim Upbringing)** [1999] 2 FCR 345 and order that the child can be raised by Shavi in whatever religion she chooses, but Tim can teach Jack about what religion he chooses during contact sessions.

✓ Make your answer stand out

■ You could refer to even more case law on religion. The cases are usefully discussed in Taylor (2009) 'Parental responsibility and religion' in R. Probert, S. Gilmore and J. Herring (eds) *Responsible Parents and Parental Responsibility*, Oxford: Hart.

■ For contrasting takes on the case law on names see Hayes (1999) 'What's in a Name? A child by any other name is surely just as sweet' *Child and Family Law Quarterly* 423 and Herring (2009d) 'The shaming of naming: parental rights and responsibilities in the naming of children' in R. Probert, S. Gilmore and J. Herring (eds) *Responsible Parents and Parental Responsibility*, Oxford: Hart.

■ The article just mentioned by Herring also contains some discussion of the ECtHR on names which could be used.

! Don't be tempted to...

■ Assume that the court will insist that the registered name of the child will be followed.

■ Talk too much about parents' rights. The courts will see these issues as about the welfare of children.

📝 Question 2

What weight is attached to the views of children when the courts make decisions about them?

Answer plan

→ Explain the significance of the welfare principle and how that relates to the wishes of children in section 1(3)(i) Children Act 1989.

→ Discuss how the maturity of the child is relevant in assessing what weight is to be attached to welfare.

→ Consider how the court will only take into account the views of a child where those views are genuinely the child's.

→ Explore how the courts will take into account the importance of the issue in determining what weight to attach to the views of a child.

→ Note that the court is willing to accept that a child may have no views on the question at hand.

Diagram plan

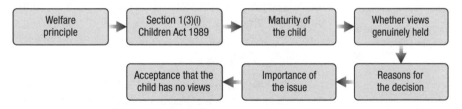

A printable version of this diagram is available from www.pearsoned.co.uk/lawexpressqa

Answer

When the court must resolve a dispute over the upbringing of a child, the key principle is the welfare principle (s. 1 Children Act 1989). However section 1(3) of the Act lists a series of factors the courts will take into account when deciding what order will best promote the welfare of the child. The first of these is 'The ascertainable wishes and feelings of the child concerned (considered in the light of his age and understanding)'.[1]

[1] It is helpful to start the essay with a summary of the key legal principles.

Before exploring further how the courts have taken into account the wishes of the child there are three reasons why a judge should take into account the wishes of a child. First, the child will know what they do and do not like and this is an important part of determining what is in his or her welfare. Second, Butler Sloss P has explained that children should be treated with respect and not as 'packages to be moved around' (**Re S(Minors)(Access: Religious Upbringing)** [1993] 1 FCR 283). Third, there is the practical point that if a child disagrees with a court order it is likely to be productive. Forcing a teenager to see a parent she does not want to see is likely to be unenforceable or simply harmful to all involved. And what is a court to do if the child refuses to comply with the order: imprison her? Fourth, a judge may decide that even if the child is making the wrong decision it will benefit the child to learn from his or her mistake.[2]

[2]It is important to make it clear to the examiner that the reasons for following children's wishes are not limited to respecting a child's right to autonomy.

In considering the wishes of the child a number of factors will be considered by the court. First, there is the maturity of the child. The older and wiser the child, the greater weight will be attached to their views. Indeed in **Re B (Minors)(Change of Surname)** [1996] 2 FCR 304 it was said it would be exceptional for a court to make an order contrary to the wishes of a teenager. In **Re S (Contact: Children's Views)** [2002] FLR 1156 Tyler J emphasised the importance of respecting young people, especially where their views were carefully thought out.[3]

[3]Giving examples from the case law will impress the examiner.

The courts will be alert to the question of whether the views expressed by the child are genuinely their own or whether they are simply being a mouthpiece for one of the parents. Clearly where that is so less weight will be attached to their views. In one case (**Re M (Intractable Contact Dispute: Court's Positive Duty)** [2006] 1 FLR 627) a 15 year-old girl and 13 year-old boy strongly opposed contact with their mother. However, it was found that they had been 'blinded' by the father's views and he had turned the children against their mother.[4] The court will also be alert to attempts by parents to bribe children and hence in **Puxty v Moore** [2006] 1 FCR 28 little weight was placed on the views of a nine year-old girl who wanted to live with her mother, after she had promised to buy the girl a pony.

[4]Giving specific examples of where this has happened makes the argument more convincing.

The courts will look at the reasons the child has for her views. Is this a thought-out decision or is it based on a misunderstanding of the facts or an unrealistic expectation about the future (**see Re M**

[5]Although these cases are usually seen to concern children's rights, they can be used in this context as they are discussing how seriously children's views should be taken.

(A Minor)(Family Proceedings) [1995] 2 FCR 90, where a girl was found to have false expectations about what life with her father would be like)? In some of the cases involving Jehovah's Witness children refusing blood transfusions (e.g. **Re E** [1992] 2 FCR 219) the court had noted that the children have had a narrow upbringing and have not had wide experience of the world.[5]

Another factor that the court will take into account is the importance of the issue at hand. We have just referred to the Jehovah's Witness cases. Where the life of the child may be at risk the courts have, so far, been reluctant to attach significant weight to the views of the child, even where found competent (**Re L** [2005] 1 FCR 421). However, in relation to minor issues it is more likely that the child's wishes will be considered.

Finally, it should be noted that the courts have accepted (e.g. **Re A (Specific Issue Order: Parental Dispute)** [2001] 1 FCR 210) that in some cases children may not have a view. They may not want to choose between their parents. In such a case the court should not put any pressure on them to reach a decision.

[6]Here there is a good summary of the key points the court will consider when looking at the wishes of children. The examiner will be pleased it is short and to the point.

To conclude, the courts do attach weight to the views of a child when deciding what order will promote the child's welfare. However, the weight attached to the child's views will depend on the maturity of the children, whether the views are genuinely held, the reasons for the views, and the gravity of the issue at hand.[6]

 Make your answer stand out

- You could refer to studies which examine the experience children have of court proceedings: see Bretherton (2002) '"Because it's me the decisions are about" – Children's experiences of private law proceedings' *Family Law* 450.

- Another issue is how children's views are presented to court. Normally a court reporter tells the court what a child's wishes are, but that may not be very reliable: see Douglas (2006) 'The separate representation of children – in whose best interests' in M. Thorpe and R. Budden (eds) *Durable Solutions*, Bristol: Jordans.

- You could explore the possibility of a claim that under article 8 of the ECHR children have a right to ensure their wishes are taken into account.

! **Don't be tempted to...**

- Assume that the welfare principle means that children's wishes only need to be followed if they are good decisions.
- Discuss the issue at a vague level and not cite specific case law examples.

Question 3

How can and should contact orders be enforced?

Answer plan

→ Set out the current modes of enforcement for contact orders: imprisonment, fines; contact activity direction; contact enforcement order; changing residence.

→ Explain how an approach based on the welfare principle and one based on the rule of law might produce different results.

→ Discuss whether it is possible to deal with injustices to mothers and fathers in this area.

→ Are there ways of assisting contact to take place? Might mediation be a solution?

→ Describe the relative powerlessness of the law in this context.

Diagram plan

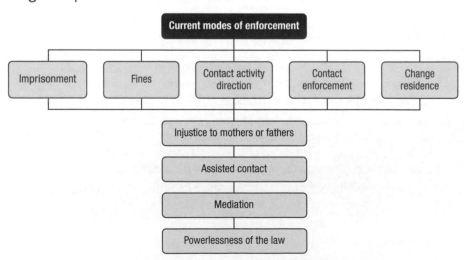

A printable version of this diagram is available from www.pearsoned.co.uk/lawexpressqa

Answer

[1]While contact disputes are typically between a resident mother and non-resident father, make it clear that that is not always the case.

[2]It is easy to get distracted from the subject of an essay. Here the focus is on enforcement and not on when a contact order should be made, so right from the start make it clear where your focus is.

[3]The examiner will want to see you considering the practical difficulties that will arise in enforcement, as well as the conceptual issues.

[4]The 2006 Act is a relatively recent reform and so the examiner will want to see you demonstrating a good knowledge of it.

For the purposes of this essay it will be assumed that the court has decided that a child will live with the mother,[1] but have regular contact with the father, that arrangement being in the best interests of the child.[2] Of course, it is possible and not uncommon for father's to have residence. However, the truth is that in most cases it is the mother who has residence and the father who is seeking contact. It will be assumed that despite the court order contact is not taking place. The court then has to decide how to enforce the contact order, if at all.

First, we will look at the range of orders that are currently available to a court. The normal order which follows a breach (especially repeated breaches) is to order imprisonment for contempt of court (**A v N (Committal: Refusal of Contact Order)** [1997] 2 FCR 475). However, it seems that this will only be done in extreme cases. As the Court of Appeal emphasised in **Re K (Children: Committal Proceedings)** [2003] 2 FCR 336 the child will suffer greatly if the mother is imprisoned and indeed it might infringe the child's right to respect for her family law. This is not to say the courts will never imprison the mother, but it will be very rare.

An alternative for the court would be to fine the mother (**Re M (Contact Order)** [1999] 1 FLR 810) for breach of the order. However, Butler Sloss P has noted that many mothers cannot afford to pay a fine (**Re S (A Child)(Contact)** [2004] 1 FCR 439) and even where she can that may end up harming the child. There is a further difficulty here too: if the mother refuses to pay the fine we are back where we started.[3]

After the Children and Adoption Act 2006 the court can make contact enforcement orders.[4] These will include ordering a resident parent to undertake unpaid work as a punishment for failing to comply with a court order. It seems that these orders are little used, perhaps because they are not seen as likely to lead to a productive result.

The 2006 Act also allows a court to make a contact activity direction which can include requiring the parties to attend assessment or mediation. The hope is that if the couple sit down and discuss this carefully they will be able to resolve the issue. However, this may be too optimistic. Only the most hardened contact disputes come to

[5]It is useful to refer to studies of contact cases in practice to highlight the real life issues that arise.

[6]The examiner will want you to make a fair presentation of the arguments on both sides. So whether you are sympathetic to fathers' groups or not make sure you account for their arguments in a reasonable way.

[7]It is helpful to refer to specific academics where you are able to.

[8]This is an important point to make in essays concerning contact and court orders.

court and they are often complex cases, involving deeply troubled families (see Trinder (2003)).[5] It is unlikely that these difficult cases will be resolved by sitting down and discussing the issue.

There has been considerable debate over the best way to deal with breached contact orders. Fathers' groups claim that the failure to enforce contact orders effectively means that their human rights are infringed. In other areas of the law breaches of court orders are enforced fiercely. That is part of the Rule of Law. Fathers' groups complain that the way in which the law works in effect means that mothers decide whether or not there should be contact, when it should be the courts.[6]

Mothers' groups also complain about the current law. They complain that insufficient attention is paid to the fact that in many cases where mothers refuse to allow contact, it is because there has been domestic violence or there is fear of abuse (see Trinder (2003)). To imprison mothers who are seeking to protect themselves or their children is harsh. Indeed Smart and Neale (1991) have complained that fathers have sought to use contact as a tool against mothers they have previously abused or terrified.[7] They also argued that the law is unfair on the allocation of responsibilities after contact. A mother who does not allow contact is vilified and threatened with imprisonment, while a father who does not contact his child does not face any punishment.

An important point in this debate has been made by John Eekelaar (2002). He warns of the danger of assuming that because contact with a father is beneficial it is beneficial to enforce it.[8] Forcing an unwilling parent to allow contact may create antagonism and tension which will not promote the welfare of the child. It may be that given the difficulty of enforcement the courts should be rather less keen on making contact orders.

A final point is perhaps that this discussion shows the weakness of law. Law cannot make everything 'all right'. Contact which is compelled by threats of court action is unlikely to be beneficial to anyone. We can encourage parties to agree contact, but where that is not mutually agreed, there may be little the law can do.

Make your answer stand out

■ Refer in more detail to some of the studies of contact disputes in practice, see Smart *et al.*, (2005) *Residence and Contact Disputes in Court*, London: DCA; Trinder (2005) *A profile of applicants and respondents in contact cases in Essex*, London: DCA.

■ Use the disputes among academics over enforcement of contact. Contrast Smart and Neale (1997) 'Argument against virtue – must contact be enforced?' *Family Law* 332 and Bainham (2003) 'Contact as a right and obligation' in A. Bainham, B. Lindley, M. Richards and L. Trinder (eds) *Children and their Families*, Oxford: Hart.

■ You could consider whether there are other ways apart from enforcement that the law might use to encourage contact to take place. See Herring (2003) 'Connecting contact' in A. Bainham, B. Lindley, M. Richards and L. Trinder (eds) *Children and their Families*, Oxford: Hart.

! Don't be tempted to...

■ Just talk about the issue in terms of children's rights.

■ Get carried away with the debates and neglect to discuss the case law and statutory provisions.

? Question 4

Ann's parents, Sophie and Mark are separating. It is agreed that Ann, aged two, should live with Sophie, but Mark seeks a contact order, which Sophie opposed. The welfare report suggests that the issue is very finely balanced, but the harms very slightly outweigh the benefits. The trial judge relying on the report declines to order contact. Mark appeals to the Court of Appeal. Consider what issues will arise in the appeal and how the court will decide them.

Answer plan

➔ Explain that the case will be governed by the welfare principle.

➔ Consider the current state of the case law and the extent to which the courts recognise rights of contact, presumptions of contact, or assumptions of the benefit of contact.

➔ Discuss the relevance of domestic violence in contact cases.

Diagram plan

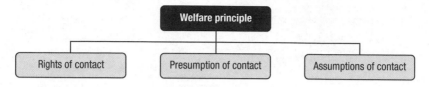

A printable version of this diagram is available from www.pearsoned.co.uk/lawexpressqa

[1]This is a key point and it is good to make it right at the start. It may seem obvious, but you still need to inform the examiner that you realise that this will be the court's starting point.

[2]This is a case where all you can do is set out the factors that will guide the court's decision, you cannot give an answer as to what the court will do for sure.

[3]The examiner will like the fact that you are aware of the way that in practice the welfare report will be seen as of central importance.

[4]Don't be afraid of suggesting that an earlier decision will be overruled or re-examined by a later case. This is especially so if you are dealing with a controversial case.

[5]The HRA plays a central role in these arguments and so the examiner will expect you to discuss it carefully.

Answer

As in all disputes over the upbringing of children the court's decision will be based on the welfare principle: the order will be made which best promotes the welfare of Ann (Children Act 1989, section 1).[1] The court will consider all of the factors listed in section 1(3). Depending on Ann's age her wishes will be a factor to be taken into account. We are not provided with all of the details of the case.[2]

The court will attach particular significance to the welfare report which is prepared to advise on the benefits and disadvantages of contact.[3] The key point in this case is that the report decides that there will be some very slight harm caused by the contact. Is that sufficient to justify not making a contact order? That depends on the extent to which the law recognises a right to contact.

In **Re L (A Child)(Contact: Domestic Violence)** [2000] 2 FCR 404, the leading case on contact orders, the Court of Appeal stated that there was not a right of contact, nor even a presumption of contact. Thorpe LJ preferred to talk, instead, of an assumption of the benefit of the contact 'from which the court embarks upon its application of the welfare principle.' This has been a controversial judgement and it could be challenged.[4]

Let us consider first the case for saying there is a right of contact. Andrew Bainham (2003) has insisted that there is a right to contact in English law, despite what the Court of Appeal stated in **Re L**. He relies on the Human Rights Act 1998 which requires courts to interpret legislation in line with the European Convention on Human Rights, in so far as is possible.[5] He points out, and this is generally accepted, that a long line of ECHR cases (e.g. **Hokkanen v Finland**; **Sahin v Germany** [2003] ECHR 340) has established that where there is family life between the child and father, then article 8(1) requires the law to protect that by ordering contact, unless there is sufficient justification for not doing so under article 8(2) (e.g. where the contact would cause notable harm to the child). In this case Mark would seek to persuade the Court of Appeal to adopt Bainham's analysis and then argue that a small amount of marginal harm from contact would be insufficient to make it necessary to justify interfering in his right under article 8(2). Under the HRA the court must ensure his right of contact is protected, and the right of contact of his child. There is nothing, he would argue, in the wording of the Children Act 1989 which requires the court to deny him his right.

However, the court may not accede to such an argument. Thorpe LJ argued that whether one follows the Human Rights Act or the welfare principle the results are the same. This is a consistent line the courts have taken (see also **Payne v Payne** [2001] 1 FCR 425). Indeed in **Re S (Contact: Promoting Relationship with Absent Parent)** [2004] 1 FCR 439 Butler Sloss P referred to the ECHR case of **Yousef v Netherlands** [2002] 3 FCR 577 where the court held that in cases of clashes between the interests of adults and children the child's rights must be paramount. She saw this as confirming there was no difference between the approaches. Although, in fairness it might be added that later ECtHR cases (e.g. **Suss v Germany** [2005] 3 FCR 666) have not used the terminology paramount and instead have talked about children's interests being of crucial importance. Even using that terminology it may be argued that under the ECHR even if contact will harm the child a little bit, as in this case, contact should be ordered.[6]

[6]The examiner will be impressed with this good understanding of the ECHR case law on this issue.

An alternative approach that Mark might try to use is to persuade the courts that there is a presumption to a right of contact. Again this was rejected by the Court of Appeal in **Re L**, although earlier in **Re M (Contact: Welfare Test)** [1995] 1 FCR 753 the court of Appeal did use the terminology of presumption. Indeed even in **Re L** itself Butler Sloss P accepted that contact was 'almost always' in the child's interests. That is borne out by an examination of the statistics on contact, which suggest it is very rare for the courts not to order contact. However, these points, it is submitted do not make a case for saying there is a presumption in favour of contact. Acknowledging that there is a presumption would mean that the

[7]A careful discussion has taken place here over the meaning of the word 'presumption'. It helps clarify what a presumption is.

courts would require sufficient evidence to rebut the presumption of contact. The fact that contact is nearly always granted does not mean that the court start with a presumption of making an order unless there is evidence to rebut it.[7]

A final approach might be to accept **Re L** and the fact that there is an assumption of the benefit of contact and argue that a report that says there is a marginal disadvantage to contact is insufficient to overcome the assumption of the benefit of contact. This argument, it is submitted misunderstands what Thorpe LJ meant by assumption in this case. An assumption he explained was 'the base of knowledge' the courts start with before looking at a particular case. He goes on to emphasise that the court must consider the benefits and disadvantages of contact in this particular case. It seems in our case that the judge did consider Ann's case and following the report found contact would not benefit her. That is an appropriate way of determining the case.[8]

[8]Again in this paragraph the examiner will be impressed by the discussion about what an assumption is and what it is that is being assumed.

All in all, it is submitted that the court was correct in its judgment in **Re L**. It was implicitly approved by the Supreme Court in **Re B** [2009] UKSC 4, where the welfare principle was highlighted as the central test, and there were warnings against the talk of rights or assumptions, misleading the courts from what should be their focus: the welfare of the child. Although that case concerned residence disputes, the same point can be made about contact cases. I would argue that the Court of Appeal in Mark's case should follow **Re L** and assert that the key question is whether contact is in the child's welfare. As the report in this case indicates that contact is not in the child's welfare, contact should not be ordered.[9]

[9]The conclusion here presents a very clear point of view and summarises the main arguments used in favour of it.

 Make your answer stand out

- Bainham's argument that there is a right of contact could be explored further. He sets his case out in Bainham (2003) 'Contact as a right and obligation' in A. Bainham, B. Lindley, M. Richards and L. Trinder (eds) *Children and their Families*, Oxford: Hart.
- You could undertake a more detailed analysis of the UK case law. For that Gilmore (2008) 'Disputing contact: challenging some assumptions' [2008] *Child and Family Law Quarterly* 285 is very helpful.
- The ECHR issues could be explored in more detail. See Choudhry and Herring (2010) *European Human Rights and Family Law* ch. 7, Oxford: Hart.
- For a feminist analysis of the law on contact see Wallbank (2010) '(En)gendering the fusion of rights and responsibilities in the law of contact' in J. Wallbank, S. Choudhry and J. Herring (eds) *Rights, Gender and Family Law*, Abingdon: Routledge.

> **!** **Don't be tempted to...**
>
> ■ Confuse a right and a presumption.
>
> ■ Focus too much on the enforcement difficulties.

🗡 Question 5

When Ingrid was born her parents were unable to care for her due to their drug use. Ingrid was cared for by her uncle, Ahmed. Ingrid is now three years old. Her mother, Susan, has formed a relationship with Barbara and has stopped using drugs. She and Barbara wish to raise Ingrid, but Ahmed wants to continue raising Ingrid himself. Susan, Barbara and Ahmed all seek residence orders. What order is the court likely to make? Advise Susan on her legal position if she and Barbara share residence, but later split up.

> ## Answer plan
>
> → Consider the orders that the court could make in this case.
>
> → Explain how the welfare principle will govern the application
>
> → Discuss the relevance of the 'natural parent presumption'.
>
> → Is it relevant that Susan and Barbara are in a same-sex relationship.

Diagram plan

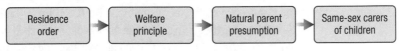

Residence order → Welfare principle → Natural parent presumption → Same-sex carers of children

A printable version of this diagram is available from www.pearsoned.co.uk/lawexpressqa

Answer

[1]This introduction helpfully sets out the key legal issue and the key principle that will be applied.

In this case Susan, Barbara and Ahmed are applying for a residence order under section 8 of the Children Act 1989. The guiding principle is the welfare principle in section 1 of that Act. The welfare of the child will be the paramount consideration.[1]

Ingrid will seek to emphasise the 'natural parent presumption' (**Re M (Child's Upbringing)** [1996] 2 FLR 441). This is the presumption that a child is best brought up by her natural parents, rather

[2]This is an important recent case and the examiner will expect you to know about it.

[3]Here you want to explain to the examiner that you are aware that a presumption is not a statement about what normally occurs, but a statement about where the legal burden of proof lies.

[4]The examiner will appreciate this recognition of the law in practice, namely that the welfare report will play a key role.

[5]Here the examiner will like the fact we have set out the arguments that will be used on both sides and provides case law that each will be able to rely on.

than anyone else. However, the significance of that principle has been greatly reduced following the decision of the Supreme Court in **Re B** [2009] UKSC 4.[2] There the Supreme Court emphasised that in residence disputes the key principle is the welfare principle. The court must make the order which will best promote the welfare of the child. Although children are normally best brought up by their natural parents their lordships said that that should not be seen as a presumption or a right.[3]

Much will depend, therefore, on the welfare report prepared in this case. If the welfare report suggests that Ahmed is best placed to raise Ingrid then, following **Re B** it is unlikely that the court will transfer residence. Similarly if the welfare report suggests that Barbara and Susan offer the best parenting, then they will be preferred.[4] It should be added at this point that the fact that Barbara and Susan are a same-sex couple will not be a relevant factor in deciding who is best at raising Ingrid (**Re G (Children)(Same-Sex Partner)** [2006] EWCA Civ 372). Further, the fact that Ahmed is a man will not be a relevant consideration (**Brixley v Lynas** [1996] 2 FLR 499). The report and court will focus on who is best able to meet the child's needs, rather than the sex or sexual orientation of the parties. In this regard Barbara and Susan may be at an advantage in being able to offer two parent figures.

A more tricky question is what the court would do if the report were neutral, in effect saying that there was nothing to choose between the applicants. Ahmed would want to emphasise the importance of the status quo which was referred to in **Re B** and **Re G (Children: Same-Sex Partner)**. This principle states that if the child is thriving in her current situation and it is not clear that she will be better off in a different situation, then she should be left where she is. He may also refer to section 1(5) of the Children Act 1989 which states that the court should only make an order if it decides that it would be better to make an order than not to. In response Ingrid may seek to rely on the natural parent presumption. Although **Re B** made it clear that the natural parent presumption carried no weight where it was shown that a child would be better off with a non-parent, she might argue that the Supreme Court did not deal with a case where the report was neutral.[5] Even if that point was accepted the court may follow the line taken in **Re H (A Child: Residence)** [2002] 3 FCR 277 where Thorpe LJ argued that a grandparent had become the natural parent by caring for the child for a long period of time.

We are asked to consider the position of Barbara if residence is granted to her and Susan. She would not be Ingrid's parent, but if a residence order was made in favour of her and Susan, Barbara would acquire parental responsibility. The House of Lords in **Re G (Children: Same-Sex Partner)** suggested that if a same-sex couple who had been caring for a child together broke up then one factor that would be taken into account would be the fact that one was the biological mother of the child.

 Make your answer stand out

- You could discuss in more detail the law's approach to same-sex couples: Reece (1996) 'The paramountcy principle: consensus of construct' *Current Legal Problems* 267 is helpful on this.
- More detail could be given on the *Re G* case. There is an excellent discussion in Diduck (2007) 'If only we can find the appropriate terms to use the issue will be solved: law, identity and parenthood' *Child and Family Law Quarterly* 458.
- You could explore a little more the possibility of giving Barbara and Susan a joint residence order. These orders are discussed in Gilmore (2006) 'Court decision-making in shared residence order: A critical examination' *Child and Family Law Quarterly* 103.

! **Don't be tempted to...**

- Place too much weight on the natural parent presumption.
- Get into too much of a debate over the benefits or disadvantages of same-sex parents.

Child protection

How this topic may come up in exams

There are few more sensitive or complex areas of law than that surrounding child protection. Social workers and courts are faced with an impossible dilemma. If a child is not removed from her parents when she should be there is a danger of serious abuse. If the child is removed from her parents when she should not be she is deprived of the chance of being raised by her parents. The media are quick to criticise both social workers and courts whether on the basis that they are 'baby snatchers' removing children unnecessarily from good parents, or 'baby neglecters' leaving children with dangerous abusive parents.

The law in this area has to strike a careful balance between enabling the protection of children at risk of harm, with protecting the rights to respect for family life for children and their parents. This tension will be at the heart of most discussion in essays. In problem questions you will need to have a good knowledge of the threshold criteria in section 31 of the Children Act 1989 and the case law which has interpreted it.

■ Attack the question

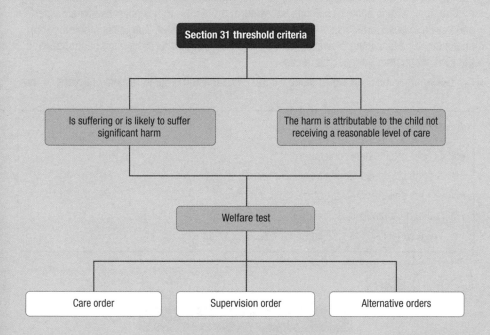

Section 31 threshold criteria

Is suffering or is likely to suffer significant harm

The harm is attributable to the child not receiving a reasonable level of care

Welfare test

Care order

Supervision order

Alternative orders

❓ Question 1

Bryony, aged 6, has bruises on her arms and legs. An expert concludes that they may have been caused deliberately, but they may be accidental. The parents (Su and Ravi) say that the bruises were either caused accidentally, or if done deliberately, were caused by her older brother, Tom, who is aged 12 and has behavioural problems. Tom is assessed by an expert and is said to pose a real risk of causing some harm to his sister. Due to his problems Tom needs careful disciplining. However, both Su and Ravi suffer depression and cannot provide the kind of constant attention he needs.

Discuss whether the court would make a care or supervision order in respect of Bryony or Tom.

Answer plan

→ Set out the threshold criteria.

→ Are the children suffering significant harm?

→ Are the children likely to suffer significant harm?

→ Is that attributable to their care?

→ Will a supervision or care order promote their welfare?

Diagram plan

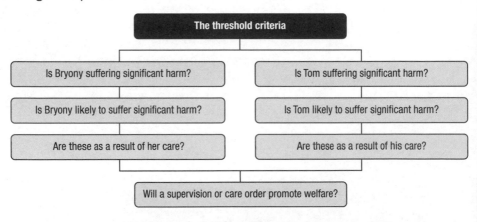

A printable version of this diagram is available from www.pearsoned.co.uk/lawexpressqa

Answer

[1]The answer starts with a summary of the key legal principle.

[2]This is an important point to make. If the local authority do not want a care order the court cannot force them to have one.

[3]Here the key case law and definitions are provided in a brief, but accurate way.

[4]This is a complex issue and the examiner will want to see you have got the law clear.

[5]Normally in family law problem questions you do not need to discuss questions of evidence, but this area is an exception because the law on evidence is central to the issue.

[6]The meaning of 'likely' is important and needs explaining carefully as done here. The examiner will be looking out for a clear definition.

Section 31 of the Children Act 1989 sets out the grounds upon which a care or supervision order can be made. We shall consider whether the threshold criteria are made and then whether a care or supervision order would promote the welfare of the child.[1] It should be added that a court can only make a care or supervision order if a local authority has applied for one, it cannot do so on its own motion.[2]

First, it must be shown that the child either is suffering or is likely to suffer significant harm. First, let us consider Bryony. The courts have explained that 'is' suffering means 'is' at the time of the first local authority intervention (rather than the time the case comes to court (**Re M** [1994] 2 FCR 871). Harm is described in section 31(9) as including ill-treatment or the impairment of health or development. Significant was said by Booth KJ in **Humberside CC v B** [1993] 1 FCR 613 to mean 'considerable noteworthy or important'.[3] Bryony currently simply has bruises. It is unlikely without further evidence that these can be sufficient to be significant harm. More likely to succeed is an argument that she is likely to suffer significant harm. In **Re H** [1996] AC 563 and confirmed in **Re B** [2008] 2 FCR 339 a court can only make an assessment that a child is likely to suffer harm based on facts. It cannot rely on assumptions. Facts must be things proved to be true on the balance of probabilities.[4] Here, the bruising is proved as a fact, but it seems it is not proved on the balance of probabilities that it was deliberate. Nor is it proved that this was caused by Tom. That is no more than speculation. Therefore the bruises cannot be relied upon as founding a claim that Bryony is likely to suffer significant harm.[5]

What about the concern that she is at risk form Tom? Here we have the opinion of an expert that Tom is a risk to his sister. But that evidence would need to be treated with care. First, the court would need to be persuaded that the view of the expert was based on facts not suspicions (**Re H**). Otherwise a suspicion could be turned into a fact by simply an expert's say so. Second, the summary of the facts state that there is a risk of causing some harm. 'Likely' in section 31 has been interpreted in **Re H** and **Re B** as meaning a real possibility, one that could not sensibly be ignored.[6] The court would need persuading that the risk amounted to that. Further, it would need to be shown there was a risk of significant harm, not just of some harm.

[7]In many cases once it is shown that there is significant harm or a risk of that there will be no difficulty in establishing it is a result of the parenting, but that is not always so, as this problem shows.

[8]This is a good point to make. If you cannot show that the parents have directly harmed the child, the local authority may be able to argue that they have failed to protect the child from harm.

[9]This is an important point to make too. It is not a question of whether the parents are doing their best, but whether they are providing a reasonable level of care.

Even if the court is persuaded that Bryony is likely to suffer significant harm it must still be shown that this is attributable to 'the care given to the child, or likely to be given to him if the order were not made, not being what it would be reasonable to expect a parent to give him' (s. 31(2)).[7] In this case it seems the risk to Bryony is not from her parents but rather her brother Tom. That would appear to be a 'knock down' argument that the threshold criteria cannot be made out. However, in **Lancashire CC v B** [2000] 1 FCR 509 although the House of Lords were willing to accept that where it was unclear whether a parent or child minder had harmed a child a care order could be made. However, that was because the child minder was *in loco parentis* and offering the kind of care a parent would offer. The question in Bryony's case would be whether or not Tom could be seen as similar to the child minder in providing the kind of care one would expect from a parent. That seems unlikely. However, this is still not the end of the argument because it could be said the risk of significant harm flows from the fact that the parents are unable to protect Bryony from the risk posed by her brother. That argument has a great chance of success but it would need to be shown that her parents had not acted reasonably in protecting her.[8] If there is little they can do then maybe they cannot be said to be failing to provide the level of care it is reasonable to expect a parent to provide.

Turning to Tom, the question is whether he is suffering significant harm or is likely to. It might be argued that although he is posing a risk to others and although his behaviour may be disruptive he himself is not suffering significant harm. However, if it could be shown that his behaviour is, for example, affecting his education, then an argument could be made that he is suffering significant harm. It could then be argued that either he is not being given the level of care it is reasonable to expect a parent to give or that the child is beyond parental control. The former requirement is objective, so that even if the parents are doing their best given their depression if it is not up to the level that a reasonable parent would give the criteria could be made out.[9]

Assuming in either Bryony or Tom's case the threshold criteria are met there is the issue of whether a care or supervision order would best promote their welfare. In this case a supervision order seems most appropriate as the family needs support and assistance rather

[10]In child protection issues it is good to take a long-term view and look to the future.

than removal of the child. A child can only be removed under a care order. So if despite the benefit of the supervision order the children are still suffering significant harm and the local authority wishes to remove them it will need to apply for a care order.[10]

 Make your answer stand out

■ Discuss the leading House of Lords decision such as *Re H* and *Lancashire* in more detail. A useful discussion of *Re H* is found in Hayes (2004) 'Uncertain evidence and risk taking in child protection cases' *Child and Family Law Quarterly* 63 and on *Lancashire* Herring (2000) 'The suffering children of blameless parents' *Law Quarterly Review* 550.

■ For a detailed discussion of the evidential issues raised look at Hoyano and Keenan (2008) *Child Abuse: Law and Policy Across Boundaries*, Oxford: OUP.

■ You could look more at the Human Rights Act issues raised.

! Don't be tempted to...

■ Forget to discuss the parental-care aspect of the threshold criteria.

■ Ignore the issues about burden of proof.

 Question 2

Assess how the House of Lords have interpreted section 31 of the Children Act 1989.

Answer plan

→ Set out the role of section 31 and the main theoretical issues.

→ Discuss *Re M (A Minor)* on 'is suffering'.

→ Explain the decision in *Re H (Minors)* on a factual basis.

→ Analyse the decision in *Re B (Children)* on the balance of probabilities test.

→ Consider *Lancashire CC* v *B* and *Re O and N (Children)* on 'unknown perpetrator' cases.

Diagram plan

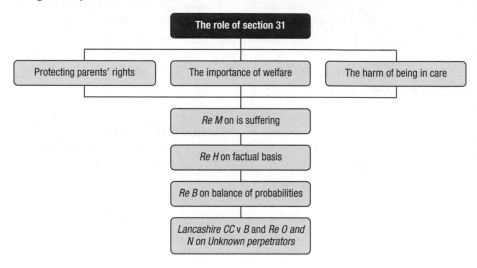

A printable version of this diagram is available from www.pearsoned.co.uk/lawexpressqa

Answer

[1] It is not worth quoting section 31. You may well be given it in the exam room in which case the examiner will give you no credit for writing it out.

Before a court can make a care order or a supervision order it must be satisfied that the 'threshold criteria' in section 31 Children Act 1989 are satisfied.[1] The court must also be persuaded that the making of the order will promote the welfare of the child. The threshold criteria, therefore, play a crucial role in that they prevent care orders or supervision orders being made simply based on what is best for the child. Not surprisingly there is substantial case law on their interpretation and the House of Lords have considered their interpretation in five important decisions. This essay will consider those decisions. When considering their significance it is helpful to consider whether they have interpreted the threshold criteria in a strict or a lax way. Interpreting them in a strict way would mean it would be harder for the courts to make a care or supervision order. If interpreted in a lax way it would make it easier. The significance of this is twofold. First, to some commentators the role of the criteria is to protect parents' rights. In effect the criteria are telling parents that unless they treat their children in way which causes or threatens significant harm their children will not be removed from them. This means that unless parents are woefully failing in their duties their children cannot be taken away simply because there is someone else who may be a better carer of the child than they are. Second, there is a question of how the threshold criteria and the welfare criterion interact. If the threshold criteria are interpreted in a lax way so that many cases satisfy them, then the courts will have more work to do at the welfare stage. Whereas if they are interpreted in a strict way it will be very likely that if they are satisfied a care or supervision order will be appropriate. In effect there is a question about the extent to which courts should have discretion about when a child should be taken into care or whether the law wants to restrict the courts' power so that even if a judge thinks that taking children into care would promote their welfare, the law will not permit the judge to make a care order.[2]

[2]It is very helpful at the start to set out the way you are going to analyse the cases. By setting out the difference between lax and strict interpretations of the threshold criteria this provides a framework you can use to discuss the case law.

In **Re M** [1994] 2 FCR 871 the key question was the meaning of the word 'is' in the threshold criterion. The issue arose in this way. The children's father murdered their mother in front of them. Social services rapidly intervened and placed them with excellent foster carers. By the time the case came to court it was difficult to say that the children were at that time suffering significant harm nor that they were likely to. However, their lordships explained that the test for the courts was whether the children were suffering significant harm at the time when the local authority intervened. Given that interpretation of the threshold criteria they clearly were satisfied.[3] That is a sensible decision, as the lordships indicated, otherwise the local authority would be prevented from obtaining an order in cases where they had put in place excellent care. In terms of whether this was a lax or strict interpretation it was a lax one, although a strict one would have made the law hard to operate.[4]

[3]Remember you must focus on the essay question. You are asked about the threshold criteria, not the use of the welfare principle once the threshold criteria are satisfied. So keep focused on the topic of the question.

[4]Here we are referring back to what we said in the introduction was our benchmark: whether the criteria were being interpreted in a strict or lax way.

In **Re H** [1996] AC 563 there were a number of questions for the court. The first was the meaning of likely. Their Lordships held that 'likely' meant that significant harm was a real possibility, a possibility that could not be sensibly ignored. This is a notably lax interpretation of the criteria. They could have held that likely meant 'more likely than not'. They also held that it must be shown on the balance of probabilities that the threshold criteria were made out. They rejected a suggestion that the criminal burden of proof (beyond reasonable doubt) should be used. However, rather confusingly, Lord Nicholls went on to say that where there was a serious allegation more evidence would be required to establish it on the

[5]This is an issue the examiner will be looking out for. It is an area of the law that is tricky and has confused many judges, let alone law students, so make sure you get it clear in your head when revising.

[6]Again, referring back to our benchmark question.

[7]Again, at the end of the discussion returning to the benchmark question.

balance of probability than a case of a less serious allegation. This dicta was reconsidered by the House of Lords in **Re B** [2008] 2 FCR 339 where their Lordships explained that Lord Nicholls was not suggesting that in cases of serious abuse the criminal burden of proof was being used. It is the civil balance of probabilities in all cases under the Children Act 1989. Rather what Lord Nicholls was trying to say was that some allegations will be inherently unlikely and they will require more evidence to establish them than others.[5] This aspect of the decision in **Re H** and **Re B** is probably best seen as a lax interpretation. Requiring a criminal burden of proof would have been a stricter interpretation but would have made it very difficult to obtain a care order.[6]

Re B also confirmed another aspect of the decision in **Re H**. That is that it can only be established that there is a risk of significant harm based on 'primary facts' proved on the balance of probabilities. Suspicions could not be relied upon. In **Re H** an older girl had alleged the father had abused her. That had not been proved on the balance of probabilities to be true, although there was a suspicion that it might have been. The court could not, however, rely on the suspicion of the abuse to make a care order in relation to the younger girl. As Lord Hoffmann in **Re B** put it, either a fact happened or it did not and there was nothing in between. A suspicion, not proved to be true on the balance of probabilities, had to be ignored. This is a noticeably strict interpretation of the criteria. As the minority in **Re H** pointed out there could be a case where there were quite a number of suspicions which together generate a real worry that a child was at a risk of significant harm. However, if this was all based on suspicions then the court could not make a care or supervision order. The majority saw the issue in terms of parental rights. Parents should not have their children removed simply on the basis of suspicions. This seems to take a strict interpretation of the threshold criteria.[7]

In **Lancashire CC v B** [2000] 1 FCR 509 although it was clear that a child had suffered harm it was not clear whether a parent or a child minder had harmed the child. In that case their lordships held that as long as it was clear that the abuse was caused by a parent or a child minder it did not matter that the court was unclear which had perpetrated the abuse. Where, however, it was unclear whether the harm was caused by a parent or someone who was not a primary carer of the child then a care order could not be made. What is significant about this interpretation of the threshold criteria is that it means that a parent could have a care order made in respect of a child even though it had not been shown that the parent was in any way to be blamed in relation to the harm. Their lordships returned to the issue in **Re O and N** [2003] 1 FCR 673 where it was emphasised that just because the threshold criteria had been made out, it did not mean that the order had to be made. In one of the cases at hand it was clear the child had been harmed by one of the parents, who had now separated. The child lived with the mother. The question for their lordships was whether at the threshold stage the suspicion that the harm might have been caused by the mother should be taken into account. It was held that at the welfare stage suspicions could be considered. In **Lancashire** the House of Lords took a notably lax interpretation of the threshold criteria in that their interpretation, as they accepted, could mean that innocent parents could have their children removed, even though they had done nothing wrong.[8] It was perhaps not as lax as it could have been because they emphasised it did need to be shown that a primary carer of the child was harming her.

In conclusion there is no consistent theme in the approach of their lordships. Sometimes they have taken a laxer line in interpreting the threshold criteria, and sometimes a stricter line. However, more often than not the laxer line has been taken. This is understandable. The courts do not want to set the threshold criteria so high that a case may occur where although it is clear a child needs protecting the threshold criteria have not been satisfied and so an order cannot be made. If the threshold criteria is set lower it is always possible to use the welfare test not to make an order where that would be too harsh on the parents. This means that the general pressure is to take a laxer interpretation of the criteria and is, by and large, what we have seen.[9]

[8]Yet again, back to the benchmark question. This repeated return to asking whether the interpretation is strict or lax gives the essay consistency and clarity.

[9]In this conclusion you give the examiner an overview of your approach to the case law.

Make your answer stand out

■ You could do more with the academic analysis of the decision. For example, Hayes (2004) 'Uncertain evidence and risk taking in child protection cases' *Child and Family Law Quarterly* 63 and Keating (1996) 'Shifting standards in the House of Lords' *Child and Family Law Quarterly* 157.

■ You could include a brief discussion of how the threshold criteria could be reformed: See Masson (2007) 'Reforming care proceedings – time for review' *Child and Family Law Quarterly*, 411.

■ For a broader discussion of how and when the state should intervene in family life see Fox Harding (1996) *Family, State and Social Policy*, Basingstoke: Macmillan.

 Don't be tempted to...

■ Simply state the decisions of the cases: you are asked to *assess*.

■ Use the criminal law burden of proof in this area: it is the civil one that applies.

✒ Question 3

Assess the impact of the Human Rights Act on the law on child protection.

Answer plan

→ Consider the significance of article 8 and particularly the way it must balance protection of family life and protecting children from harm.

→ Explain the principle of proportionality as developed in the interpretation of article 8.

→ Discuss the duty on the state to protect children found in articles 3 and 8.

→ Analyse the procedural protections found in articles 6 and 8

Diagram plan

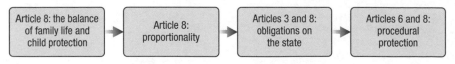

| Article 8: the balance of family life and child protection | → | Article 8: proportionality | → | Articles 3 and 8: obligations on the state | → | Articles 6 and 8: procedural protection |

A printable version of this diagram is available from www.pearsoned.co.uk/lawexpressqa

Answer

[1]This introduction has set
the debate in the context
of the wider debate over
the relevance of the HRA in
family law. The examiner will
like the fact that you are not
seeing the subject made up of
separate 'boxes'.

When the Human Rights Act 1998 was passed there was considerable debate over how much of an impact it would have on family law (see Fortin (2009a) and Herring (1999)). In fact, its impact has been much less than might have been expected. However, child protection is one area where it seems that the Act has made a noticeable difference. This essay will seek to set out the significance of the Act in this area.[1]

[2]Students sometimes rather loosely talk of the right to family life, but the language of Article 8 is the right to respect for family life, which is not the same thing.

The starting point is article 8. In paragraph one this sets out that children and parents have the right to respect for their family life.[2] This means that any intervention by the state in family life (e.g. by removing the child from the family, or requiring the family to permit a social worker access to their home) will infringe their rights. However, such an interference can be justified under paragraph 2 of Article 8. It is necessary to show that the interference is in accordance with the law and is necessary in the interests of the child.[3] In weighing up whether an interference in the rights of parents is justified in order to protect the welfare of the child the European Court has said that the interests of the child will be crucial (**K and T v Finland** [2000] 3 FCR 248). This means that where the child is suffering serious harm an interference will be readily justified. However, two points need to be emphasised here. The first is that any interference must be in accordance with the law. A local authority cannot simply remove a child on the basis that the child is at risk, it must act in accordance with a court order or other legal authority (**Re V** [2004] 1 FCR 338). Second there is the issue of proportionality, which we need to discuss further.[4]

[3]The examiner will want to see a clear explanation of the way that paragraph 2 accepts that a breach of the right to respect for family life can be justified.

[4]The examiner will be pleased to see this careful analysis of when a breach of article 8.1 may be justified.

In **K and T v Finland** the European Court of Human Rights explained that if it is to be shown that the interference in the right to respect for family life in article 8(1) is necessary under article 8(2) then it must be proved that the intervention is proportional. There are, in fact, two concepts here: first that the risk facing the child is sufficiently severe to justify an interference and second that there is no less interventionist way that can adequately protect the child.[5] In **K and T v Finland** itself, a baby was removed from her mother shortly after her birth. The European Court found this disproportionate. Although there were legitimate concerns about the mother, there may have been less interventionist ways of protecting

[5]Some concepts are complex and breaking them down into a number of separate points can help explain them.

[6]This is a useful phrase to remember for revision. You cannot be expected to recall lengthy quotes, but try and remember a few short ones.

[7]The examiner will be looking out for this issue. This is a very important part of the impact on child protection of the HRA.

[8]Normally you do not need in family law exams to be too worried about procedural issues, but this is an exception because the HRA has had a dramatic impact.

the child (e.g. through close supervision). The English courts have adopted this language of proportionality (**Re C and B** [2000] 2 FCR 614). Therefore if a local authority is seeking a care order it will need to show that a less interventionist supervision order will not adequately protect the child (**Re C and B**). In **Re N** [2000] 1 FCR 258 Bracewell J held that a care order can only be made if there is a 'pressing social need for intervention' and that the care order is proportionate to that need.[6]

Another important aspect of the Human Rights Act is the positive obligation placed on the state.[7] Under article 3 the state has an obligation to protect children from a risk of torture or inhuman or degrading treatment. This is an absolute right and the state cannot justify an interference by reference to any matter. However, the state is only required to act in a reasonable way. It means that if a local authority knows or ought to know that a child is suffering serious abuse then it is obliged to protect the child from harm (**E v UK** [2002] 3 FCR 700; **Z v UK** [2001] 2 FCR 246). A failure to protect the child could lead to a claim against the local authority by a child under the Human Rights Act 1998. Even if the dangers facing the child are less than sufficient to amount to torture or inhuman or degrading treatment, there are obligations to protect children from interference with their right to respect for their private life under article 8. This could include lower level physical or emotional abuse.

One area of the law where the HRA has had a significant impact is in relation to procedural protection.[8] These arise from articles 6 and 8. They apply both to the procedure to be followed before an application is made to a court for an order and also to how parents are involved in decisions concerning a child who has already been taken into care. In **W v UK** (1988) 10 EHRR 29 the European Court explained that the decision-making process of a local authority had to be sufficient to ensure that parents had an adequate opportunity to make their views known and for them to be taken into account by the local authority. This is not to mean that in an emergency a local authority cannot immediately apply for a court order. But it means the local authority must ensure that parents are adequately involved in the process. This means that parents should be shown a copy of any report prepared by an expert so they can comment on it (**Re C** [2007] 3 FCR 288); they should be informed of important meetings concerning their children and invited to attend (**McMichael v UK**

[9]The examiner will want to see that you appreciate that only very rarely will the court allow a parent to succeed in a claim against the local authority. Even where there has been a breach, the courts are often willing to find that the later involvement of the parents rectified the earlier lack of respect for their rights.

[1995] 2 FCR 718); and the parents have access to legal advice and representation during care proceedings (**P, C, S v UK** [2002] 3 FCR 1). Where parents are not adequately involved this may amount to a breach of their human rights and damages may need to be paid (**Re L** [2004] 1 FCR 289). That said, the courts have made it clear that they will be looking at whether the parents' procedural rights were adequately protected during the process seen as a whole, so a single failure to involve parents adequately, may be insufficient to justify a damages claim if generally the procedure did adequately protect their rights (**Re J** [2006] 2 FCR 107).[9]

[10]This conclusion neatly summarises the main issues you have discussed in the essay.

To conclude, we have seen that there are a number of important ways in which the Human Rights Act has affected the law on child protection. First, there is the notion of proportionality. Second, there is the obligation on the state and local authority to protect children who are at risk of abuse and thirdly there is the protection of procedural rights for parents during decision-making in this area.[10]

 Make your answer stand out

- Use more decisions of the European Court and the national courts. A helpful discussion can be found in Choudhry and Herring (2010) *European Human Rights and Family Law* ch. 8, Oxford: Hart.
- You could refer to the writing of Felicity Kaganas, who has argued, somewhat contrary to the general view, that the HRA has had little impact in this area. See Kaganas (2010) 'Child, protection, gender and rights' in J. Wallbank, S. Choudhry and J. Herring, *Rights, Gender and Family Law*, Abingdon: Routledge.
- A good point to add would be that many of the difficulties in child protection result not from problems with the law, but a lack of funding.

! Don't be tempted to...

- Forget the emphasis on flexibility of the HRA, especially in the procedural context.
- Exaggerate the significance of human rights, it is still the Children Act which is the starting point for all litigation in this area.

Question 4

Critically examine the decision of the House of Lords in *Re S; Re W* ([2002] UKHL10) and consider its impact on the balance of power between courts and local authorities in the area of child protection.

Answer plan

→ The key issue.

→ The role of care plans.

→ The approach of the Court of Appeal.

→ The approach of the House of Lords.

→ The human rights angle.

→ Subsequent developments.

Diagram plan

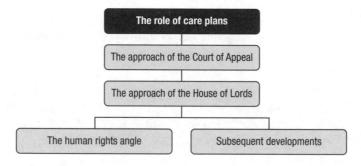

A printable version of this diagram is available from www.pearsoned.co.uk/lawexpressqa

Answer

[1]Start by setting out the legal principles behind the decision.

When a local authority applies for a care order it is required to prepare a care plan.[1] This sets out what the local authority intends to do with the child if the care order is made. It might, for example, state that the child will be removed and placed with foster carers. Or it might state that the child will remain with the parents, but under close supervision from the local authority. When the court decides whether or not to make the care order it will pay special attention to the care plan. Following the Human Rights Act 1998

(HRA) and the significance attached to proportionality the care plan can play a crucial role. However, there is nothing to stop a local authority deciding to depart from the care plan once a care order has been made. It was that issue which was crucial in this case.

[2]You are asked to discuss the decision of the House of Lords and you should focus on that, but the Court of Appeal decision needs explanation because it provides the background for the House of Lords decision.

[3]This is an important point to make. It is not a legal point, but the law must operate against the realities of the world and lack of money is a constant problem in childcare services.

The Court of Appeal stated that it was unhappy with the fact that care orders had been made by courts on the basis of a care plan, but subsequently the local authority departed radically from the care plan.[2] The court explained that this was normally as a result of budgetary constraint, rather than any deceptiveness by the local authority.[3] The solution proposed by the Court of Appeal was that when making a care order a court could star various items on the care plan (e.g. where the child was to live or crucial services which were to be provided by the local authority). The Court of Appeal stated that if the local authority wished to depart from one of the starred care items it would need to return to the court to seek permission to do so. The Court justified its approach by referring to the Human Rights Act. The court accepted that there was nothing in the language of the Children Act which justified its approach, but argued that the Human Rights Act required the court to read in such a jurisdiction to ensure that any state intervention was proportionate.

The House of Lords rejected the approach taken by the Court of Appeal. The primary reason was because they held that the Court of Appeal had misused the Human Rights Act 1998. The HRA could be used to interpret legislation, but the Court of Appeal had used it to insert new sections and thereby amend legislation.[4]

Their lordships went further and claimed that the approach of the Court of Appeal undermined a cardinal principle of the Children Act 1989. That was that the court should operate as a gateway into care, but that once a care order was made it was for the local authority and not the court to decide how the care order should be implemented. The court had the job of deciding whether or not a care order should be made and the local authority had the job of deciding how to look after the child in care. The approach of the Court of Appeal had blurred their roles. Critics of the decision of the House of Lords (e.g. Herring (2002)) have responded that, in fact, the Children Act does not suggest there is such a clear division of responsibilities.[5] There are quite a number of issues over which the local authority must seek court permission in relation to a child in care: for example, terminating contact between a child and family; changing a child's name; or changing a child's religion.

The House of Lords did go on to consider the human rights angles. The argument that had persuaded the Court of Appeal is that if a local authority was free to depart from the care plan then it could make a disproportionate interference in the child or parents' article 8 rights, without there being a remedy. The House of Lords were adamant that if a local authority did act disproportionately in implementing the care plan there were remedies available. This could be a claim under section 7 of the Human Rights Act against a local authority or a judicial review of the local authority's decision. Lord Nicholls accepted it might be thought that this might not be adequate to protect the rights of children in care, especially where their parents were not willing to bring proceedings. Also because it can be very difficult to establish that a local authority were acting unreasonably for the purposes of judicial review.[6]

[6]You could go on here to discuss the problems with '*Wednesbury* Unreasonableness' which is used in judicial review cases, but you probably don't have the space to do that.

Since this decision there were some amendments to the Children Act 1989, sections 26 and 31 by the Adoption and Children Act 2002.[7] These require the local authority to produce a care plan whenever it applies for a care order. It also requires the local authority to ensure that the implementation of care plans are internally reviewed. This is well short of the judicial supervision of the implementation of care orders the Court of Appeal imagined.

[7]Your focus is on the actual decision, but what happened afterwards in the law can be a helpful way of considering the decision reached.

It is noticeable that nearly five years after the House of Lords decision the Court of Appeal in **Re S and W** [2007] EWCA 232 considered the issue again. This fact itself indicates judicial unhappiness with the current lack of judicial control on the implementation of care orders. The Court of Appeal emphasised that a court could not amend a local authority's care plan. The court had either to make a care order on the basis of the proposed care plan or decline to make a care order. At most the court could ask the local authority to reconsider the case.

[8]This is a practical but important point. The examiner will be pleased you are aware of the practical problems for lawyers working in this area.

The issue which is rather hidden in these decisions is money.[8] When a local authority does not implement a care plan that is commonly because the local authority is short of money. While a court may be in a good position to decide what is best for a particular decision, it cannot realistically determine the best way for the local authority to use its budget for all the children who are in care. The strongest argument in favour of the House of Lords' approach is that the court is not in a position to interfere in monetary decision by a local authority. Perhaps the real message from the case law is that children in care are not receiving the kind of care they should receive because of lack of money for social service budget.

✓ Make your answer stand out

- Refer to the academic commentary on these decisions, e.g. Herring (2002) 'The human rights of children in care' *Law Quarterly Review* 534.
- You could explore further the significance of Human Rights Act reasoning.
- The decision could be put in the wider context of finding the balance of power between the courts and local authorities; see Dewar (1995) 'The courts and local authority autonomy' *Child and Family Law Quarterly* 15.

! Don't be tempted to...

- Assume that if a care order is made a child must be removed from the parents.
- Believe that judicial review is necessarily an adequate remedy.

Question 5

Albert is aged three. He suffers from a severe learning disability. His mother, Betty, is aged eighteen and also suffers from a mild learning disability. She finds it very frustrating to look after Albert and has hit him on several occasions. Social workers dealing with her case are concerned that Albert is not developing as well as he could. Advise the local authority on what orders might be appropriate.

Answer plan

→ Set out the threshold criteria and consider whether they are met in this case.

→ Explain the effect of a care order and discuss whether it is appropriate here.

→ Explain the effect of a supervision order and explore whether it is appropriate in this case.

→ Might a family assistance order be useful in this case?

Diagram plan

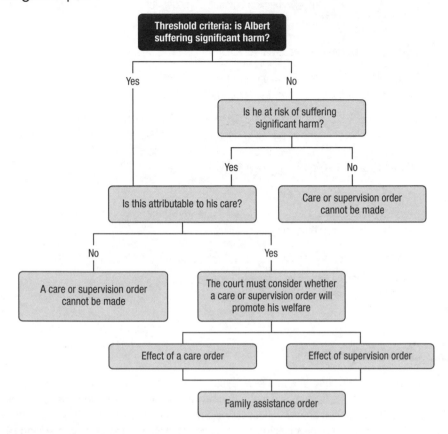

A printable version of this diagram is available from www.pearsoned.co.uk/lawexpressqa

[1]This introduction tells the examiner how you are going to approach the question.

[2]The examiner may have put this in as a trap. A weak student might think that having learning difficulties is suffering. You need to make it clear to the examiner that you are not tempted to make this error.

Answer

This essay will consider whether the threshold criteria have been made out. Then the alternative orders will be considered to see which is most appropriate for this case.[1]

The fact that Albert is suffering from learning difficulties cannot itself be regarded as meaning that the threshold criteria are satisfied.[2] Although harm can include impairment of development (s. 31(9) Childrens Act 1989), it could not be shown that that harm was attributable to care he was receiving or him being beyond

3Remember you need to
show not only that the child is
suffering or is likely to suffer
significant harm but that this
is attributable to the lack of
reasonable parental care. A
common error is to forget
that both of these need to be
shown. Make it clear to the
examiner that you have not
made that error.

parental control (s. 31(2)(b) Childrens Act 1989).[3] However, the local authority might rely on the hitting by Betty. It might depend on how severe the hitting is. Section 54 of the Children Act 2004 means that parents are permitted to use corporal punishment on children, but only so long as the injuries do not involve actual bodily harm or a more serious harm. Even if the injuries are not currently severe, it might still be relied upon as evidence that Albert is at risk of suffering significant harm.

If the threshold criteria are satisfied the court must, considering the welfare principle in section 1 of the Children Act 1989, decide whether to make a care or supervision order. These are the key differences between the two orders.

- A child can only be removed from a family under a care order. If the court thinks Albert should be removed immediately then a care order must be made.

- If the child is to stay with the parents then either a care or supervision order can be made. However, under a care order a child can be removed without referring the matter back to a court. If a supervision order is made then the local authority will need to apply for a care order if they wish to remove the child.

4Setting out the clear
differences between the
orders is an important part
of answering this question.
Using bullet points is a
perfectly acceptable way of
doing this.

- Under a care order a local authority acquires parental responsibility, but they do not under a supervision order (**Re V (Care or Supervision Order)** [1996] 1 FLR 776).[4]

5The examiner will like the
fact that having listed the
differences you are then
considering which ones will
be particularly significant for
the case you are looking at.

That last point may be significant in this case.[5] If Betty is unable to make appropriate decisions about Albert's medical, social or educational care, then it may be appropriate for the local authority to be given a care order so that they can acquire parental responsibility and thereby make those decisions. On the other hand the court will also be mindful for the principle of proportionality (**K and T v Finland** [2001] 2 FCR 673) meaning that the court must make the less interventionist order that will adequately protect Albert.[6] In this case, therefore, it will need to be shown that either gaining parental responsibility or the ability to remove Albert without further court order is necessary. A court may be persuaded that it is worth trying a supervision order first and seeing whether Betty, with support and advice, can provide a reasonable level of parenting for Albert (**Re C and B** [2000] 2 FCR 614).

6It is good to bring in the
ECtHR case law where
appropriate.

[7]Students often forget to discuss family assistance orders, so it will be useful to include them in this essay. It is likely to mean your essay will be a bit different from other answers.

A family assistance order can be ordered under section 16 Children Act 1989.[7] It requires a local authority officer to 'advise, assist and (where appropriate) befriend any person named in the order'. This is designed to offer help and assistance to a family and is particularly useful where there is a need to assist the parent with parenting skills. It therefore seems well suited if in this case what is needed is help for Betty to look after Albert. However, these orders are rarely made and can only be made with Betty's consent. The maximum length of the order is six months. It may be that if Betty is willing to receive the help the court will not think it necessary to make an order.

In conclusion, the most likely order in this case is a supervision order, providing the threshold criteria can be met. If not then a family assistance order may be appropriate. Finally, it should not be forgotten that a local authority can supply assistance on a voluntary basis if the parent does not object.

 Make your answer stand out

- Look in more detail at the differences between a care order and supervision order. Hoyano and Keenan (2008) *Child Abuse: Law and Policy Across Boundaries*, has an excellent discussion, Oxford: OUP.
- You could look at the notion of proportionality in more detail.
- Make more use of arguments under the Human Rights Act. See Choudhry and Herring (2010) *European Human Rights and Family Law* ch. 8, Oxford: Hart.

! Don't be tempted to...

- Assume that if the threshold criteria are made out the court will automatically make a care order.
- Believe that a local authority can only offer services if there is a court order. It can act on the basis of consent if necessary.

10

Adoption and special guardianship

How this topic may come up in exams

Essay questions in this area are likely to focus on two main issues. The first is the current use of adoption and special guardianship. It is important in such essays to make clear you appreciate that the current use of adoption is very different from how it was used in the past. The second theme of essays for this topic is on the differences between adoption and special guardianship.

Problem questions are also likely to feature two main issues. The first are the circumstances in which an adoption order can be made. In particular the circumstances in which parents' consent to adoption can be dispensed with. Here it is important to be familiar with the changes made to the law in the Children and Adoption Act 2006. The second is how the court decides whether to make an adoption order or a special guardianship. Here you will need a good knowledge of the legal differences between them.

■ Attack the question

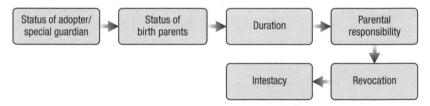 Question 1

What are the differences between adoption and special guardianship?

Answer plan

→ Start by summarising the essential difference between the status of adopter and a special guardian.

→ Explain the different status of the birth parents following adoption or special guardianship.

→ Set out the differences in the duration of adoption and special guardianship.

→ Consider the differences in the parental responsibility of an adopter and of a special guardian.

→ Examine the differences in the law on revocation of special guardianship and of adoption.

→ Analyse the differences in treatment of adoption and special guardianship in cases of intestacy.

Diagram plan

```
Status of adopter/   →   Status of         →   Duration   →   Parental
special guardian         birth parents                         responsibility
                                                                     ↓
                         Intestacy         ←   Revocation
```

A printable version of this diagram is available from www.pearsoned.co.uk/lawexpressqa

Answer

[1]This introduction sets out well the legal basis for special guardianship and explains why it was introduced. This provides a useful starting point for the discussion.

The status of special guardianship was created by the Adoption and Children Act 2002. It was designed to provide a middle path between making an adoption order and just a residence order: providing a special guardian with fewer rights than an adopter, but more rights than the holder of a residence order. However, the precise differences between special guardianship and adoption are complex.[1]

First, there is the status offered. On adoption the adopter becomes a parent for all purposes. However, a special guardian is not a parent. Although they will acquire many of the rights of the parent, they are not given that status (**Re S (A Child) (Adoption or**

[2]It is good in essay questions of this kind to provide practical examples of cases where the differences matter.

[3]This is good practical down-to-earth advice on when adoption may be less appropriate than special guardianship.

[4]This examiner will be pleased to see you highlighting how this is not just a theoretical issue but in some cases has significant practical implications.

[5]You will get marks for going into the detail here, rather than just saying that there are limits on parental responsibility we have gone on to give precise examples.

Special Guardianship Order) [2007] 1 FCR 271. This is one of the reasons why when a child is to be cared for permanently by a family member special guardianship is preferred. It might, otherwise, be confusing for a child to have, say, a grandparent, who is also a parent. However, this point does not mean it is never appropriate for a relative to be permitted to adopt (**Re J (A Child) (Adoption or Special Guardianship Order)** [2007] 1 FCR 271).[2] Certainly a special guardianship would be more appropriate for an older child who wanted to retain the link with their birth family.[3]

Second, there is the status of the birth family. On adoption the child ceases to be a child of the birth family, but that is not so in a case of special guardianship. One significance of this is that special guardianship is less of an intervention in to the article 8 rights of the birth family and so may be more easily justified than an adoption order (**Re S (A Child) (Adoption or Special Guardianship Order)** [2007] 1 FCR 271). It also means that in cases where a child has a strong link with a sibling or grandparent, that may steer the court towards a special guardianship order.

Third, there is the duration of the order. Adoption lasts for life, but a special guardianship order ceases when the child reaches the age of 18. This may be of significance if the child has a disability and the parents will need to be involved in their care beyond the age of 18.[4]

Fourth, on adoption the birth parents cease to have parental responsibility, but they retain it in cases of special guardianship. Although special guardians acquire parental responsibility, as do adopters, there are some limitations on it. In relation to removal from the jurisdiction, changing name, consent to adoption and major medical procedures the consent of the birth parents is required in addition to that of the special guardians. Further, as the birth parents retain parental responsibility they can apply for a section 8 order without leave, challenging the decision of a special guardian.[5]

Another difference between special guardianship and adoption relates to revocation. Unless there are truly exceptional cases an adoption order is irrevocable (**Webster v Norfolk CC** [2009] EWCA Civ 59). However, a special guardianship can be revoked on application to the court based on the welfare of the child. Of course, a court will be reluctant to revoke one, but it will be easier to justify doing so than revoking an adoption order.

[6]The examiner will be pleased to see this point. Although intestacy may be an issue for those who do not know the law, once you are informed of it you can escape from the intestacy rules by making a will.

A final difference concerns intestacy. If adopters die their adoptive children will have autonomic rights of succession, that would not be true for children whose special guardians die. Of course, this is unlikely to be a significant factor because the special guardians could make a will ensuring there is a gift to the child in question, if necessary.[6]

[7]Here the summary reminds the examiner of the key points you have made in the essay.

To summarise, both adoption and special guardianship offer ways of giving a formal status to those undertaking long-term care of a child, there are significant differences between the legal rights provided by them.[7]

 ## Make your answer stand out

- You could refer to some of the academic studies on how special guardianship is being used in practice: e.g. A. Hall (2008) 'Special guardianship: themes emerging from case law' *Family Law* 244; J. Masson (2010) 'A new approach to care proceedings' *Child and Family Social Work* 3.
- More detail could be provided on the case law on special guardianship. See Herring (2009a) *Family Law* ch. 11, Harlow: Pearson.
- Another angle is to look at how local authorities are these days trying to use family members to care for children who cannot be looked after by their families. See Argent (2009) 'What's the problem with kinship care?' *Adoption and Fostering Journal* 6.

! Don't be tempted to...

- Assume that special guardians get the same parental responsibility as adopters.
- Avoid a discussion of the practical issues which are involved.

Question 2

Assess the legal effect of an adoption order.

Answer plan

→ Explain the impact of an adoption order on parenthood.

→ Summarise the effect of an adoption order on parental responsibility.

→ Set out the impact of an adoption order on birth parents, particularly in the areas of marriage and succession.

→ Consider the impact of an adoption order on inheritance, citizenship and discrimination.

Diagram plan

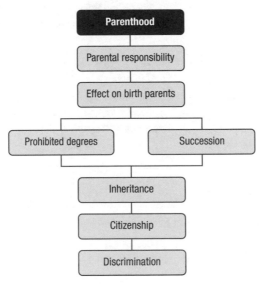

A printable version of this diagram is available from www.pearsoned.co.uk/lawexpressqa

Answer

[1]Although this is a short introduction it does enough: it provides a basic overview of the shape of the essay.

This essay will start by setting out the current law on the effect of an adoption order, before going on to consider whether the current law is appropriate.[1]

On adoption a child becomes the 'legitimate child of the adopter or adopters' (s. 67 Adoption and Children Act 2002).[2] This means that the adopters acquire the status of parents and also acquire parental responsibility. This means that adopters can make all the decisions about a child that a natural parent can, including whether or not to appoint a guardian.[3] The impact of the adoption order on the birth family is that it extinguishes their parental status for nearly all purposes and it extinguishes their parental responsibility. For example, it means that an adopted child cannot inherit property from their birth parents based on the rules of intestacy. An adopted child will acquire British citizenship if the adopter is a British citizen.

There are a few exceptions to these basic principles.[4] First, a child is still within the prohibited degrees of relationship with her birth parents for the purposes of marriage. So an adopted child would not be permitted to marry his blood brother or sister, even though they may no longer be formally brother or sister. Second, a child can retain the nationality he or she had as a result of birth and this will not be automatically removed by the adoption. Third, adoptions also do not affect the right to succeed peerages.

The legal results of adoption, as set out above, reflect the so called 'transplant model' of adoption, whereby the adopters are transplanted into the shoes of the natural parents.[5] However, there are those who question whether it is the appropriate model for adoption today. First, there is the point that most adoptions now are not of children, but rather of older children. In the past adoption was typically used in cases of unmarried mothers, who wanted their child adopted to avoid the embarrassment of having a child out of wedlock. Nowadays adoption is used as part of the care proceedings, and is a service for children rather than a service for infertile couples. This means that birth parents nowadays often still want to be involved in the child's life, at least to some extent. Further, the child will know their birth parents, and so an attempt to pretend that the adopters are their birth parents will be doomed to fail.[6]

Second, the courts are increasingly open to the idea of the birth family keeping contact with the child (**Re T (Adoption: Contact) [1995] 2 FLR 251**).[7] This does not fit easily with the transplant model. If it is beneficial to the child still to see their birth family, it is unlikely to be appropriate to sever all links between the child and birth family.

Third, with older children being given to adopters for adoption, then the issue of state support for adopters is an important one. The provision of services for adopters does not sit well with the overall transplant model. The Adoption and Children Act 2002 does allow for the payment of financial support to adopters. However, if the state is to pay, and therefore to some extent, supervise the parenting of adopters, that makes them less like 'normal parents' and more like foster carers.[8]

[8]This is an important point in practice and you will get marks for noting it.

Finally, a significant proportion of adoptions are those involving mothers and step-fathers adopting the mother's child. Adoption seems a rather cumbersome method of achieving that goal. The Adoption and Children Act 2002 enables a step-parent to be given parental responsibility for the child. That seems a more appropriate mechanism for recognising the link between child and step-parent than adoption.

There is, therefore, little doubt that the transplant model of adoption seems a little out-dated. It seems to present a fiction to the child, when the truth as to parenthood will be known to the child. It also assumes that birth parents will have no role to play in the child's life, when, in fact, increasingly it is imagined that the birth family will be involved in the child's life. It also does not seem appropriate in cases where the adopters are to receive support from the local authority and adopters are closer in position to foster carers. Finally, it seems inappropriate in cases of step-parent adoption. Perhaps the time has come to produce a definition of adoption which reflects the current practice of adoption.[9]

[9]This conclusion brings out the central themes of the essay well.

 Make your answer stand out

■ Make more use of the academic articles looking at adoption. See Lewis (2004) 'Adoption: The nature of policy shifts in England and Wales' *International Journal of Law, Policy and the Family* 235

■ You could discuss more of the human rights perspectives on adoption. See Harris-Short (2008) 'Making and breaking family life: Adoption, the state and human rights' *Journal of Law and Society* 28.

■ Consider further the objections made to the transplant model of adoption. See Dey (2005) 'Adapting adoption: A case of closet politics' *International Journal of Law, Policy and the Family* 289.

🖎 Question 3

Discuss the circumstances in which an adoption order can be revoked.

Answer plan

→ Explain that the marriage of parents will revoke an adoption.

→ Discuss when exceptional circumstances will cause an adoption to be revoked.

→ State that another adoption will revoke an earlier one.

→ Consider the different policy issues involved in this area.

Diagram plan

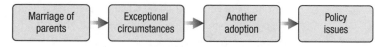

A printable version of this diagram is available from www.pearsoned.co.uk/lawexpressqa

Answer

[1]This brief summary tells the examiner how you are going to go about answering the question.

Once an adoption order has been made the law is very reluctant to allow its revocation. We shall be examining the policy reasons for this later on. First, we shall consider the current law.[1]

One circumstance in which an adoption order can be revoked is where a child has been adopted by one of his parents, and the parent then marries the other parent of the child. They can apply to have the adoption revoked under section 55 Adoption and Children Act 2002.[2] The reason why they might wish to do that is that they can then be parents by virtue of being natural parents, rather than through adoption. Needless to say this provision is rarely invoked.[3]

[2]Refer to the specific statutory provisions where appropriate.

[3]It is rarely invoked which is why it is a good idea to keep the discussion brief.

[4]The exceptional circumstances ground is the most important circumstance in which an adoption may be revoked and so it is worth discussing that in detail.

More significant is the ability to appeal against an adoption order if there are exceptional circumstances.[4] However, the courts have shown that it is very rare that an adoption order will be revoked. In **Webster v Norfolk CC** [2009] EWCA Civ 59 an adoption order was made in respect of three children after doctors became convinced that injuries caused to one child were non-accidental. Although the parents denied the allegation the court was persuaded by the doctors' evidence and made a care order and later an adoption order. However, several years later it transpired that the doctors had made a mistake and the injuries were caused by scurvy, rather than deliberate assault. The Court of Appeal held that this was not sufficiently exceptional to justify revoking an adoption order, especially several years after it had been made.[5]

[5]This might seem a lot of space to spend on summarising the facts of the case, but it is the leading case on the issue and the facts have to be explained to understand its significance.

This decision shows that the courts will be very strict in interpreting exceptional circumstances. Central to the finding of the Court of Appeal's reasoning was that on the basis of the evidence before the court the correct decision had been made, and further there was nothing wrong in the procedures used in the making of the adoption order. This may distinguish **Re K (Adoption and Wardship)** [1997] 2 FLR 230 where an English woman had adopted a child found in Yugoslavia. In that case it was found that the procedures leading to the making of the adoption in Bosnia had been deeply flawed: there had been no Guardian ad Litem used to represent the child's interests and inadequate evidence about the existence or views of the birth family had been presented.

To complete the picture it might be added that a new adoption order could revoke an existing one. So, in a scenario such as **Webster**, it would have been open, had the court been so minded, to make an adoption order making the birth parents the parents.

[6]You have been asked to discuss the law and so you will lose marks if you just set out what the law is.

So, why are the courts so reluctant to revoke adoption orders?[6] In **Webster** the Court of Appeal held it was important to ensure that adoptive parents had the security of knowing that their status as parents could not be removed on the basis of a finding that there was an error in the making of the adoption order. Arguably this does not give sufficient weight of the fact that in this case the natural parents had had their security of parenthood challenged by having their children removed, without justification. Another aspect of the **Webster** decision which is controversial is that it was said not to be based on the welfare principle. It might be questioned why the welfare principle, which normally applies in cases involving children (s. 1 Children Act 1989), was not held to govern the decision in that particular case.

 Make your answer stand out

- Use academic criticism of the *Webster* decision more. See, e.g. Herring (2009c) 'Revoking adoptions' [2009] *New Law Journal* 377.
- Consider in more detail some of the case law. See the discussion in Harris-Short and Miles (2007) *Family Law* ch. 13, Oxford: OUP.
- Consider further how a human rights challenge may be made to the current law.

! Don't be tempted to...

- Simply state the law and not discuss it.
- Assume that the courts will be generous in interpreting 'exceptional circumstances'.
- State that the welfare principle will govern the law on revoking adoptions.

? Question 4

Zia is aged 10. She was taken into care as a result of the drug addiction of her parents (Billie and Vi). She was placed for adoption with Mary and Sue who have entered a civil partnership. Billie and Vi object to the adoption because they do not approve of same-sex couples. They also believe that they have much to offer Zia in the future. Zia wants to live with Mary and Sue, but does not want to be adopted because she loves her grandparents, and does not want to lose the connection with them. Consider what the local authority will need to demonstrate if an adoption order is made.

Answer plan

→ Explain that the court will make the adoption if it considers that the adoption is in the best interests of Zia.

→ Consider some of the factors the court will take into account: Zia's wishes; the effect of the order on her life; and her relationships with other relatives.

→ Explain the need for parental consent before an adoption order can be made. Discuss whether in this case the need for consent might be dispensed with.

Diagram plan

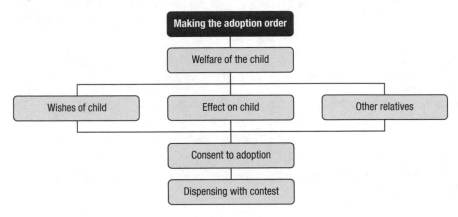

A printable version of this diagram is available from www.pearsoned.co.uk/lawexpressqa

[1]This introduction tells the examiner that you are aware of the overall legal structure of decision-making for adoption orders. It also informs the examiner how you are going to approach the question.

[2]In adoption questions, start with the welfare test before considering parental consent.

[3]You could list all the factors in section 1(4) but you probably don't have time. So focus on those that are particularly relevant.

Answer

There are two stages to the making of an adoption order under the Adoption and Children Act 2002. First, the court must be persuaded that the making of the adoption order will promote the welfare of the child. Second, either the parents of the child must consent, or the consent of parents must be dispensed with.[1]

Considering first the issue of whether making the order will promote Zia's welfare.[2] The court will want to consider the welfare report prepared on her and the assessment of her placement with Mary and Sue. Section 1(4) of the Adoption and Children Act 2002 provides a list of factors that the court will take into account in particular when determining whether or not to make an adoption order.[3] The court will consider Zia's welfare not just during her childhood but for her lifetime (**Re P (Children)(Adoption: Parental Consent)** [2008] 2 FCR 185). Of particular relevance in this case will be the following.

First, Zia's views are an important factor to take into account (s.1 (4)(a) Adoption and Children Act 2002). The court will consider her understanding and maturity. They will also want to be persuaded that these are Zia's own views. If they are this will argue strongly against an adoption order. In **Re M (Adoption or Residence Order)** [1998] 1 FLR 570 the views of a 12-year old, namely that

[4]This is a good example from
the case law which is similar
to the question you have
at hand. The examiner will
approve of your selection of
case law if the cases have
similar facts to the one you
are discussing.

[5]Here the examiner will be
pleased to see you applying
this factor to the case.

[6]As is common in family law
problems it is not possible to
provide a definite answer, but
the examiner will want you to
express a view as to what you
think is the most likely result.

[7]In a problem question
where it is not obvious what
route the court will take it is
best to list all the possible
alternatives.

she wanted to retain formal links with her siblings, led to the court making a residence order, rather than an adoption order.[4]

Second, the court will consider 'the likely effect on the child (throughout her life) of having ceased to be a member of the original family and become an adopted person'. If Billie and Vi are able to offer Zia supportive parenting in the future, it may not be sensible to make an adoption order ending their link with her.[5] However, the court will not want to stay away from an adoption order based on speculation that the family have something to offer her in the future (**Re H (Adoption: Non-Partial)** [1996] 1 FLR 717).

Third, the courts are specifically asked in section 1(4)(f) of the Adoption and Children Act 2002, to consider Zia's relationship with her relatives and whether the relationship with them is likely to continue. Assuming that Zia has a good relationship with her grandparents and Zia wants to retain her link with them, then a special guardianship may be more appropriate than an adoption order.

It seems on balance the factors point to a special guardianship or simply a residence order, rather than an adoption order.[6] That is especially so when the Human Rights Act 1998 is borne in mind. It must be shown that adoption is necessary in order to protect the child (**Johansen v Norway** (1996) 23 EHRR 33). It seems here that a special guardianship can provide the security Zia needs, without severing the links with the birth family. For completeness it might be added that the fact that Mary and Sue are a same-sex couple will not affect the court's analysis (Zia has no objection) and indeed a same-sex couple can adopt a child (s. 1 Adoption and Children Act 2002).

If, despite these points, the court decides that adoption is appropriate then Billie and Vi will need to consent or their consent must be dispensed with.[7] Under section 1 of the Adoption and Children Act 2002 their consent will be dispensed with if the welfare of the child requires it. The court will therefore consider the various factors already listed. However, in order to dispense with parental consent it must be shown that the dispensing was required in order to promote the welfare of Zia. In **Re P (Placement Orders: Parental Consent)** [2008] EWCA Civ 535 it was held the word 'required' indicated that dispensing of consent was required. If, therefore, the court decides it is very much in the welfare of Zia to be adopted, they will dispense with parental consent.

To conclude, it is suggested that in this case special guardianship may be the most appropriate course. It is in line with Zia's wishes and will enable her to retain her link with her grandparents.

Make your answer stand out

- You could discuss more of the human rights arguments. See Harris-Short (2008) 'Making and breaking family life: Adoption, the state and human rights' *Journal of Law and Society* 28.
- More detail could be provided on the case law on adoption. See Herring (2009a) *Family Law* ch. 11, Harlow: Pearson.
- Consider in more detail when consent may be dispensed with. See Choudhry (2003) 'The Adoption and Children Act 2002, the welfare principle and the Human Rights Act 1998' *Child and Family Law Quarterly* 119.

! Don't be tempted to...

- Suggest that parental consent can be dispensed with simply because that would be in the welfare of the child.
- Forget the option of a residence order.

Question 5

When will the consent of parents to adoption be dispensed with?

Answer plan

→ Set out the requirements for an adoption order.

→ Consider the impact of the Adoption and Children Act 2002.

→ Analyse in detail the word 'requires'.

→ How might the Human Rights Act impact on the issue?

→ Natural parent presumption.

Diagram plan

A printable version of this diagram is available from www.pearsoned.co.uk/lawexpressqa

Answer

Before an adoption order can be made the court must be persuaded that an adoption order will be in the child's welfare (s. 1 Adoption and Children Act 2002). It is also necessary to have the consent of all parents with parental responsibility and any guardians. Consent must be given 'unconditionally and with full understanding of what it involve[s]' (s. 52(2) Adoption and Children Act 2002). If that consent is not forthcoming the court can dispense with consent. This essay will discuss the circumstances in which the consent can be dispensed with.[1]

[1] This paragraph sets the scene for the essay and shows the examiner that you are aware of the context in which the issue arises.

The Adoption and Children Act 2002 provides two circumstances in which consent can be dispensed with. The first is where the parent or guardian cannot be found or is incapable of giving consent (s. 52(1)(a)). This could be used where a baby has been abandoned and no one knows its parentage (**Haringey v Mr and Mrs E** [2006] EWHC 1620 (Fam)). It might also be used if a father has left the family and no one knows where he has gone.[2]

[2] This ground for dispensing with consent is rarely used and there is not much to say about it. It is, therefore, appropriate to keep the discussion brief.

The second, and more commonly used, is that 'the welfare of the child requires the consent to be dispensed with (s. 52(1)(b) Adoption and Children Act 2002). In this provision the Act significantly changed the law from the previous position, in the Adoption Act 1976.[3] Under the 1976 Act a parent's consent could be dispensed with if they were unreasonably withholding their consent to the adoption. The change in terminology from asking whether the parents are acting reasonably in withholding their consent to asking whether the child's welfare requires dispensing with consent requires a subtle shift in focus from the parents' reasons for refusing to consent to the welfare of the child. This point was emphasised in **Re R (Placement Order)** [2007] EWHC 3031 (Fam) where Muslim parents objected to adoption as being contrary to

[3] Your focus is on the current law, but here the examiner will expect you to compare the new law with the old.

[4]This is a good use of the case law to illustrate the point made and show the examiner you have understood it.

[5]The examiner will be pleased to see this focus on the wording of the statute.

[6]It is often helpful to bring in an approach based on the Human Rights Act 1998.

[7]Remember that the House of Lords is now the Supreme Court.

[8]This conclusion brings together the key points well.

their religious beliefs. The court held that the question was about the child's welfare, not the reasonableness of the parents' religious beliefs.[4]

One issue which has troubled commentators is how the test for dispensing with parental consent differs from the general welfare test (is the adoption order in the welfare of the child?) which the court will consider first. The key, it is suggested, lies in the word 'requires'.[5] It is not enough just to show that the adoption will be in the welfare of the child, but it must be shown that it is strongly enough in the welfare of the child to require dispensing with consent. In **Re P (Placement Orders: Parental Consent)** [2008] EWCA Civ 535 the Court of Appeal noted that the word 'requires' suggested that there was an imperative to dispense with the consent, rather than it simply being desirable.

This conclusion could also be supported by reference to the Human Rights Act 1998.[6] The European Convention on Human Rights, article 8, requires respect for family life unless it is necessary to justify interference. Further there is the principle of proportionality whereby it must be shown that there is no less serious intervention which could adequately protect the child. This suggests that adoption against parental wishes must be shown to be necessary, not just desirable.

The courts might also place weight on the 'natural parent' presumption. Although this presumption has been greatly weakened by **Re B (Children)** [2009] UKSC 4, the Supreme Court did accept that generally children were better brought up by their natural parent, even though in a particular case the court must focus on what is in the best interests of the particular child.[7]

To conclude, this essay has shown that before a parent's consent to adoption can be dispensed with it must be shown that the parent cannot be found or lacks the capacity to consent, or that the welfare of the child requires the consent to be dispensed with. It has been argued in this essay that the word 'requires' indicates that it must be shown that adoption is significantly in the welfare of the child. This is appropriate because adoption terminates all legal links between child and the birth family. To justify such a dramatic order it must be shown to be required in the child's welfare.[8]

Make your answer stand out

■ For more discussion on the human rights arguments and especially claims that the rights of parents are not adequately protected. See Harris-Short (2008) 'Making and breaking family life: Adoption, the state and human rights' *Journal of Law and Society* 28.

■ Consider in more detail the changes in the law brought about by the Adoption and Children Act 2002, see Eekelaar (2003) 'Contact and the adoption reform' in A. Bainham; B. Lindley, M. Richards and L. Trinder (eds) *Children and Their Families*, Oxford: Hart.

■ Consider the alternatives to adoption, especially special guardianship.

! Don't be tempted to...

■ Assume that consent will be dispensed with as long as the welfare condition is met.

■ State we know for sure how the courts will interpret the provisions.

Bibliography

Anitha, S. and Gill, A. (2009) 'Coercion, Consent and the Forced Marriage Debate in the UK' *Feminist Legal Studies* 295.

Archard, D. (2004) *Children, Rights and Childhood*, London: Routledge.

Argent, H. (2009) 'What's the problem with kinship care?' *Adoption and Fostering Journal* 6.

Autchmuty, R. (2008) 'What's so special about marriage? The impact of Wilkinson *v* Kitzinger' *Child & Family Law Quarterly* 479.

Bailey-Harris, R. (1998) 'Dividing the assets on breakdown of relationships outside marriage: challenges for reformers' in R. Bailey-Harris (ed.) *Dividing the Assets on Family Breakdown*, Bristol: Jordans.

Bainham, A. (1998) *Children: The Modern Law*, Bristol: Jordans.

Bainham, A. (2001) 'Men and women behaving badly: Is fault dead in English family law?' *Oxford Journal of Legal Studies* 219.

Bainham, A. (2003) 'Contact as a right and obligation' in A. Bainham, B. Lindley, M. Richards and L. Trinder (eds) *Children and their Families*, Oxford: Hart.

Bainham, A. (2006) 'The rights and obligations associated with the birth of a child' in J. Spencer and A du Bois-Pedain (eds) *Freedom and Responsibility in Reproductive Choice*, Oxford: Hart.

Bainham, A. (2008a) 'Arguments over parentage' *Cambridge Law Journal* 322.

Bainham, A. (2008b) 'What is the point of birth registration?' *Child and Family Law Quarterly* 449.

Bamforth, N. (2007) '"The benefits of marriage in all but name?" Same-sex couples and the Civil Partnership Act 2004' *Child and Family Law Quarterly* **19**, 133.

Borkowski, A. (2004) 'Wilful refusal to consummate: "Just excuse"' *Family Law* 684.

Bradney, A. (1994) 'Duress, family law and the coherent legal system' *Modern Law Review* 499.

Bretherton, H. (2002) '"Because it's me the decisions are about" – Children's experiences of private law proceedings' *Family Law* 450.

Burton, M. (2008a) *Legal Responses to Domestic Violence*, London: Routledge.

Choudhry, S. (2003) 'The Adoption and Children Act 2002, the welfare principle and the Human Rights Act 1998' *Child and Family Law Quarterly* 119.

Choudhry, S. and Herring, J. (2006a) 'Domestic Violence and the Human Rights Act 1998: A New Means of Legal Intervention' *Public Law* 752.

Choudhry, S. and Herring, J. (2006b) 'Righting domestic violence' *International Journal of Law Policy and the Family* 1.

Choudhry, S. and Herring, J. (2010) *European Human Rights and Family Law*, Oxford: Hart.

Choudhry, S., Herring, J. and Wallbank, J. (2010) 'Welfare, rights, care and gender in family law' in J. Wallbank, S. Choudhry and J. Herring (eds) *Rights, Gender and Family Law*, Abingdon: Routledge.

Cooke, E. (2007) 'Miller/McFarlane: law in search of a definition' *Child and Family Law Quarterly* 98.

Davis, G. and Murch, M. (1988) *Grounds for Divorce*, Oxford: Clarendon Press.

Day Sclater, S. (1999) *Divorce: A Psychological Study*, Aldershot: Dartmouth.

Day Sclater, S. and Piper, C. (1999) *Undercurrents of Divorce*, Aldershot: Ashgate.

Deech, R. (2009) 'Divorce – A disaster?' *Family Law* **39**, 1048.

Dewar, J. (1995) 'The courts and local authority autonomy' *Child and Family Law Quarterly* 15.

Dewar, J. (1998) 'The normal chaos of family law' *Modern Law Review* **61**, 467.

Dey, I. (2005) 'Adapting adoption: A case of closet politics' *International Journal of Law, Policy and the Family* 289.

Diduck, A. (2003) *Law's Families*, ch. 1, London: LexisNexis, Butterworths.

Diduck, A. (2007) 'If only we can find the appropriate terms to use the issue will be solved: law, identity and parenthood' *Child and Family Law Quarterly* 458.

Diduck, A. and O'Donovan, K. (2007) *Feminist Perspectives on Family Law*, London: Routledge.

Diduck, A. and O'Donovan, K. (2007) 'Feminism and families: Plus ça change?' in A. Diduck and K. O'Donovan (eds) *Feminist Perspectives on Family Law*, London: Routledge.

Douglas, G. (2006) 'The separate representation of children – in whose best interests?' in M. Thorpe and R. Budden (eds) *Durable Solutions*, Bristol: Jordans.

Eekelaar, J. (1991a) 'Parental responsibility: State of nature or nature of the state' *Journal of Social Welfare and Family Law* 37.

Eekelaar, J. (1991b) *Regulating Divorce*, Oxford: Clarendon Press.

Eekelaar, J. (1999) 'Family Law: Keeping us on Message' *Child and Family Law Quarterly* 387.

Eekelaar, J. (2000) 'Post-divorce financial obligations' in S. Katz, J. Eekelaar and M. Maclean (eds) *Cross Currents*, Oxford: OUP.

Eekelaar, J. (2002) 'Contact – over the limit' *Family Law* **32**, 271.

Eekelaar, J. (2003) 'Contact and the adoption reform' in A. Bainham, B. Lindley, M. Richards and L. Trinder (eds) *Children and Their Families*, Oxford: Hart.

Eekelaar, J. (2006a) *Family Life and Personal Life*, Oxford: OUP.

Eekelaar, J. (2006b) 'Property and Financial Settlements on Divorce' *Family Law* **36**, 754.

Farson, R. (1978) *Birthrights*, London: Penguin.

Fineman, M. (2004) *The Autonomy Myth*, New York: The New Press.

Finnis, J. (1994) 'Law, morality and "sexual orientation"' *Notre Dame University Law Review* 1.

Fortin, J. (1996) 'Re F: the gooseberry bush approach' *Modern Law Review* 296.

Fortin, J. (2006) 'Accommodating Children's Rights in a Post Human Rights Era' *Modern Law Review* 299.

Fortin, J. (2007) 'Children's Representation through the looking glass' *Family Law* 500.

Fortin, J. (2009a) *Children's Rights and the Developing Law*, London: Butterworths.

Fortin, J. (2009b) 'Children's Right to Know Their Origins – Too Far, Too Fast?' *Child and Family Law Quarterly* 336.

Fox Harding, L. (1996) *Family, State and Social Policy*, Basingstoke: Macmillan.

Freeman, M. (1985) 'Towards a critical theory of family law', *Current Legal Problems* **40**, 179.

Freeman, M. (1999) 'Not such a queer idea. Is there a case for same-sex marriage?' *Journal of Applied Philosophy* 1.

Freeman, M. (2003) 'The State, Race and Family in England Today' in J. Dewar and S. Parker (eds) *Family Law Processes, Practices, Pressures*, Oxford: Hart.

Freeman, M. (2007) 'Why it remains important to take children's rights seriously' *International Journal of Children's Rights* 5.

Gardner, S. (2008) 'Family Property today' *Law Quarterly Review* 422.

George, R. (2008) '*Stack* v *Dowden* + Do As We Say, Not As We Do?' *The Journal of Social Welfare and Family Law* 49.

George, R., Harris, P. and Herring, J. (2009) 'Pre-Nuptial Agreements: For Better or For Worse?' *Family Law* 934.

Gilligan, C. (1982) *In a Different Voice*, London: Harvard University Press.

Gilmore, S. (2003) 'Parental responsibility and the unmarried father – a new dimension to the debate' *Child and Family Law Quarterly* 15.

Gilmore, S. (2006) 'Court decision-making in shared residence order: A critical examination' *Child and Family Law Quarterly* 103.

Gilmore, S. (2008) 'Disputing contact: challenging some assumptions' *Child and Family Law Quarterly* 285.

Gilmore, S. (2009) 'The limits of parental responsibility' in R. Probert, S. Gilmore and J. Herring, *Responsible Parents and Parental Responsibility*, Oxford: Hart.

Glennon, L. (2008) 'Obligations between adult partners: Moving from form to function?' *International Journal of Law Policy and Family* **22**, 22.

Hall, A. (2008) 'Special guardianship: themes emerging from case law' *Family Law* 244.

Harding, R. (2007) 'Sir Mark Potter and the Protection of the Traditional Family: Why Same Sex Marriage is (Still) a Feminist Issue' *Feminist Legal Studies* 223.

Harris, N. (2009) 'Playing Catch-up in the Schoolyard? *Children* and Young People's "Voice" and Education Rights in the UK' *International Journal of Law, Policy and the Family* 73.

Harris-Short, S. (2008) 'Making and breaking family life: Adoption, the state and human rights' *Journal of Law and Society* 28.

Harris-Short, S. and Miles, J. (2007) *Family Law*, Oxford: OUP.

Hasson, E. (2003) 'Divorce Law and the Family Law Act 1996' *International Journal of Law, Policy and the Family* 338.

Hayes, H. (1999) 'What's in a Name? A child by any other name is surely just as sweet' *Child and Family Law Quarterly* 423.

Hayes, M. (2004) 'Uncertain evidence and risk taking in child protection cases' *Child and Family Law Quarterly* 63.

Hayward, A. (2009) 'Family values in the home' *Child and Family Law Quarterly* 242.

Herring, J. (1999) 'The Human Rights Act and the welfare principle in family law – conflicting or complementary?' *Child and Family Law Quarterly* **11**, 223.

Herring, J. (2000) 'The suffering children of blameless parents' *Law Quarterly Review* 550.

Herring, J. (2002) 'The human rights of children in care' *Law Quarterly Review* 534.

Herring, J. (2003) 'Connecting contact' in A. Bainham, B. Lindley, M. Richards and L. Trinder (eds) *Children and their Families*, Oxford: Hart.

Herring, J. (2005) 'Why financial orders on divorce should be unfair' *International Journal of Law Policy and the Family* 218.

Herring, J. (2009a) *Family Law* 4th edn, Harlow: Pearson.

Herring, J. (2009b) *Older People in Law and Society*, Oxford: OUP.

Herring, J. (2009c) 'Revoking adoptions' *New Law Journal* 377.

Herring, J. (2009d) 'The shaming of naming: parental rights and responsibilities in the naming of children' in R. Probert, S. Gilmore and J. Herring (eds) *Responsible Parents and Parental Responsibility*, Oxford: Hart.

Herring, J. (2010a) 'Money, money, money' *New Law Journal* 300.

Herring, J. (2010b) 'Relational autonomy and family law' in J. Wallbank, S. Choudhry and J. Herring (eds) *Rights, Gender and Family Law*, Abingdon: Routledge.

Herring, J. (2010c) 'Sexless Family Law' *Lex Familiae* **11**, 3.

Herring, J. and Taylor, R. (2006) 'Relocating relocation' *Child and Family Law Quarterly* **18**, 517.

Holt, J. (1975) *Escape from Childhood*, London: Dutton.

Hoyano, L. and Keenan, C. (2008) *Child Abuse: Law and Policy Across Boundaries*, Oxford: OUP.

Jones, C. (2010) 'The identification of "parents" and "siblings"' in J. Wallbank, S. Choudhry and J. Herring (eds) *Rights, Gender and Family Law*, Abingdon: Routledge.

Kaganas, F. (2010) 'Child, protection, gender and rights' in J. Wallbank, S. Choudhry and J. Herring (eds) *Rights, Gender and Family Law*, Abingdon: Routledge.

Keating, H. (1996) 'Shifting standards in the House of Lords' *Child and Family Law Quarterly* 157.

Lacey, N. (1993) 'Theory into Practice? Pornography and the Public/Private Dichotomy', in A. Bottomley and J. Conaghan (eds) *Feminist Theory and Legal Strategy*, Oxford: Blackwell.

Lewis, J. (2004) 'Adoption: The nature of policy shifts in England and Wales' *International Journal of Law, Policy and the Family* 235.

Lim, H. (1996) 'Mapping Equity's Place: Here be Dragons' in A. Bottomley (ed.) *Feminist Perspectives on the Foundational Subjects of Law*, London: Cavendish Press.

Lind, C. (2008) 'Responsible fathers: paternity, the blood tie and family responsibility' in J. Bridgeman, H. Keating and C. Lind (eds) *Responsibility, Law and the Family*, London: Ashgate.

Lowe, N. and Douglas, G. (2006) *Family Law*, Oxford: OUP.

Lowe, N. and Murch, M. (2001) 'Children's participation rights in the family justice system' *Child and Family Law Quarterly* 137.

Lyon, C. (2007) 'Children's participation and the promotion of their rights' *Journal of Social Welfare and Family Law* 99.

Maclean, S. and Maclean, M. (1996) 'Keeping secrets in assisted reproduction – the tension between donor anonymity and the need of the child for information', *Child and Family Law Quarterly* **8**: 243.

Madden Dempsey, M. (2006) 'What Counts as Domestic Violence? A Conceptual Analysis' *William and Mary Journal of Women and the Law* **12**(2), 301.

Madden Dempsey, M. (2007) 'Towards a feminist state: What does 'effective' prosecution of domestic violence mean?' *Modern Law Review* **70**, 908.

Madden Dempsey, M. (2009) *Prosecuting Domestic Violence*, Oxford: OUP.

Masson, J. (2006) 'Parenting by being; parenting by doing – In search of principles for founding families' in J. Spencer and A. Du Bois-Pedain *Freedom and Responsibility in Reproductive Choices*, Oxford: Hart.

Masson, J. (2007) 'Reforming care proceedings – time for review' *Child and Family Law Quarterly* **19**, 411.

Masson, J. (2010) 'A new approach to care proceedings' *Child and Family Social Work* 3.

McCandlass, J. and Sheldon, S. (2010) 'The Human Fertilisation and Embryology Act 2008 and the tenacity of the sexual family' *Modern Law Review* 175.

Mears, M. (1991) 'Getting it wrong again' *Family Law* **21**, 231.

Miles, J. (2005) 'Principle or pragmatism in ancillary relief' *International Journal of Law, Policy and the Family* 242.

Miles, J. (2008) 'Making sense of need, compensation and equal sharing after Miller; McFarlane' *Child and Family Law Quarterly* 378.

Mullender, A. (2005) *Tackling Domestic Violence: Providing Support For Children Who Have Witnessed Domestic Violence*, London: Home Office.

Murray, A. (2008) 'Guidelines on Compensation' *Family Law* **38**, 756.

O'Donovan, K. (1988) 'A right to know one's parentage' *International Journal of Law, Policy and the Family* 27.

O'Donovan, K. (2005) 'Flirting with academic categorisations' *Child and Family Law Quarterly* 415.

Olsen, F. (1998) 'Asset Distribution after Unmarried Cohabitation: A United States Perspective', in R. Bailey-Harris (ed.) *Dividing the Assets on Family Breakdown*, Bristol: Jordans.

O'Neill, O. (2002) 'Children's rights and children's lives' *International Journal of Law Policy and the Family* 24.

Parkinson, P. (2005) 'The Yardstick of Equality: Assessing contributions in Australia and England' *International Journal of Law, Policy and the Family* **19**, 163.

Price, F. and Cook, R. (1995) 'The donor, the recipient and the child – human egg donation in UK licensed clinics', *Child and Family Law Quarterly* 7: 145.

Probert, R. (2002) 'When are we married? Void, non-existent and presumed marriages' *Legal Studies* 398.

Probert, R., Gilmore, S. and Herring, J. (eds) (2009) *Responsible Parents and Parental Responsibility*, Oxford: Hart.

Rasmusen, E. (2002) 'An economic approach to adultery law' in A. Dnes and
   R. Rowthorn (eds) *The Law and Economics of Marriage and Divorce*, Cambridge: CUP.
Raz, J. (1986) *The Morality of Freedom*, Oxford: OUP.
Reece, H. (1996) 'The paramountcy principle: consensus of construct' *Current Legal
   Problems* 267.
Reece, H. (2003) *Divorcing Responsibly*, Oxford: Hart.
Reece, H. (2006) 'The End of Domestic Violence' Modern Law Review 69, 770.
Reece, H. (2009) 'The degradation of parental responsibility' in R. Probert, S. Gilmore and
   J. Herring (eds) Responsible Parents and Parental Responsibility, Oxford: Hart.
Richards, M. (1994) 'Divorcing children: Roles for parents and the state' in M. Maclean and
   J. Kurczewski (eds) *Families, Politics and the Law: Perspectives for East and West Europe*,
   Oxford: Clarendon Press.

Schneider, E. (1994) 'The violence of privacy' in M. Fineman and R. Myktiuk (eds) *The Public
   Nature of Private Violence*, London: Routledge.
Sevenhuijsen, S. (1997) *Citizenship and the Ethics of Care*, London: Routledge.
Smart, C. *et al.* (2005) *Residence and Contact Disputes in Court*, London DCA.
Smart, C. (1989) *Feminism and the Power of Law*, London: Routledge.
Smart, C. and Neale, B. (1997) 'Argument against virtue – must contact be enforced?'
   Family Law 332.
Smart, C. and Neale, B. (1999) *Family Fragments?*, Cambridge: Polity Press.

Taylor, R. (2009) 'Parental responsibility and religion' in R. Probert, S. Gilmore and J. Herring
   (eds) *Responsible Parents and Parental Responsibility*, Oxford: Hart.
Trinder, L. (2003) 'Working and not Working Contact after Divorce', in A. Bainham,
   B. Lindley, M. Richards and L. Trinder (eds) *Children and Their Families*, Oxford: Hart.
Trinder, L. (2005) *A profile of applicants and respondents in contact cases in Essex*, London: DCA.
Turkmendag, I., Dingwall, R. and Murphy, T. (2008) 'The removal of donor anonymity in
   the UK: The silencing of claims by would-be parents' *International Journal of Law, Policy
   and the Family* 283.

Wallbank, J. (2009) '"Bodies in the Shadows" Joint Birth Registration, parental responsibility
   and social class' *Child and Family Law Quarterly* **21**, 267.
Wallbank, J. (2010) '(En)gendering the fusion of rights and responsibilities in the law of
   contact' in J. Wallbank, S. Choudhry and J. Herring (eds) *Rights, Gender and Family Law*,
   Abingdon: Routledge.
Wong, S. (2004) 'Cohabitation and the Law Commission's Project' *Journal of Social Welfare
   and Family Law* 265.

Index